*This book is dedicated to my son,
James Ashley Shepherd, who has no idea
how to use Pro Tools . . . yet.*

Acknowledgments

The author would like to thank the following for their contributions and assistance:

My wife Annette and the rest of my family for allowing me to do this, John McDaniel at Sonic Arts for technical guidance, Doug Thornton my technical soul-brother, Bob Uphaus at Red Echo Post for a world of expertise, John Rotondi at Enterprise Post for an expert opinion, John McKay for amazing work on *The Lord of the Rings,* Bob Reardon at Waves, Richard Diehl for some interesting photos, Philip Rodriguez the foley man, Claudia Cook at Digidesign, Valarie Schwan at USC photo archives, Zac Wheatcroft at Bias, Joe Milner at Puget Sound, Kaleo Willess at Dolby Laboratories Inc., Marti D. Humphrey (a. k. a. Dr. Sound), Fred Hecht, Keith Roberts, and Ryan Limke at Lightborne for being cool, and Mark Garvey, Kevin Harreld, and Andy Shafran for this opportunity.

About the Author

Ashley Shepherd is a graduate of the Berklee College of Music. He has been in the music and recording industry for 20 years, garnering several gold and platinum records. An ADDY® award recipient for original music, he has produced and recorded for major labels, network TV, national commercials, independent films, games, Internet sites, and international corporations.

Currently, Ashley is completing his new studio facility located in a historic church in Newport, KY, that will cater to music, film, and multimedia. He also writes manual content for Steinberg's Nuendo software in addition to continuing to produce original music and to record audio for film and video. For more information, visit his Website at www.picturemusic .com and his studio at www.audiogrotto.com.

Contents

Introduction. xiii

Chapter 1
Film, Video, and Multimedia Technology 1

A Brief History of Motion Pictures and Film Sound. 1
Thomas Edison's *The Sneeze*. 1
Sound Technology in the 1920s 2
Disney's *Fantasia* 3
Film Sound Formats 7
Television and Video Recording. 9
Sound in *Star Wars* and *Apocalypse Now* 10
Internet Video 10
HDTV. 11
Digital Multimedia Formats. 13
QuickTime. 13
MPEG Codecs 14
DV Codec 14
H.264 and the MPEG-4 File Type 15
Avid Video 16
Flash and Shockwave 16

Chapter 2
Audio for Film, Video, and Multimedia 17

The Components of a Soundtrack 17
Dialogue and Narration 17
Foley Sounds 20
Sound Effects. 22
Music 23

How Does Pro Tools Help?. 25
   The Non-Linear, Non-Destructive Editing Model. 25
   QuickTime Movie Support 25
   Automation, Automation, Automation 26
   Multi-Channel Mixing 27
   The Standard in Hollywood. 27
Project Workflow. 28
   Pre-Production (Planning and Preparing). .28
   Production (Filming and Recording on a Set or on Location) 34
   Post-Production (Re-Recording, Sweetening, Editing, and Mixing). 36

Chapter 3
Synchronization and SMPTE Time Code   43

Synchronization Basics 43
   Positional Reference 44
   Playback Rate 44
Origin and History of Time Code 46
   Film 46
   NTSC versus PAL. 47
   Color versus Black and White 48
Parameters of Time Code 49
   Frame Rates. 49
   Frame Count 50
Current Usages and Practices. 52
   To Drop or Not to Drop? 53
   2-3 Pull-Down 54
SMPTE Time Code Scenarios. 59
   NTSC Video to NTSC Video 59
   Film to NTSC Video. 60
   Film to Film. 61
   24p HD to Video 62
   True 24fps HD to Film (or 24p HD) 62
   Film to 24p HD 63
   HD to Just About Anything. 63

Chapter 4
Getting Started with Pro Tools and Video   65

Hooking Up Your Equipment 65
   Typical Equipment Setups 66
   Audio Clock Source 69

Digidesign's Sync HD and Sync I/O 69
Third-Party Synchronizers 70
SMPTE Time Code Reader, MIDI Interface 71
9-Pin Machine Control 71
MIDI Machine Control (MMC) 78
Video Playback Monitors 80
Creating a New Video Session 84
Choosing Sample Rate and Bit Depth .84
Choosing Frame Rate and Frame Count 85
Choosing Session Start Times. 86
Importing Video Files 88
Opening QuickTime Movies 89
Capturing DV Video from Tape. 90
Multiple Video Tracks and Regions (HD and DV Toolkit Only) 99
Changing Movie Offsets 100
Checking Sync 103
Importing Audio from QuickTime Movies 103
Examining Lip Sync 103
Time Code Burn-In Window 104

Chapter 5
Recording to Picture   107

Using Audio from the Set (Production Audio) 107
EDLs. 108
Conforming EDLs. 110
Importing OMFI Files 117
Recording from Production DAT Tapes 124
Digital Field Recorders 127
Recording Dialogue and Narration. 134
Replacing Existing Dialogue (ADR) .135
Recording Voiceovers and Narration .142
A Note About Animation Dialogue 144
Creating Rough Tracks for Video Editing 145
Recording Action Sounds (Foley) 147
Using a Foley Stage. 147
Using FX Libraries 150
On Location 151
Creating Sound Effects 153
Using Field Recordings 153
Sound Effects Libraries 154

Using Synthesizers and Samplers 155
Importing the Score and Incidental Music 159
Importing from CD, DAT, or Tape 159
Importing from CD-ROM 159
Importing Multi-Channel Music 161
MP3 Files 161
Backing Up Your Data! 161
Backup Plan 163
Mass Storage Media 166

Chapter 6
Editing to Picture   169

Setting Up Pro Tools Sessions for Editing .169
Seeing the Information You Need 169
Edit Grouping 180
Using Counters and Rulers 186
Using Grid Values 191
Using Memory Locations 195
Creating Memory Locations 195
Using the Cue List to Create Markers 197
Recalling Markers and Memory Locations 199
Aligning Regions to Markers 205
Using Nudge Commands 206
Setting Nudge Values 206
Aligning Regions to Video Frames 207
Subframe Nudging 209
How to Use Sync Points 210
Creating a Sync Point 210
Using Sync Points and the Grid 211
Playlists 212
Conforming to Picture Changes 215
Virtual Katy 216
Manual Rebalancing 217

Chapter 7
Processing Audio Using Audiosuite Plug-Ins   223

Operation of Audiosuite Plug-Ins 223
Reversing Files 224
Time Compression/Expansion 230

Audiosuite Time Compression/Expansion 231
Trimmer Tool Compression/Expansion 234
Pitch-Changing 235
Digidesign's Time Shift Plug-In 236
Aligning Dialogue 236
Noise Reduction and Restoration 240
Surgical EQ 248

Chapter 8
Mixing to Picture in Pro Tools   249

Stereo and Surround Formats 249
Encoding and Decoding with Dolby Technologies 249
Preparation for Mixing 252
The I/O Setup 252
Speaker Systems and Layouts 258
Loudness Calibration 264
Bass Management 269
Film-Style Mixing Workflow 276
From Edit to Print Master 277
Pre-Mixes or Pre-Dubs 278
Mixing Dialogue 282
Mixing Foley 285
Mixing Effects 286
Mixing Music 286
LFE Channel 288
Using Automation While Mixing 289
Levels 289
Automating Panning 291
Automating EQs 291
Building Dynamics 294
Control Surfaces 295
TDM and RTAS Plug-In Delay Compensation .298
Delay Compensation for Pro Tools LE Systems 298
Automatic Delay Compensation in Pro Tools HD 301

Chapter 9
Delivery of Master Recordings   303

Mix Stems 303
Reference Levels 303

The Purpose of Reference Levels and Tones 304
Using Reference Levels 306
Recording a Mix on a VTR 310
Using Digital Connections 310
Using Analog Connections 312
Creating Multi-Channel Surround Masters 313
Bouncing to QuickTime Movies 314
Creating an Audio File or Data CD Master 314
Redbook Audio CDs 316
Preparing Audio Files for Internet Streaming .317
Archiving and Backing Up the Final Mix 318
Mix Stems: Dipped or Not Dipped 318
Pro Tools Data 319
Harness the Power of Cinema 319

Appendix A 321
Appendix B 325

Index 327

Introduction

Welcome to the exciting world of creating sound for film, video, and multimedia. Pro Tools is the professional standard for creating dynamic and provocative soundtracks for movies, television, and a variety of Internet media, including Flash movies.

This book will help you master the features in Pro Tools that allow you to deal with the complexities of taking a multimedia project from creation to completion. The book begins by looking at the different facets that make up a soundtrack and how they are organized. Next, you'll explore how you begin a project and learn about the people you will interact with as a sound engineer. You'll review all of the relevant visual technology that you will encounter along the way. You will then explore the specific tasks one by one and learn how to use Pro Tools to easily create all the audio necessary for any multimedia project.

Sound for picture is a terribly complex task fraught with technical traps that can leave audio engineers pulling their hair out. Pro Tools has the features you need in order to conquer these projects. With this book, you will be prepared for the challenges involved and have an understanding of how Pro Tools will help you get through them.

Music recording engineers will find helpful explanations of film and video technology and how they relate to the audio studio. Film and video editors looking to do more complex audio productions will learn how to export projects into Pro Tools for advanced editing and mixing capabilities. Web designers and programmers will be introduced to the world of multi-track audio and digital mixing.

Pro Tools is capable of so many audio tasks but is particularly well suited to audio post-production. It has become an international standard in the audio post-production community. This book teaches you how to use Pro Tools to its fullest advantage as an audio for video tool and helps you understand the complete creative process for audio in film, video, and multimedia.

What You'll Find in This Book

This book is designed as a specific guide to producing audio for film, video, and multimedia using Pro Tools. It is not meant as an introductory tutorial on Pro Tools itself. A basic working knowledge of the software is needed prior to reading this book. You will be examining advanced features in Pro Tools and how they are applied to film, video, and multimedia specifically.

After reading this book, you will know how to do the following:

- Work with SMPTE time code and its variations in Pro Tools.

- Synchronize Pro Tools with videotape, QuickTime movies, and other audio sources such as digital field recorders.

- Record narration, dialogue replacement, foley, and special effects.

- Mix audio down to multi-channel formats.

- Print your final mix onto a VTR, DAT, audio CD, or QuickTime file.

- Work with directors, editors, and production sound mixers/recordists.

- Interchange audio data between Pro Tools and video editing software such as Avid's Media Composer and Final Cut Pro.

- Use cue sheets to create marker lists into Pro Tools in order to place audio events quickly.

- Use pitch shifting to create unique sound effects.

- Use EQ to correct for mic placement.

- Remove unwanted noise from production audio.

- Place audio to specific time code positions.

- Use Pro Tools in a laptop for location recording.

- Calibrate and use reference levels.

- Calibrate multi-channel sound systems for proper monitoring.

- Organize your project workflow in Pro Tools.

- Integrate your work into larger productions.

- Use automation to create a dynamic and compelling mix.

- Back up and archive your data.

Who This Book Is For

The book will be helpful to any of the following professionals:

- Music engineers moving into the field of audio for film, video, and multimedia.

- Film and video editors wanting to create more complex audio productions than is possible in current generation video-editing software.

- Independent film makers who are planning on doing all of their post-production in-house.

- Musicians composing for film, TV, and Internet media.

- Web designers who want to add dynamic sonic content to their Web pages.

- Anyone who wants to know how to use Pro Tools to create stunning, professional, and creative audio for their films, commercials, music videos, Flash movies, Web pages, corporate media, animation, and much more.

How This Book Is Organized

This book contains nine chapters:

Chapter 1: "Film, Video, and Multimedia Technology." This chapter starts with a brief history of the audio visual arts, beginning with Thomas Edison's kinetoscope and ending with today's Internet streaming video technology. It includes an extensive discussion of SMPTE time code and its variations.

Chapter 2: "Audio for Film, Video, and Multimedia." You'll get a tour of all the different aspects involved in creating audio for multimedia. This chapter will get you comfortable with how things are typically done. You will learn how Pro Tools' unique feature set is well matched for this task and follow a mock project workflow from beginning to end in order to familiarize yourself with many of the terms and concepts you will use throughout the book.

Chapter 3: "Synchronization and SMPTE Time Code." This chapter is dedicated to a thorough explanation of SMPTE in its many formats and uses. The origin and history of time code and how it is used will be explored to give some background as to why SMPTE is so strange and varied. Synchronization concepts and details are covered. You learn about how Pro Tools handles all of this gracefully and with precision.

Chapter 4: "Getting Started with Pro Tools and Video." This chapter covers all the necessary equipment you need in order to use Pro Tools with video. I'll get you up and running by creating a new session, importing video and audio files, and checking sync between audio and video.

Chapter 5: "Recording to Picture." This chapter shows you how to record each element of a soundtrack from dialogue and foley sounds to special effects and music. Each element will be covered in detail including mic setups, organization of multiple takes, and the process of importing existing audio.

Chapter 6: "Editing to Picture." This chapter is chock full of useful tips and shortcuts to help get your audio trimmed and timed efficiently. Pro Tools has many unique features that help you move audio around precisely and quickly.

Chapter 7: "Processing Audio Using Audiosuite Plug-Ins." This chapter explores processing of audio outside the mixing environment, including noise reduction, vocal alignment, time stretching, pitch shifting, and special effects.

Chapter 8: "Mixing to Picture in Pro Tools." Here you will learn about multi-channel mixing formats and how to set up Pro Tools to mix in surround sound. You will learn how to calibrate a multi-channel monitoring system using Waves plug-ins, in accordance with Dolby guidelines. I'll also talk about using automation to fix problems and create a dynamic mix.

Chapter 9: "Delivery of Master Recordings." This chapter deals with getting your mix back together with the master video, film, or Internet media. Film mixing formats are extensively covered here. This is a critical step in the process and I'll break it down for you.

Appendix A contains a storyboard script for the fictional commercial discussed in Chapter 2, and Appendix B shows a graphical representation of how sound recordings move through the post-production process.

1 Film, Video, and Multimedia Technology

Duro the course of this book, I'll show you how to create complete audio productions for film, video, and multimedia. In order to better show how Pro Tools fits into the historical context of movie making, the first part of this chapter offers a brief history of motion picture and sound technology and how it has evolved over the years.

In the current information age, motion pictures and audio have entered the digital realm. The latest technology allows you to use programs like Pro Tools to create all forms of multimedia. I will review some of this relevant technology as it applies to Pro Tools.

A Brief History of Motion Pictures and Film Sound

People have been creating sound for motion pictures for over a century. Although the technology of recording sound has inevitably changed over the years, it is interesting to note that much remains the same. As with many modern-day inventions, sound technology all started with Thomas Edison.

Thomas Edison's *The Sneeze*

"My plan was to synchronize the camera and the phonograph so as to record sounds when the pictures were made, and reproduce the two in harmony.... We had the first of the so-called "talking pictures" in our laboratory thirty years ago."—Thomas Edison, 1925.

The talking picture he was referring to is called *The Sneeze*. Edison (see Figure 1.1) filmed Fred Ott, a man who worked in his Newark laboratory, sneezing and recorded the sound onto one of his sound discs. The film and the sound recording were then played back together to make one of the first audio/visual works ever created. *The Sneeze* is only a few seconds long, but the ideas demonstrated by it are the foundations of modern multimedia. Edison went on to create many more films and even built a special building that allowed sunlight to be controlled in a way that was conducive to filming. Throughout the early 1900s, other attempts were made to synchronize sound with motion pictures, but few of these attempts were very successful.

Figure 1.1 Thomas Edison with an original Kinetoscope, one of the first motion picture cameras.

Sound Technology in the 1920s

In 1922, The German inventors Josef Engl and Hans Vogt invented the *Tri-Ergon* process. This process was an optical audio recording made onto the film itself, allowing sound and movies to be played together. It was accomplished by using a photoelectric cell to transduce sound vibrations into light waves that could be printed onto the edge of the film in a photographic process. When the film was replayed, another photoelectric cell read the light patterns off the film and output an electrical waveform that could be amplified and fed to speakers in the theater.

In 1926, the Fox Film Corporation developed another sound-on-film technique, called *Movietone*, and began making newsreels with sound. The launch of Charles Lindbergh's trans-Atlantic flight to Paris was one of the first Movietone newsreels.

In the early 20s, Bell Laboratories developed a sound-on-disc system using 33 1/3rpm discs called *Vitaphone*. Warner Brothers first used the technology in the release of the movie *Don Juan*. It was the first major release of a film that replaced the traditional orchestra with music from the Vitaphone system. However, there still was no dialogue in this movie.

Warner Brothers released the first "talkie," *The Jazz Singer,* in 1927. No dialogue was written for the film, so its star, Al Jolson, improvised a few lines, and that marked the end of silent movies. Warner Brothers continued to push the boundaries of sound in film with the release in 1928 of *Lights of New York,* the first all-dialogue feature film. In that same year, Walt Disney created the entire soundtrack for *Steamboat Willie* in post-production, including dialogue, sound effects, and music.

The 1920s ushered in most of the technological innovations that shape the world of film sound to this day. All of the elements of the soundtrack were created, in some form, during that first decade of film sound. The tools have changed, but the basic goals of creating entertaining motion pictures have remained the same. Just think what Walt Disney might have done with Pro Tools!

Disney's *Fantasia*

Walt Disney continued his innovation in film and audio techniques with the landmark production of *Fantasia.* Starring Mickey Mouse (along with many other animated characters), *Fantasia* choreographed animation to classical music. To facilitate a truly immersive experience, the Disney technicians came up with many new methods and equipment for recording sound. Multi-track recording was used for the first time to capture an orchestra and then overdub additional instruments, creating a many-layered soundtrack. John Volkmann, the recording engineer for *Fantasia,* used eight optical recorders to capture the orchestra—six machines recorded different sections of the orchestra, and a distant microphone on the seventh and the eighth recorders captured a balanced mix of the whole orchestra. This method gave Volkmann the ability to recombine the levels of each section in the orchestra or even re-record or overdub them if need be. Later, a ninth click track was added as a guide for animators to follow. Cues could be given as to what action should be taking place, and the animators would have accurate timing down to each frame of film. The 42 days it took to record the music for *Fantasia* used nearly half a million feet of sound film!

As there was no such thing as time code or electronic synchronization in the 1930s, a different mechanical method was used to synchronize the nine optical recorders. The same sprockets that insert into the holes on the edges of film in order to keep it positioned and running at the correct speed could be linked mechanically between machines in order to synchronize them physically, as seen in the Moviola machine in Figure 1.2. Once the sound film had been placed on the machine and aligned to the sprockets, it would stay in sync with the other optical recorders connected to it. This way, many machines could be linked to create as large a tape machine as needed. This type of synchronization is still used in the film industry today, although digital technology such as Pro Tools is rapidly taking over.

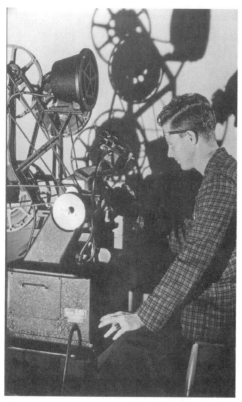

Figure 1.2 A very early film-editing machine called a Moviola. This type of machine is still in use today, although it is rapidly being replaced by non-linear digital editing systems.

A special playback system called *Fantasound* was invented specifically for *Fantasia*. The system employed two projectors. The first projector had the visual images on it, as well as a mono mix of the entire soundtrack as a backup. The film in the second projector, which was mechanically synchronized to the first, was printed with four mono optical tracks (see Figure 1.3). Track one had control information, in the form of various frequency tones and amplitudes that were used to modulate the volumes of certain speakers during the show. Tracks two, three, and four contained the audio for the screen left, screen right, and screen center speakers, respectively. In addition, there were three other sources—called house left, house right, and house center—placed behind the audience. These channels were derived from the screen left and right channels and were modulated by the control track as well. Thus, the first surround-sound system was born.

Because the optical recording process did not offer much in the way of dynamic range, each signal was recorded as loud as possible, in order to reduce the noise level during

Figure 1.3 A piece of modern film showing the stereo optical tracks at the edge of the film. Notice how holes in the film go over the sprockets, helping to align and synchronize the motion of the film through the projector.

playback. To achieve the dynamics needed by the film's orchestra conductor, Leopold Stokowski, the control track was implemented to vary the output levels to each speaker in accordance with the dynamics specified using voltage-gain amplifiers. This was a very early form of noise reduction and a precursor to modern mixing automation. Today, technology such as Dolby SR provides noise reduction in more sophisticated ways.

William Garity, chief engineer for Disney at the time *Fantasia* was being made, was charged with creating a device that would simulate motion of a sound source back and forth across the screen. He theorized that fading levels between two speakers would create the desired effect. With that in mind, he designed a three-way differential circuit that allowed mixing down to a three-track master. The device was dubbed *the panpot*. It required six people, conducted by Stokowski, to operate all the panpots and adjust the levels while mixing the film. Stokowski had all the level and pan markings in his score, and he conducted the mixdown session as a film-scoring session would be done today. As the VU meter had not yet been invented, a special three-color oscilloscope was used to maintain the proper recording levels.

Fantasia's 54-speaker system was so expensive that only two were ever installed in theaters, one in New York's Broadway Theater and the other in the Carthy Theater in Los Angeles, at a cost of $85,000 each. The premier showing of *Fantasia*, on November 13, 1940, did not use a complete Fantasound system. Because of certain technical factors, a live sound engineer mixed the surround speakers during the screening. The Fantasound system used only during the final "Ave Maria" sequence, and, for the first time, an audience was wrapped in 360-degree sound.

Due to the high cost of the Fantasound system, a smaller version was created that could travel around the country. It filled up half a freight car and weighed 15,000 pounds. It was called "Fantasia Road Show" and was used in only 14 theaters during the tour.

Fantasia has been re-released in various formats five times in the last 50 years. The first re-release, in 1942, had a mono mix and was edited down by 43 minutes. In 1956, *Fantasia* was released in its entirety with a four-track magnetic format. In 1982, the soundtrack was re-recorded using a digital format. Although the fidelity of the 1982 recording is better, many fans of the movie considered the performance to be inferior to the original. So, in 1990, Disney restored both the picture and the soundtrack from the original masters. Because the optical recordings had been lost, the 1956 magnetic masters were used. Months were spent researching the original notes about the mix before Disney's Terry Porter was able to re-create the Fantasound mix for the modern 70mm Dolby six-channel surround format seen in theaters. This mix was also used to create the DVD master of the film.

Fantasia must be considered the most important film with respect to technical achievement in film sound. The innovations generated by its creation have fathered many of the techniques still used today in one form or another. It was an amazing accomplishment in animation, audio technology, and entertainment. Its high quality and creative value are still evident today.

Innovations in the Creation of *Fantasia*

1. Multi-track recording using synchronized optical recorders

2. Overdubbing of different parts by the orchestra

3. Click track used by conductor and animators to choreograph animation and audio mixdown

4. Multi-channel surround playback system

5. Panpot used to move sounds across the screen

6. Control track on film used to regenerate dynamics from optical recording—that is, noise reduction

7. Use of oscilloscope to monitor recording levels—predecessor to the VU meter

Film Sound Formats

During the 1950s, film went through many different sound formats. The fear of losing audiences to television drove the film industry to adopt many new film formats using wider screens and more channels of audio to "wow" the viewers and stay competitive. The wide-screen formats of today are a direct result of this competition.

Following is a list of some of the many film formats used in the last 50 years, along with a brief description of related size and audio formats.

- **Cinerama (1952–1962):** Three projectors and eight audio channels played back from a 35mm magnetic film audio tape with a seven-track headstack similar to the machine in Figure 1.4. Abandoned in 1963 due to high costs.

- **Cinemascope (1953–1967):** Used anamorphic technique to achieve widescreen aspect ratio. Four-channel magnetic audio on the edge of the film, plus a mono

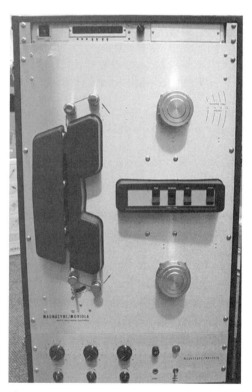

Figure 1.4 A 16mm, magnetic film, audio recorder. The Magnasync Moviola TP1710.

optical track. This format was replaced by Panavision, with a stereo optical soundtrack with Dolby noise reduction.

- **Warnerphonic (1950s):** Used another machine with sprocketed, magnetic film that was mechanically synchronized with the projector. Cinemascope's combined film made this format obsolete.

- **Todd-AO (1955–1992):** *Oklahoma* was the first film released in the Todd-AO format. Invented by Michael Todd and the American Optical Company, it was printed on a 70mm piece of film with the audio occupying 5mm of that width. There are five speakers behind the screen—left, mid-left, center, mid-right, and right—and a mono surround speaker behind the audience.

- **Dolby Stereo (1976–present):** 35mm with two-track, matrix-encoded optical sound. Left, center, right, and mono surround.

- **Dolby Discrete Six-Track (1976–present):** 70mm, 6-track magnetic master with left, mid-left, center, mid-right, right, and mono surround channels.

- **Dolby "Baby-Boom" Six-Track (1977–present):** 6-track magnetic master with left, center, right, mono surround, and a low-frequency effects channel (LFE).

- **Dolby "Split-Surround" Six-Track (1979–present):** 6-track magnetic master with left, center, right, left surround, center surround, right surround, and LFE channels. The Big Daddy!

- **Dolby Digital (1992–present):** 35mm, 5.1 optically encoded digital using AC-3 compression. Left, center, right, left surround, right surround, and the ".1" LFE channels.

- **DTS (1993–present):** 35 or 70mm with accompanying proprietary CD that is synchronized to an optically encoded time code track on the film print. Includes Dolby Stereo compatible optical track as a backup. Same 5.1 channel configuration as Dolby Digital.

- **SDDS (1993–present):** 35mm optically encoded 7.1 with left, mid-left, center, mid-right, right, left surround, right surround, and LFE channels. The Big Mama!

Analog Backup Note that with any of the digital film audio formats there will usually be a Dolby Stereo analog track printed on the film as a backup, in case of any failure of the digital system and for compatibility with older theaters.

Television and Video Recording

In 1940, the first TV station began broadcasting in Chicago. The first television sets showed images in black and white only. Throughout the 1940s, different systems for color television were tried, and finally, in 1953, the Federal Communications Commission (FCC) approved a system that was backwards-compatible with the existing black and white system, so that even though the signal was broadcast in color, a black and white TV would still display the picture. This meant that people who already owned black and white TV sets would not have to buy new ones. The system is called the National Television System Committee (NTSC) color video standard and is the same system we use now for analog broadcast television. Figure 1.5 shows a camera from the early days of TV. Note the tubes used inside.

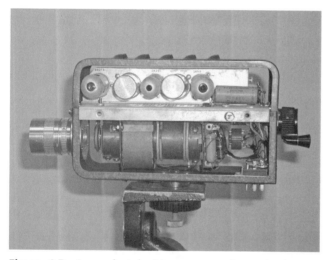

Figure 1.5 An early television camera from the late 1950s; a Blonder-Tongue TVC-1-C Vidicon camera head.

Also during the early 1950s, teams were developing techniques to record the images from television cameras onto magnetic tape. In 1952, Ampex played back the first recognizable image from a video tape recorder. Throughout the rest of the 1950s and 1960s, many video recording, editing, and synchronization systems were developed, creating a maze of incompatible standards. In 1969, the Society of Motion Picture and Television Engineers (SMPTE) created the standard time code that we use today to synchronize videotape machines and identify tape locations. Chapter 3, "Synchronization and SMPTE Time Code," is dedicated to SMPTE time code, its uses, and its variations.

Sound in *Star Wars* and *Apocalypse Now*

The debut of *Star Wars,* in 1977, changed the world of film sound with Ben Burtt's groundbreaking sound effects. The use of manipulated sounds in *Star Wars* was very unique and identifiable—for example, Burtt created an entire language of mechanical and electrical sounds for the small robot R2-D2. The use of cable vibrations to create the TIE fighter sounds was another innovation. *Star Wars* signified a departure from the traditional method of capturing the performance of the music or actors to creating new sounds by manipulating the recordings of other sounds. The simplest method used to do this is changing the speed and pitch of a recording. When a sound is slowed down greatly, it can begin to sound like something completely new and different. This way, the sound engineer is not limited to realistic sounds. Movies such as *Star Wars* enlarged the palette of sound engineers could use.

As sound engineers became more creative, their role evolved into that of a sonic artist rather than just a technician. In response to this role change, the title of "Sound Designer" was introduced, and it really did accurately describe what these people were doing. The first person to be credited as a sound designer in a film was Walter Murch, for *Apocalypse Now.*

During the 1970s, Dolby Laboratories created new sound formats, including a low-frequency effects (LFE) channel, in response to the wide sonic palette that movies like *Star Wars, Apocalypse Now,* and *Close Encounters of the Third Kind* contained. *Apocalypse Now* was released in Dolby Split Surround. With six discrete channels for left, center, right, left surround, right surround, and LFE, Dolby Split Surround is the predecessor to Dolby Digital, the 5.1 surround format we hear on DVDs and in home theaters today. Movie theater sound has evolved even further, using 6.1 and even 7.1 systems. Other standards include extremely large-format screens such as Imax and its wrap-around cousin Omnimax, both of which have hi-fidelity, multi-channel sound systems.

Internet Video

With the advent of the Internet, video technology entered a new era. The ability to transmit moving images across Internet connections has been a continual motivating force behind the advancement of video technology. In just a few short years, it has evolved from the early herky-jerky clips to entire movies streaming over broadband connections. Figure 1.6 shows a frame from a Flash movie, a popular format for Internet media. A slew of audio and video *codecs* have been created to improve the quality of movies and music transmitted via the Internet and other digital media.

What Is a *Codec*? Codec is short for compression/decompression algorithm. When audio/visual data is sent over the Internet or placed on a CD-ROM, it is typically compressed (using a specific compression scheme, or *codec*) in order to get more information in the same amount of space. Some examples of AV codecs are MPEG-2, AVI, H.264, HDV, and mp3 (for audio only).

As multimedia technology evolves, file types and codecs will become obsolete, and new ones will be created. This is happening everyday. A great deal of confusion arises around this subject, primarily due to rapid changes in the technology. Working with digital video and Pro Tools will always keep you on the bleeding edge of multimedia. Try to read up on the subject using the Internet to keep current on the technological trends.

Figure 1.6   A frame from a Flash movie called *The Fly Family,* for which I helped create the audio.

HDTV

In the mid-1970s, the Japanese company NHK started developing a new broadcast technology that would be much higher in quality than the current television system. The results of the research and development were astounding and were the foundation of our present-day digital TV. In 1975, Francis Ford Coppola was introduced to an early HDTV system in the basement of NHK while visiting Japan. He envisioned that films would eventually be made entirely digitally and that the creative process would benefit greatly from this use of technology. He was not wrong. Today, Mr. Coppola's vision is a reality. All new television sets sold today are required to have HD broadcast tuners built-in. Many network shows are being produced in HD, not to mention all the sporting events are shot in HD. February of 2009 marks the end of analog television broadcasts as mandated by the FCC. At that point, only digital HDTV signals will be available over the public airwaves. However, standard definition (NTSC) video can still be broadcast via HDTV signals and will continue to be into the future until the older equipment has been replaced throughout the industry.

HDTV is capable of generating images that are wider than a traditional television picture. The dimensions of these images are expressed as a ratio of the width to the height, called the *aspect ratio*. Analog broadcast television has an aspect ratio of 4:3. HDTV is capable of a 16:9 aspect ratio, as seen in Figure 1.7. This advancement in television technology reflects the desire to emulate the film industry—HDTV is trying to compete with an experience that until now has been available only in theaters. The image quality of HDTV is amazing, and with its ability to deliver high fidelity sound, many feel that the home theater sight and sound experience now rivals that of commercial theaters.

The HDTV broadcast standard includes specifications for the delivery of six channels of surround sound in the form of Dolby AC3. AC3 is a surround format that is currently used on DVDs to provide discrete 5.1 channel sound. This compressed format can also be used for transmission of HDTV audio via satellite, cable, or local broadcast.

Figure 1.7 The Samsung LTM405W LCD screen is capable of displaying HDTV signals with a resolution of 1280 × 768 pixels. It uses the 16:9 aspect ratio, which can accommodate the wider aspect ratios of theatrical film releases. This screen is 40 inches wide.

An increasing number of films today are created with HD cameras and editing equipment and then transferred to film for presentation in theaters. Certain theaters have already seen the future of digital projection systems capable of projecting high-quality large images. *Star Wars: Attack of the Clones* was actually filmed, edited, and, in some theaters, projected entirely in the digital domain. The era of digital cinema is soon upon us. One of the added benefits of digital cinema is that the image does not degrade after repeated viewings.

From Thomas Edison's first experiments with films such as *The Sneeze* to George Lucas and *Attack of the Clones,* audio-visual technology has enjoyed a century-long evolution at a breakneck pace that shows no signs of slowing down.

Digital Multimedia Formats

In today's information age, motion pictures and sound have moved into the digital domain. The expansion of the Internet has fueled technological development at a furious pace, bringing us movies over the Web, a true theatrical experience in the home, and portable music and video players in our pockets. This technology enables more people to create and experience multimedia without a large investment in highly specialized equipment. A desktop or even laptop computer or iPod will work just fine. With that in mind, these next sections focus on the specific multimedia technology you will use with Pro Tools.

QuickTime

QuickTime is a cross-platform software technology developed by Apple Computer for playback and creation of multimedia content. It is also the media player format supported by Pro Tools. Any movie or video that you would like to import directly into Pro Tools must be in a QuickTime-compatible format. QuickTime supports many different codecs, including MPEG, AVI, Sorenson, Cinepak, Flash, DV, and others.

QuickTime supports a long list of file formats. Each file format can contain multiple streams of multimedia. These streams may contain audio, video, or even text and graphics. With audio and video streams, it becomes necessary to compress the data in order to create file sizes that are smaller and more appropriate for the Internet. Codecs are used to accomplish this. Each codec (MPEG-2, Sorenson, Cinepak, H264, and so on) has its own specialized way of compressing video data. Each codec has its advantages and disadvantages. Some reduce the file size a great deal, but also sacrifice the video quality. Others have excellent video quality but might have a larger file size or require a great deal of processing power to decompress.

In order for Pro Tools to be able to play a video file, five things must be present:

1. QuickTime must be installed on the host computer.

2. QuickTime must support the file type of the video.

3. The codec used within the video file must be installed on the host computer.

4. Pro Tools must also support that particular file type and codec.

5. Certain codecs will require specialized hardware to play back the file, including Avid video. Detailed information on video hardware is found in Chapter 4, "Getting Started with Pro Tools and Video."

QuickTime Pro Upgrade I recommend purchasing the QuickTime Pro upgrade, which will allow you to convert the various video file formats and codecs into ones that will work best with your system. It is an inexpensive upgrade that will save you a great deal of time when dealing with various video files and Pro Tools.

MPEG Codecs

MPEG stands for Motion Picture Experts Group. The MPEG group was formed in the late 1980s by the International Standards Organization (ISO), headed by Leonardo Chiariglione. The ISO's job was to create standard methods of coding audio and video into compressed, digital formats. The term MPEG is used to denote a whole family of audio and video compression algorithms developed by MPEG. They are MPEG-1 (which includes the mp3 audio format), MPEG-2 (which is used for DVD and HDTV encoding, among other things), and MPEG-4 (a next generation codec, including the H.264 algorithm). MPEG-3 was originally intended as an extension of MPEG-2 for use with DVDs but was eventually merged entirely into MPEG-2. Don't confuse it with the "mp3" audio format, which is short for MPEG-1, Layer 3. All of the MPEG codecs are supported in the latest version of QuickTime. The MPEG-2 format requires the purchase of additional software to work in QuickTime.

Windows Media Player Documents (WMV) Windows Media Player documents are not compatible with QuickTime and cannot be used in Pro Tools. This is a common AV format for PCs and Internet movies. These files must be converted into QuickTime movies before importing into Pro Tools. There are third-party solutions that allow QuickTime to play WMV files, but they will not work with Pro Tools.

DV Codec

DV is a confusing term, as it is used for many things, including as a generic designation for "digital video." The technical term refers to an international standard created for consumer, semi-pro, and professional digital video equipment, including DV (consumer camcorders), DVCPRO, and DVCAM. The unique aspect of DV equipment is its ability to digitally transfer audio and video over the IEEE 1394 interface commonly known as Apple's Firewire or Sony's iLink. This technology was originally developed by Apple Computer and adopted in 1995 by the International Standards Organization as IEEE-1394-1995. This combination has allowed desktop computer users to import high-quality video into their computers and then edit and process it all within a digital environment. Straight transfers between DV equipment using the 1394 interface are perfect digital clones. The quality of DV video is very high, and it is well suited to audio studios because of its low cost.

Audio post-production studios sometimes receive video on DV tapes. It is possible to use a consumer camcorder like the one in Figure 1.8 to transfer DV movies into a Pro Tools computer for use in audio post-production. I go into detail on this subject in Chapter 4.

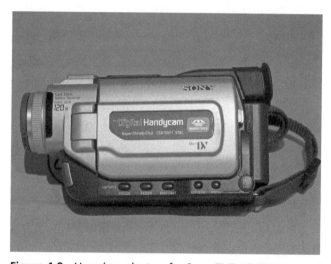

Figure 1.8   Here is a photo of a Sony TVR-17 DV camcorder that uses the iLink IEEE 1394 interface to connect to desktop computers and other DV equipment. I use this camcorder to capture DV files into the Pro Tools computer and then view the movie on a regular TV monitor.

H.264 and the MPEG-4 File Type

One of the latest multimedia file types is the MPEG-4 standard, which includes the H.264 video codec, also known as AVC (Advanced Video Coding). This standard has provided users with a next-generation multimedia codec that has increased video quality at all resolutions and is scalable in terms of the amount of data compression that is used. Pro Tools supports the use of MPEG-4 and H.264/AVC video files.

Avid Video

Digidesign's parent company Avid has a long history in developing video-editing work-stations and the video formats and codec that work with them. Pro Tools is capable of playing back certain varieties of Avid video if the Avid Mojo video hardware is part of the Pro Tools system. The Avid Mojo system is covered in greater detail in Chapter 4.

Flash and Shockwave

Two Internet media worth mentioning are Flash and its big brother Shockwave, both developed by Macromedia. These are very popular technologies for adding motion and graphic elements to Websites and CD-ROMs without requiring large amounts of band-width. Flash files amount to moving slide shows or, technically speaking, vector graph-ics that appear as animation and can contain embedded video as well. The ability to time certain visual events with audio files constitutes a form of multimedia that is becoming more common on the Web. I have created many soundtracks to go with flash movies and Websites that entail all the aspects of a full-blown film or video pro-duction. The specific needs of Flash movies and Shockwave files are discussed in Chapter 4 and in Chapter 8, "Mixing to Picture in Pro Tools."

2 Audio for Film, Video, and Multimedia

Before we get to the specific directions for using Pro Tools to create audio for film, video, or multimedia, let's consider the different aspects of this type of audio production and how they work together. In this chapter, I break down the soundtrack into components and describe each in detail. I also describe each step in an imaginary production of a commercial in order to show you a real-world example of how it's done.

The Components of a Soundtrack

Creating a soundtrack is perhaps the most complicated audio engineering task you can take on. You must not only capture dialogue (words spoken by people on-screen) and narration (words spoken by someone off-screen), but also the sounds people make on-screen as they move around, called *foley* sounds. Foley sounds include footsteps, doors opening and closing, papers rustling—you get the idea. Then there are imaginary sounds, such as the sound a spaceship makes traveling through the vacuum of space. I consider this an imaginary sound because sound cannot travel in a vacuum. Such sounds are called *special effects,* and they include bigger-than-life sounds like the unrealistic gunshots and body punches in the movies and on TV. Last, but certainly not least, is music. Music can take the form of the score or background music, environmental music such as the jukebox in *Happy Days,* and incidental music such as songs playing over the ending credits or in a music video.

Dialogue and Narration

Dialogue and narration make up the most important element in any soundtrack except for a music video. In order to communicate information and emotional content effectively, speech must be clearly heard. Taking the time to perfect dialogue and narration tracks will pay dividends later, when they are combined with other elements of the soundtrack.

Production Audio

Dialogue consists of what the characters say while they are on-screen or within earshot of the camera's point of view. A member of the film crew, usually the production sound mixer, will record the dialogue into a standalone audio recorder or, in the case of video production, directly into the camera itself. This is called *production audio*—that is to say, any audio recorded during the filming phase of a project. Production audio includes *wild takes*, or recording while the camera is *not* filming. These takes of dialogue, background ambience, and sound effects can be used later in post-production.

The audio recorders used for field recording traditionally have been either Nagra 1/4″ analog tape decks or portable DAT machines. However, in today's digital environment, using a recorder capable of generating data files—such as the Fostex PD-6 shown in Figure 2.1 and the Zaxcom DEVA—is becoming a popular alternative to traditional methods. Transferring files from one of these data recorders into Pro Tools or into a video-editing system is a simple process of copying data directly off a DVD disc or through a direct connection to the field recorder, thereby eliminating a time-consuming, real-time transfer. The day of an all-digital production chain from source to delivery is here now. Pro Tools has embraced this technology and has unique tools for importing audio from the latest field recorders. These tools are discussed in Chapter 5, "Recording to Picture."

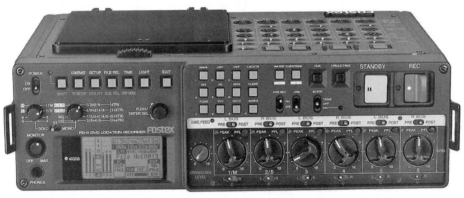

Figure 2.1   The Fostex PD-6 DVD Field Recorder is capable of recording six tracks of 48kHz audio or two tracks of 96kHz audio directly to standard DVD-RAM discs.

Re-Recorded Dialogue, or ADR

Many times production audio becomes unusable because of environmental noise such as passing cars, airplanes, dogs, or some other sound. Equipment failure can also wreak havoc during filming, causing loss of audio. The solution to these problems is "dialogue replacement." Commonly referred to as ADR (automatic dialogue replacement), it is the process of re-recording parts or all of the dialogue in a certain scene or take in which the original audio is unusable. The actors and actresses (called the *talent*) who performed in the scene come into the recording studio and record the lines needed. They do this by watching the original footage and listening to themselves talking in order to maintain what is called "lip sync." If you've seen *Lord of the Rings: Fellowship of the Ring* or *The Two Towers* then you've seen movies that are mostly ADR dialogue. Due to the nature of modern visual special effects, there is often a lot of noise on a film set, rendering the production audio useless. ADR can also be used to enhance the emotional performance of a character. Dialogue replacement can also be used to edit profanity out of a scene. We've all seen this done badly, as when we hear "shucks" but we see the actor's lips saying something quite different!

Narrator/Voiceovers

Narration and voiceovers are simply the voice of the announcer. Sometimes this can take the form of one of the on-screen characters either narrating part of the story or talking to himself. Voiceovers are usually recorded in a studio similar to the one shown in Figure 2.2. Timing is particularly important to voiceovers. A tenth of a second can make a big difference in a 15-second TV spot. Talented voiceover artists can adjust their speed to fit certain timings within tenths of a second! It can sometimes be necessary for an engineer to edit out breaths and spaces in order to make a voiceover fit. Have you ever wondered how they get all the disclaimer information in car ads spoken so quickly? Fast talkers and good editors!

Figure 2.2   This is a typical voice-recording studio with an isolation booth. All types of dialogue may be recorded in a studio like this. The key elements are a neutral acoustic quality that can lend itself to a variety of voice recording and suitable isolation from outside noise.

Voices for Animation

Animation is a special case when it comes to dialogue recording. As there is no filming of characters on a set or at a location, there is no production audio to use. With animation, the dialogue is always recorded first. Animators then will use the finished dialogue to create the different expressions and make the animated mouths move in sync with the words.

With the advent of computer-generated animation, certain action scenes may be animated before the dialogue is recorded. The talent can watch their animated characters moving on-screen while they read their lines, kind of like ADR recording. Then, later, animators can superimpose the expressions and mouth movements derived from the recorded dialogue onto the already-moving bodies of animated characters. You can see an example of this in the movie *Shrek*. Certain scenes began as animated bodies, and then the actors read their lines while watching the bodies' movements. Finally, the animators created facial expressions and mouth motions that matched the dialogue and had the computer place them on the bodies of the characters.

Foley Sounds

Foley is a term used to describe the re-created sounds caused by characters as they move around in a scene. The name originates from the man who invented the process, Jack Foley, who worked for Universal Pictures during the transition from silent movies to the early "talkies." Foley would be called in to record sound effects tracks for silent movies that were being converted into talking pictures. As the silent movie had no audio to begin with, Foley would have to create all the action sounds for the entire movie. His technique of watching the film and reenacting the action moves is the basis for foley recording as we know it today. An example of a modern foley studio is shown in Figure 2.3.

Figure 2.3 Enterprise Post's foley studio. Notice the pits used to contain different materials used for making footsteps and other sounds.

Foley Artists and Stages

In order to add these re-created action sounds to a scene, you first need a person capable of simulating the scene using props that will make the correct sounds. These people, like Philip Singer, pictured in Figure 2.4, are called *foley artists*. Next, you need a space filled with the appropriate props where the foley artist can view the scene while recording footsteps, clothing sounds, door openings, and such. This is called the *foley stage,* and it can be quite an interesting place to see. For instance, during the recording of a fight scene you might see telephone books used for body punches or a staple gun used to imitate a real gun. We'll explore the foley stage in depth in Chapter 5.

Figure 2.4 Philip Rodrigues Singer, a foley artist, hard at work on the foley stage.

Creating Foley with Sampling and FX Libraries

When budgets are tight and you don't have access to a foley stage, sound effect libraries can help you put a foley track together. However, it can be quite tedious to use the same 14 footsteps on a CD for an entire movie! Placement of each footstep must be done one by one. Samplers can be used to make the most of pre-recorded sounds. For instance, a sampler can pitch footsteps up or down to provide variations and help them sound more realistic. Samplers can also be played in real-time, allowing for quicker placement to the picture.

Foley from Wild Production Audio

Often it can be advantageous to gather foley sounds on location at the film shoot in order to capture the ambience of that space. This way, footsteps and other foley elements will have the same ambience as the dialogue for that scene. Plus, you can use unique items such as very large doors or fixed mechanical items that you can't drag into a studio. Be aware that sets might not be built out of material that sounds right. For example, plywood floors might be painted to look like marble, but on-screen you want to hear the footsteps as if they *are* walking on marble. Real-life locations like the one in Figure 2.5 provide the best opportunity to capture ambience and sounds that will match the scene that was shot there.

Figure 2.5   Here I am on location, gathering sounds of American Bison for use in a museum exhibit in Florida. I recorded these sounds directly to a laptop computer for easier importing into Pro Tools.

Sound Effects

Any sound that could not realistically be made by one of the characters on-screen can be considered a sound effect, such as the sounds of cars, boats, and planes. Sound effects have a powerful impact on the way viewers react to a movie or video. Because they are not usually recorded during filming, they can be altered to change the mood or pace of a scene. In this way, they become part of the creative design of a film or video.

Sound Design   The term *sound design* refers to the creative aspect of recording and mixing audio. Just as a film has a "look" to it, it also has a "sound" that is consistent throughout the movie. Creating the sonic texture and character is the job of the sound designer. Usually there is a sound designer credit given in movies, and sound designers can even win Oscars.

Sound design has become a staple of film-making, television, and even commercials. Usually, music provides the first clue, but a *sound effect* could also be what first tells you what show you're watching. Whenever you hear that hammer-hitting effect on TV, you know one of the *Law & Order* series shows is about to come on.

There are three basic categories of sound effects; the following subsections describe each category.

Ambience

Ambience is the background sound of a scene. If you filmed in an open field, you would expect to hear the sound of a gentle breeze and maybe some crickets and a bird or two in the distance. Well-executed ambience tracks can really help create the effect of envelopment and "being there" for the viewer.

Bigger than Life Sounds

Explosions, explosions, explosions... Most explosions you see and hear in the movies and TV don't sound the way explosions do in real life. Real explosions are usually dull thuds that don't have a lot of drama to them other than the destruction they cause. In a movie, the audience needs to feel the power of something like that without actually being there. Augmenting these sounds so they are bigger than life can help the drama become real to the viewer. Take, for example, the movie *Backdraft*. The sound of the fire in that movie is not realistic at all. There are sounds of wolves and bears mixed in with other things in order to create the sound of a living creature out of the fire. Even though the fire is not alive, the sound designer wants us to think of it as evil and menacing, thereby heightening the drama.

Imaginary Sounds

Sound effects can also be imaginary, like ghostly sounds, laser blasts, and rockets that make sounds in space. They can also be enhancement or augmentation of sounds that characters might make. Consider the machine-like sounds of R2-D2 in *Star Wars*. As we don't know what a real robot might sound like, its sounds are, in essence, imaginary. However, they also function as the foley sound of R2-D2's character. I would consider them sound effects first, rather than foley. The lines are blurred in a case like this, but for the purposes of this book, let's consider any imaginary sound to be an effect.

Music

Music is one of the most important layers of any soundtrack. Film composers watch the edited video in a studio like the one in Figure 2.6 and then create original music that follows the video. Music helps set the tone and emotion for any scene. It can also be the

Figure 2.6 The music composition suite of Douglas Thornton at Postscores. Film scores, jingles, and other musical pieces are created here, using Pro Tools.

only sound element in, for instance, a music video. There are four basic varieties of music in a soundtrack.

- **The score.** The background music you hear in films and commercials is called the *score*. This music is composed to fit the picture specifically and can really add to the story through the emotions we feel as listeners.

- **The jingle.** The jingle is a piece of music that is composed specifically for a commercial. Typically, the music includes lyrics and singing that relate to the product or service being advertised. When vocals are present, the jingle is usually in the foreground as the focus of the soundtrack. When the vocals are not in the mix, the music functions like a score. It is in the background supporting the dialogue and any other sounds that are present.

- **Environmental music.** Music that is part of the actual scene is called *environmental music*. This takes the form of radios in cars, music in bars, and elevator music, among other things. Environmental music must sound as though it is emanating from the visual image itself. There are many ways this can be done in a mix, for instance, running the music through a small speaker in the studio and recording that to emulate music from a clock radio.

- **Soundtrack music.** Soundtrack music is similar to the score in the sense that it is emanating from somewhere other than inside the picture. Usually, soundtrack music is some form of popular music that is placed during a section without dialogue, such as the ending credits or maybe an action sequence. The song is the main focus rather than the dialogue or effects. A music video is the best example of soundtrack music as, in a music video, there is usually no other audio except the song itself.

By this point, you might be asking yourself, "This is all fine and good, but how does Pro Tools fit in?"

How Does Pro Tools Help?

Pro Tools is the ultimate audio tool for post-production. Let's go over a few key features of Pro Tools that make this process so much easier.

The Non-Linear, Non-Destructive Editing Model

The traditional method of using an analog tape machine to record dialogue, foley, sound effects, and music required a painstaking process of recording each sound separately. Editing audio meant cutting up the tape itself, rearranging it, and piecing it back together again by hand. Working on long-format projects required many reels of tape and hours of rewind and fast-forward time.

Using Pro Tools, you now have the ability to change when and how sounds are played back without permanently altering or destroying the original audio. You can instantly move from the end of a long piece to the beginning. You can effortlessly create perfect duplicates of a sound and place them wherever you like. You can save different versions of your work without losing the original. You can snip, clip, cut, and paste pieces of audio, rearranging them in limitless ways, all in the digital realm and without any loss of quality.

Think about the difference between the word processor I'm using right now and traditional pen and paper. Pen and paper are linear and destructive methods of writing. The word processor is non-linear and non-destructive. Analog recording is linear and destructive. Pro Tools is non-linear and non-destructive.

QuickTime Movie Support

Usually when creating soundtracks, you must watch the video or film in sync with audio and be able to quickly locate different sections of a scene. Pro Tools can be synchronized to QuickTime movies without the need for costly additional hardware. When a QuickTime movie is imported into Pro Tools, a window is created that allows you to watch the video while Pro Tools is playing, as shown in Figure 2.7. Whenever playback begins, the video runs right along in sync. Wherever you click the Selector tool in the timeline, the QuickTime movie will immediately jump to that point and display that frame of video. Each time you move a region in the timeline, the video window shows you what image coincides with the beginning of the audio region. If you were placing the sound of a glass hitting the floor, each time the region was moved you could see which frame is the one where the glass actually touches the floor. That way, the crashing sound begins right when the glass hits. This is just one example of how Pro Tools makes it convenient to work with movies and video. In Chapter 5, I discuss these possibilities in depth.

Figure 2.7 The QuickTime movie window in Pro Tools.

Automation, Automation, Automation

Pro Tools has extensive automation features that help polish the production when it comes time to mix your project. Pro Tools allows automation of almost every parameter involved in mixing, from level and pan controls to plug-in parameters such as reverb time and EQ settings. Figure 2.8 shows an example of volume automation displayed over the waveform. Being able to tweak very minute details can save the day and your project. Mastering the automation modes will give you key skills that will put your productions ahead of the competition.

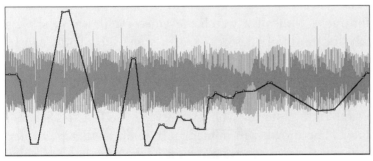

Figure 2.8 View of an automation playlist in Pro Tools.

Multi-Channel Mixing

In addition to automation, Pro Tools has the capability to mix to many different formats, such as good old stereo, Quad, LCR, LCRS, 5.1 (as shown in Figure 2.9), 6.1, and even mega-surround with 7.1. In today's world of ever-changing audio/video formats, this type of flexibility is a must. For a detailed explanation of mixing formats, see Chapter 6, "Editing to Picture." In that chapter, you learn how to set up Pro Tools to mix to these varied formats.

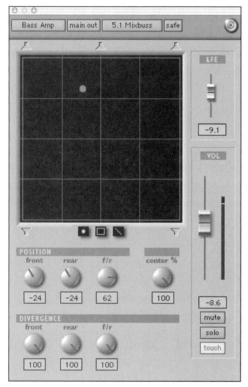

Figure 2.9   A surround-sound panner in Pro Tools.

The Standard in Hollywood

Pro Tools has become the standard DAW used in the film industry. It has been used in nearly every major motion picture released in the U.S. over the past five to ten years, including extensive use in *Star Wars Episode I*. The entire audio post-production community is familiar with Pro Tools. As a Pro Tools user, you have an advantage in being able to interchange audio directly with other studios and work with the popular Avid video editing systems quite easily. I will go into detail on the subject of interchanging files in Chapter 4, "Getting Started with Pro Tools and Video," and in Chapter 7, "Processing Audio Using Audiosuite Plug-Ins."

Project Workflow

Let's follow a sample project through all the phases of creation. Let's say you're the post-production audio engineer. A production company has hired you to complete the audio production once the video shoot and edit have been completed. Someone else will handle the recording of audio during the shoot. You are in charge of anything that needs to be recorded after the shoot, editing all the audio, and mixing everything into a final, complete format.

The whole process can be divided into three main phases: *pre-production* (the planning stage), *production* (usually referred to as filming or videotaping), and *post-production* (editing and mixing). Even though Pro Tools is primarily used in post-production, it is important to understand all the phases, as they will affect what you do in post-production. Decisions made at the beginning of a project can have a profound effect on the final result. Let's begin with the planning, or pre-production, phase.

Pre-Production (Planning and Preparing)

During pre-production, the key creative and technical people meet in person or by phone to discuss several issues, including scheduling, deadlines, scripts, creative content, technical personnel, talent, and budgets. Scripts and storyboards are put together so that everyone can get an idea of what the project calls for.

What Is the Project Going to Be?

First you need to know what it is you're going to create. Is it a short film? A commercial? A feature length movie? A Flash movie for the Internet? A corporate training film? All of these projects have different needs and special considerations to keep in mind.

For the purposes of our example, let's imagine your project is going to be a 30-second TV commercial for SuperSuds soap. You already know the length by definition. That's a good start. You also know the commercial will be for television broadcast and will probably be mixed in stereo. You will not need surround sound. You are going to be selling something, so vocal clarity is very important. In TV commercials there is usually some music and at least some dialogue in the form of narration and/or on-screen characters. You have extracted this much information just by knowing what kind of project you're working on. Amazing!

Next, it's a really good idea to know who is going to be watching this commercial. Having this information can be helpful in how you approach each step in recording and mixing. If the commercial is for kids, for instance, things are going to be more active in the mix and probably not very subtle. If the commercial is for senior citizens, maybe a more pleasant and smooth sound is the way to go. You get the idea.

Who Are You Working With?

As you will be working with several people very closely on this project, it's a good idea to get to know them and understand what their jobs are. Usually a meeting will be held including everyone involved with the project. At that meeting, a script will be presented (check it out in Appendix A) that will describe the commercial in detail. It will have descriptions of the scene, characters, written dialogue, and cues for sound effects and music. Now is the time to discuss this project with other members of the creative and technical staff. Discussing the project is important for several reasons. First, you must learn about the creative vision and overall concept that the others have. Learning the vision for the commercial can give you ideas and help you add to its overall effectiveness. Next, you need to discuss technical requirements for each phase of the production. This can be a real headache later if standards are not agreed to early on.

Your opinions about this commercial might differ from others involved. A meeting can eliminate potential conflicts before they occur. Each member of the team has to work together in order to create the final product. Your job as the post-production sound engineer is but one piece in the puzzle. Creative meetings help the puzzle fit together perfectly.

Here is a list of the primary players involved in creating this fictional commercial:

- **The Producer.** Simply put, the producer is the boss. Typically, a producer runs the business side of the project, dealing with budgets, hiring or firing people, and overseeing the whole project. In the end, producers are responsible for everything. They "produce" the finished product, in our case a commercial. The producer of our fictitious commercial is Susan. She drinks a lot of coffee.

- **The Director.** The director plays a more creative role than the producer and is in charge of keeping all the technical people working together. The director takes a guiding role during filming, controlling how the talent acts out the script and determining what angles the camera shoots from. A director is also involved in the editing of the footage and in the audio editing and mixing. He will oversee your work and guide you so that the creative vision remains consistent throughout the entire production. Get to know the director and what he expects from you. For our soap commercial, the director's name is Jack, and he's a really nice guy. He wears sunglasses and is glued to his cell phone 24/7.

Who's in Charge?   In this example I have simplified the supervisory roles to include only a producer and a director. In reality, there may be several other persons involved in directing and controlling the creative process. The client themselves (SuperSuds) might be directly involved in the creation of a television commercial. The ad agency that they hired to create the commercial might also work with you directly. The permutations of creative control in a situation like this are almost endless. For this example, the producer will function as a manager of all the people involved, and the director will function as the single person with creative control. The politics of this job are going to be easy!

- **The Production Sound Mixer.** The person who records the audio during filming is the production sound mixer. It is a good idea to meet this person and find out how she will record this commercial. Is she planning to use lavalier mics or shotgun boom mics? Will she record to DAT or into the camera in the case of video? What SMPTE time code format will be used? These are questions worth asking at the beginning of a project so that there will be less confusion later. Ideally, the sound mixer will take notes during filming that can be used later in post-production. The notes will typically list which take occurred at what time code number and other useful information, such as what mic is on each channel. The sound mixer for our project is Jodie, and she eats sushi all the time. For our project, Jodie is going to use a combination of lavalier and boom mics and record directly into the camera, as this will be a video shoot. The time code will be 29.97fps non-drop frame.

- **Video Editors, Film Editors, and Web Designers.** A video or picture editor handles the technical aspects of editing the different scenes and camera angles together with the corresponding production audio. When the editor has finished at least a rough edit of your commercial, he will give you the edited audio (in some form) and a video for you to use in post-production. The transfer process can be simple or terribly complex and difficult. It is a good idea to establish a relationship with the video editor and understand how you will exchange audio and video with him. Our video editor is Justin, and he likes cinnamon-raisin bagels. He'll be editing on an Avid system (see Figure 2.10). When dealing with Internet media, the Web designer functions as a video editor. She will create the moving images that you will work with. Flash movies and other Internet media have special requirements that we discuss in Chapter 7.

How Will You Exchange Audio?

In order to work efficiently and reduce the amount of mistakes and confusion, standards for exchanging audio throughout the project must be agreed upon by the technical personnel involved. In today's digital world, you are presented with a maze of options when transferring audio between workstations. Each phase of a project might require

Figure 2.10   A video-editing suite. This one has several workstations, allowing graphics generation to take place alongside the video editing. Usually a video editor will work with an assistant who helps by loading tapes, editing graphics, and getting lunch!

a different audio format because of equipment variances, personal preferences, and availability. Gradually the audio exchange process is becoming more streamlined, and A.E.S. (the Audio Engineering Society) is working on new standards that will help. Many manufacturers are currently using the Broadcast Wave format; it allows transfers of audio and edit data easily across different platforms.

Let's take a look at the audio exchange possibilities.

- **Acquisition.** Acquiring and gathering audio is the first step, and the format you choose can speed up or slow down the rest of the project. As far as filming is concerned, the audio format is determined by the recording machine. DAT tapes have been used for many years, but the ability to record directly to hard disk on location using devices like the DEVA recorder (shown in Figure 2.11) or even by running Pro Tools on a laptop has rapidly taken over as the standard recording method. The TV show *Survivor* used a Pro Tools Digi 001 system to capture audio on location. A multi-channel system like that allows you to record multiple microphones without mixing them together, thereby giving you flexibility later on. This makes it very easy to transfer those files to another Pro Tools workstation for later editing.

You will always need to get sounds outside of the filming process for use as sound effects and foley. Because DAT machines are a dying breed these days, using a hard disk or solid state field recorder would be preferable for this. When recording, be aware of what file format you're using. The native file format for Pro Tools is

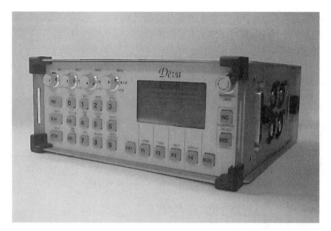

Figure 2.11 The Zaxcom DEVA hard disk field recorder uses the Broadcast Wave file format as one available option.

Broadcast Wave (BWF/WAV) or AIFF. Consider what format the video editor might prefer.

As Justin is using an Avid system, the native supported file formats are the same.

- **Audio and Video Interchange.** The next format issue is the interchange of audio between the video system and Pro Tools. The simplest way of accomplishing this interchange is to record the audio out of the video editing system onto a synchronized tape machine and then record that into Pro Tools. As long as proper sync was maintained throughout the process, you now have a mixed version of the audio from the video editor. However, due to the complex nature of your task, this might not be good enough. It is often necessary to have all the source audio files that the video editor used and the information necessary to play portions of those audio files in the correct order so that the audio will be in sync with the picture. This editing information is called an *edit decision list,* or *EDL.* You will need a method of transfer that brings across all the source audio files and necessary EDL information so that every editing and mixing option is available to you after the transfer.

Session Data and the EDL   Each Pro Tools session contains six main items, as shown in Figure 2.12:

- The Session Document or Pro Tools File. (There may be more than one! Here, there are three versions of the SuperSuds 30-second soap commercial.)

- Audio files (in a folder).

- Fade files (in another folder).

- Region groups (in yet another folder).

- Session file backups (in the fourth and final folder).

- WaveCache.wfm (this file contains the waveform graphical data for the audio files).

The Pro Tools session document contains all the information necessary to place all or portions of each audio file in the timeline at certain locations. This information comprises the *edit decision list*, or EDL. It also contains mixing information such as volume, pan, and plug-in settings for EQ and compression. The same is true for video editing software—it must have an EDL in order to know how to play back the video and audio clips. When transferring audio and video data between different editors, it is necessary to also transfer EDL information so that the receiving editor will have the information necessary to play the audio and video back in the proper sequence.

> ▶   Audio Files
> ▶   Fade Files
> ▶   Region Groups
> ▶   Session File Backups
>   SuperSuds Soap 30 –02.ptf
>   SuperSuds Soap 30 –03.ptf
>   SuperSuds Soap 30.ptf
>   WaveCache.wfm

Figure 2.12   The elements of a session. Here is what you will find inside a Pro Tools session folder.

Back to the list of formats, the most common way to transfer audio between platforms involves using AAF files (Advanced Authoring Format). AAFs are multimedia files that can contain the audio data, EDL data, and video data in one standardized format. Created by Avid, Digidesign, and other media software companies, AAF files are a new standard used throughout the industry. If the video system does not support AAF or the older OMF files, things can get complicated quickly. I'll talk more about AAF files, OMF files, and other methods of interchange in Chapter 5. For now, Justin agrees that you should use AAF files for interchange.

- **Delivery.** Once you have completed a final mix of the commercial, it must be put back together with the edited video on the master tape. This is typically called the layback process, or "laying back to tape." Because our commercial is for broadcast video, you will be laying back to videotape. Justin will record, or *lay*, his finished video edit on a tape, and then your mix will be recorded onto the same tape in sync with the video in order to create the finished master. For this to work, you and Justin must be using the same standards in time code, tape format, and synchronization. Our master tape format for this commercial will be Digital Betacam, using 29.97fps (frames per second) non-drop SMPTE time code. In the case of film, you would have to create a master tape, maybe in a surround format, that can be converted into an optical track for the film print. This is quite a bit more complex, and I'll talk more about film mixing in Chapter 3, "Synchronization and SMPTE Time Code."

■ **Backup and Archival.** You must protect yourself from loss of data throughout the project. Hard drives crash, and the power occasionally goes out. Backing up daily and keeping copies of your sessions can reduce downtime (and expense!) due to data loss. Once you have completed the project, you need to back up and archive the data in case the producer, Susan, wishes to change something later, or in case the SuperSuds Soap Company wants to use the same commercial next year but change the voiceover. There are many possibilities for backing up your data. You read about them in Chapter 8, "Mixing to Picture in Pro Tools." Backup scenarios depend greatly on the hardware you have available. In our imaginary situation, you have a Mac G5 with a DVD burner that will back up to DVD data discs. Justin thought that was a good idea. We'll bring him some bagels next time we see him.

Production (Filming and Recording on a Set or on Location)

The production stage of a project primarily involves filming. Unless you are the production sound mixer, there is not much to do on the set. Nevertheless, other tasks need to be accomplished during this phase.

Keeping in Contact with the Film Crew

During filming you should stay in contact with the film crew to find out how everything is coming along, perhaps even stopping in at a convenient time to actually see how they are recording. Many things can change while filming—the script could be revised, or the whole thing could change creative directions. You never know. It's a good idea to talk to the sound mixer or the director during this period. If the script has changed, now would be a good time to get a current copy.

You have talked to Jodie, and everything seems to be running smoothly on the set. A couple of lines in the script have changed, and our director, Jack, now wants a special sound effect for the soapsuds that you will have to create. Good thing you talked to her, because now is a good time to start creating any special effects.

Creating Cue Lists from Scripts

Now that you have an up-to-date script, let's put together a list of every audio event that is going to happen in the project. This is called a *cue sheet* or *cue list*. You can read through a written script and get a good idea of what sounds will be needed and where—for example, the opening of a door when a character enters the scene, or car sounds if there is a car in the script. You don't need to list absolutely everything, such as rustling clothes and individual footsteps, unless they are specific to the scene. You just want an idea of what the major sound events will be. Storyboards are even more help in this regard because they provide a visual indication of some of the action and can give you more clues as to what the sound requirements are.

Animation Dialogue

Animation is always a special case. During the production phase of an animated production, the first thing you must do is the recording of the dialogue, so that animators can draw the facial expressions and mouth movements of the recorded speech. This way, you are creating the production audio in the studio and not on a set. You learn more about this in Chapter 4.

Gathering Environmental Audio

You can use your laptop, field recorder, or DAT recorder to record sounds necessary for any special effects, ambience, and anything else you find on the cue sheet. Ambience is certainly an important sonic area to cover. In this case, you need the background sound of a farmyard, including all the animal noises. Some of these sounds you might find in a sound effects library, but certain ones you might prefer to record yourself in order to make them sound really sharp. The "soapy suds" sound effect is one that should also be really unique, according to our director. You could try setting up a tub of suds in the studio and recording different sudsy sounds, for example.

Let's say you decide to record the background ambience of the farmyard, as you've checked the effects library, and nothing in it seems to fit. As the original filming location is in a high-traffic area, it isn't suitable for ambience recording due to the high level of background noise from a nearby highway. You've arranged a time to go to another barnyard that has the animals you need and where the ambience will be appropriate. You might want to use a microphone with a wind baffle, such as the one shown in Figure 2.13.

Good. I feel like we're getting some real recording done here. Bagel, anyone?

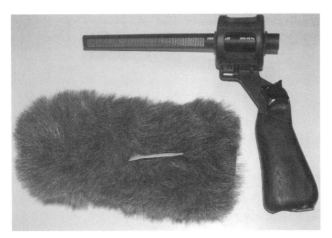

Figure 2.13 The Sennheiser MKH-416 is a popular shotgun microphone used to record dialogue, ambience, and other sounds on the set. It has a very tight, hyper-cardiod pickup pattern that is useful in minimizing unwanted noises from the recording.

Post-Production (Re-Recording, Sweetening, Editing, and Mixing)

The video shoot went well. You've just had a meeting with Jack, and he feels positive that you have a great commercial in the making. You played him your super-sudsy sound, and he loves it and feels it will add a new dimension to the *spot* (a term commonly used to refer to a commercial). Now, it's time for post-production. Post-production is where everything is put together. All of the different camera takes and angles are edited and combined with text and graphics. You record voiceovers, sound effects, and any other audio needed and then assemble them so that they work well with the picture. Let's discuss the cue list first.

Finalizing Cue Lists

Once the video is edited, at least as a *rough cut,* you can look at it and refine your cue list. It's a good idea to do this as soon as possible in order to eliminate any sounds that aren't needed and to determine whether any new sounds should be added. Now, the job is laid out for you.

Transferring Audio from the Video Editor

Justin has provided us with an AAF file as he agreed to do back in pre-production. This AAF file can be translated into a Pro Tools session using Digitranslator. This piece of software reads the AAF file and extracts audio files, EDLs, and even crossfade and automation data. It will then create a Pro Tools session. This session should have all of the edits that the video editor made to the production audio and any additional audio tracks such as scratch tracks containing music, effects, and/or voiceovers. Often, directors will have the video editor put in these temporary sound elements to help the editing process. They can be used as a guide for placing final sound elements.

Record Any Additional Audio

Our AAF file contains dialogue from the production audio and the reference video only. You have translated the AAF into a Pro Tools session and opened it up to see what's there. Everything looks good, but the audio ends around 19 seconds into the spot. After looking at the script again, you realize that the voiceover starts at about 19 seconds. Because Jack and Justin adjust the timing of the video edits to any dialogue that occurs, you need to record the voiceover now so they can continue editing.

The following list explores how you record each audio element in the production. Once this is done, you can start editing everything to fit the video.

- **Voiceovers.** Jack has told you that the announcer's lines need to last for eight seconds in order for the video edit to work well. This was also planned out during the pre-production phase. It is your job now to make sure that the voiceover fits this space. The voiceover talent is very professional, and within a few takes you have what you need for the ending. The take that Jack liked is 8.5 seconds long, so you need to edit out one breath and change some spacing to make it fit. (You'll find out how to do this in Chapter 5.) Because the final voiceover file is relatively small, you have emailed it to Justin in order to keep us on schedule. This has saved a decent amount of time. Pretty cool, eh? Now, Justin owes you lunch.

- **ADR dialogue replacement.** While filming, the farm was quiet enough that all of the dialogue was usable except one piece. The line that both farm boys say together when they come running up to their mother was too far off the boom mic to sound good. You need to replace that line with a new one recorded in the studio using a process called ADR.

  You'll need to get the actors that played the farm boys back in the studio to do this. Jack has made some calls and found out that both of them are busy on another gig and won't be available for two days. You don't have that much time, and as there is only one line that needs replacing, Jack has decided to use other actors to read the line for the boys. You should have no problem creating the illusion that the voices you use are actually the same as the boys on film. This sort of thing happens often when a director likes an actor's face but not his voice. In our case, we are doing this for more practical reasons. In Chapter 5, I will go into detail about how to set this session up and get perfect lip sync, even using talent that was not in the original filming.

- **Foley and sound effects.** Next, you must record and edit the foley sounds and any special effects, such as the "soapy suds" sound you created in pre-production. You will use your cue sheet as a checklist for this step. First, you need barnyard ambience, including chickens, goats, horses, dogs, and miscellaneous birds. The base ambient track that you recorded on location has the general ambience of a rural setting, including wind in the trees, occasional bird chirps, and a couple of distant dog barks. That covers some of what you need. The specific chickens, goats, and horses you will have to get from a sound effects library. The sounds from the library can be placed wherever you choose, which will be helpful in keeping the dialogue clear. You don't want a goat "baaahing" over one of the mother's lines, do you?

  Even though the script does not specifically say it, you will need the screen door sound when the mother comes out of the house, her footsteps across the lawn, and the boys' running footsteps as they approach her. The end of the commercial shows the family standing outside. You could put more ambience there, but the music and voiceover will overshadow this, and they are really the focus at that point. Don't forget the soapy suds sound when the mother dunks her laundry in the tub. This is a signature sound that will really stand out in the mix. In Chapter 5, I'll go into detail on how to record foley and use a sound effects library to enhance your soundtracks with a high level of detail.

- **Music.** Music plays an incredibly important role in film, video, and all sorts of multimedia. It can establish a mood, set the pace, and highlight the action in many ways. In our commercial, the SuperSuds music, or jingle, has been adapted into a country style by the composer. Her name is Shirley, and she lives in Nashville, so the jingle has a real down-home country sound to it. Shirley has mailed us a CD of the finished music that you will import into Pro Tools and use at the end, during the voiceover. Sometimes music will come in different formats. For instance, Shirley has sent us several variations of her jingle. The first is with a full band and has singing all the way through it. It's 30 seconds long. Next, she has the instrumental version of the first. Third, there is an acoustic version that has no drums or bass guitar in it. She sent that one with and without vocals. And finally, she sent a version that is the vocals only or a'capella version.

You can use these versions to create alternate mixes to suit your needs. In this case, the music plays only during the last 11 seconds of the commercial, and the singing occurs only on the last line, "SuperSuds, for that country-fresh scent." You will have to edit pieces of different versions together in order to create the one you need for this spot. Many times, the music will be recorded specifically for a given script and will not need editing, but in our case the music was written some time ago, before this script was even conceived. Chapter 4 contains all the details about music editing and mix stems.

Editing Audio to Picture

Now that you have all the elements recorded or imported into Pro Tools, it's time to edit them to picture. This involves synchronizing Pro Tools to the edited video and aligning all the audio regions so that they occur at the right times, in sync with the action. This is where Pro Tools really shines. There are so many helpful tools for this phase that it makes me feel all warm and fuzzy inside just thinking about it.

You can't begin to edit to picture if you don't have a picture to look at. The video editor must supply a finished edit of the video for you to work with. This could come in the format of a videotape or a digital movie file such as a QuickTime or MPEG file.

You have two choices for synchronization: You can lock Pro Tools to an external video playback device (a tape machine, hard disk video player such as the Doremi V1, or another computer running software such as Virtual VTR) using SMPTE or you can use the Import Movie function in Pro Tools itself to synchronize a digital movie file to the audio in Pro Tools. The second option is becoming the preferred way of working these days. Digital files can be sent via the Internet, and no expensive tape deck is required to play them back. Pro Tools is also much quicker and more efficient when working with digital files than with videotape. In pre-production, you decided to use a QuickTime format for video synchronization. Justin has put a QuickTime file of the finished commercial on a CD-ROM and had it sent to your studio. We'll get him some extra bagels for this.

Once you have imported this movie file into Pro Tools (much, much more on this in Chapter 4), it might be helpful to put in some markers to indicate where sounds are supposed to go. This way, you have a visual indicator of certain key times during the commercial. You can do this on-the-fly as Pro Tools is playing, or you can manually enter time code numbers to specify locations where markers will be placed (Chapter 6 has more details on this). By creating markers you can put your cue list into Pro Tools—doing so will help you remember everything you need to do in order to finish the commercial. Granted, a 30-second spot might not have that many cues to remember, but in longer-form material such as feature films, the cue list could be a book unto itself. Managing a cue list like that can be a formidable task.

You can now use these markers to place your audio roughly where it needs to be in relation to the video image. Then you can watch the spot to see if any timings need to be changed. If they do, you can use the nudging feature to move audio in set increments to correct the timing. Chapter 6 will go into great detail on all the ways to bounce, nudge, trim, and edit your audio.

Now that everything is in place and you've double-checked your cue list, you should get Jack, the director, to come in and approve everything before you begin mixing. Jack liked everything you did, but he wanted fewer animal noises in the beginning. He decided the goat sound had to go, as it didn't exactly say "clean and fresh." You have obliged him and now are ready to mix all the tracks together.

Mixing Down Tracks to Picture

Now all of these elements must be combined to produce a finished soundtrack. The finished product should have clarity, smoothness, and believability, so that the viewer is drawn into the commercial and mesmerized into buying SuperSuds. It must also conform to broadcast standards so that it can be used by TV stations without altering the recording levels.

You will watch the finished video in sync with the session to see how it all sounds together. You will adjust levels of different tracks so that each element is in balance with all the rest, and the overall level does not exceed the standards you have to abide by. (There's much more about broadcast standards and film mixing conventions in Chapter 7.) For any anomalies in each track, you can use the powerful automation available in Pro Tools to compensate. What used to take several operators and a console the size of a banquet table can now be done by one person using a keyboard and a mouse. Amazing!

Once you have mixed the commercial to your satisfaction, you need to get Jack and Susan and perhaps Justin to come listen to your work and see what they think. It's always a good idea to get a fresh opinion on something that you've been working closely on for any amount of time. Jack feels the music at the end is too loud, causing the voiceover to lose clarity. You adjust the level to his liking and save the session. After he leaves, you try returning the level of the music but applying some careful EQ adjustments in order to create more space for the voiceover. You save this session using a different name in case Jack doesn't like your new EQ method. You now have two versions of the mix, and you'll have Jack and Susan listen to them both and decide which one will be the final version.

Delivering Master Recordings (Layback)

The next day, it is time to record the final mix onto the master videotape. This tape will be used to create the copies that go to each TV station that is airing the commercial. This is an important step because it is the last time you will have any control over the audio before the audience hears it.

First, you get both the producer and director (Susan and Jack, respectively, or whomever has creative control, be it the client, ad agency, and so on) in for a decision on which version of the mix will be the final one. You play each mix for them without telling them what the differences are. That way, they can make a more objective decision. Both Jack and Susan agree that the mix with your new EQ setting on the music sounds fuller without losing clarity in the voiceover at the end. Great, you are now ready to record the final mix onto the master videotape. This process is typically called *layback* or *laying* the mix *back* to tape.

In pre-production you determined what the format of the master tape was going to be, allowing you to now prepare a mix that will be compatible with the format you've chosen. As the master is on Digital Betacam, you will use a digital connection to the video tape deck at a sample rate of 48kHz and a bit depth of 20 bits. You will be locked to 29.97 non-drop time code for synchronization. You record the mix on videotape and then listen to it to make absolutely sure that everything was recorded to tape correctly. Once you have heard the result and the record tab on the tape has been switched to the safe position, you can relax, knowing that your job has been well done. Let's go have one of those bagels with Justin. He still owes you lunch!

Layback at the Video Studio   In this chapter I am describing the layback process that would occur if your studio had layback capability and the decision was made to layback the audio there. Typically, laybacks are performed at a video post-production facility. You would be required to provide a completed mix in whatever format the video facility requires. I go over all of these possibilities in Chapter 9, "Delivery of Master Recordings."

This chapter was designed as a general overview in order to give you a big-picture view of what's involved in a multimedia project. Now that you have a basic understanding of how audio production is handled as far as workflow, the issue of synchronization must be addressed. In order to understand synchronization, you need a comprehensive understanding of SMPTE time code. The next chapter addresses all aspects of SMPTE and how it is used in audio post-production.

3 Synchronization and SMPTE Time Code

In film and video two different media, visual and auditory, must be experienced together. In order to create sound that works seamlessly with visuals, you need two playback systems—one strictly for audio and another strictly for video. These two systems must be capable of playing back together in perfect time. The process of making two or more distinct audio or visual systems play back together is called *synchronization*.

Synchronization is a basic principle of working with audio for video and film. Any alteration of the audio must be done in the context of the visual image. It wouldn't be possible to establish and control the relationship between the two media without synchronization. A thorough mastery of the concepts and practices of synchronization will become invaluable as you get deeper and deeper into audio post-production. This chapter is devoted to synchronization theory, techniques, and real-world practices that you will use every day when creating sound for films and video.

Synchronization Basics

As I said, synchronization is the process of keeping two or more audio or visual systems running at the same speed and with the same relationship to each other. Keeping audio in sync with video means playing both together from the same point without either one moving faster or slower than the other. It is crucial to do this with a high degree of accuracy and repeatability, as every single edit and mix move you perform must be matched up with a certain action on-screen.

Two things are necessary for accurate sync. The first is a positional reference, or the "where-in-time." The second is a playback rate, or "how fast." I like to use the analogy of cars on a two-lane highway. The positional references are the mile markers on the side of the highway that tell you where on the road you are. The playback rate is the speed of the car, for instance 65 mph. If you know what mile marker you're at and how fast you're traveling, it's easy to get another car moving along in sync with your car. Think of the audio as one car and the video as a second car in the next lane. If either car speeds up or slows down, the two cars will no longer be in sync. The drivers of these two cars must be in constant communication with one another in order to maintain the correct speed and position. With Pro Tools and digital audio, this communication is handled in two ways—one for positional information and the other for speed reference.

Digital audio is based on a sampling frequency that determines how often the analog audio is digitally sampled and turned into numeric information. The source of this sampling frequency is referred to as the *digital clock* and is required for proper operation of any digital audio device. If the sampling frequency or clock *speed* is changed, the speed at which audio is played back will change accordingly. If the clock speed increases, digital audio will play back faster and higher in pitch. If the clock speed slows, audio will play back slower and lower in pitch. Thus, the sampling frequency can control the speed of the audio. This is how the speed reference for synchronization is communicated when using Pro Tools.

Positional Reference

You must assign unique numbers to each segment of audio and video in a project in order to know exactly where you are at any given point in either medium. For instance, bars and beat numbers can be used to identify locations in a piece of music. In visual systems, each frame of film or video must be given a unique number. This is accomplished through the use of SMPTE (Society of Motion Picture and Television Engineers) time code.

Every frame of film or video in an AV project may have a specific SMPTE time code number assigned to it. SMPTE time code is the standard method by which you get positional references in audio, film, and video (see Figure 3.1). SMPTE time code represents time in an eight-digit number with colons separating each time value for hours, minutes, seconds, and frames (00h:00m:00s:00f). A frame of SMPTE can be as small as 1/60th of a second or as large as 1/24th of a second, depending on how fast the film or video is moving. I'll discuss the different frame rates in more depth in just a bit. For now, understand that SMPTE time code numbers are positional references—they tell you where you are in a soundtrack or film.

Playback Rate

The second thing you need to know to achieve accurate synchronization is how fast the frames are moving. In my highway analogy, this relates to the speed of the two cars. In film and video, the playback rate is the frame rate. In digital audio, the playback rate is the sample rate or sampling frequency. The speed relationship between the audio and video must remain the same in order to be in sync. Otherwise, the audio will either slip ahead of or behind the video.

Figure 3.1 An SMPTE readout displaying 1 hour, 11 minutes, 45 seconds, and 24 frames.

Several standard frame rates for film and video are commonly used. They are as follows:

- 24 frames per second for film

- 25 frames per second for European or PAL video

- 29.97 frames per second for NTSC color video

- 30 frames per second for audio only or old B&W television

- 23.976 frames per second for HD video that converts to NTSC video

- 59.94 frames per second for HD video that converts to NTSC video (29.97 × 2) (often mistakenly referred to as 60fps)

- 60 frames per second for HD video at its highest standard speed

In digital audio, the rate at which sound is played back is not measured in frames but in samples. Each sample of audio is a unit of information, or slice of time, much in the same way that each frame of film or video is a single snapshot of time, although an audio sample is exponentially smaller in duration. The rate at which samples are played back (the *sample rate*) is usually expressed in kilohertz (abbreviated kHz); multiplying the kilohertz number by 1,000 results in the number of samples per second—for example, 44.1kHz represents a rate of 44,100 samples per second.

There are several sample rates commonly used in audio production. They are as follows:

- **44.1kHz:** The standard music sample rate. This is used to create the commercial music CDs people buy everyday.

- **48kHz:** The video and film standard. Professional digital video formats such as Sony's Digital Betacam use this sample rate.

- **88.2kHz:** Hi-res music sample rate for audio CDs. Easily converts to 44.1kHz.

- **96kHz:** Hi-res sample rate for music and video; it is a multiple of 48kHz and is easier to convert.

- **192kHz:** Super hi-res sample rate for demanding recordings such as orchestral, jazz, and archival recordings. Currently impractical for film and video due to large file sizes, but may be used in the near future.

To sum up, in order to synchronize audio and video, you must know the positional information, in the form of SMPTE time code and playback speed. Audio and video must start from the same position and play back at the same rate in order to maintain perfect sync. This might sound simple, but as you will see, it can get quite complicated once you consider all the variations in SMPTE formats and playback rates.

Origin and History of Time Code

In order to better understand the variety of SMPTE formats, let's take a look at how time code developed and eventually turned into the SMPTE format.

Film

In the early days of film, scenes were filmed from beginning to end with one camera and in one complete take. Film scenes paralleled the way plays on stage were viewed. The only editing that would take place would be to cut all the scenes together in the correct order. The high-speed edits and rapid-fire cuts that are the norm today were simply not used in early film.

Gradually, as filmmakers began to explore the new medium, new techniques of filming caught on. Soon, scenes were filmed in multiple takes using different camera angles, in order to capture the action in new and exciting ways. These new filming techniques made the editing process much more complicated, as each scene had multiple edits throughout. Keeping track of all the pieces of film and where they went became an arduous process. Film editors needed a system that allowed them to keep notes about their editing and exchange that information with other editors. They began to write on the edge of the film, placing notes and then numbers to help the editing process. This evolved into the use of "feet and frames" as a measuring tool. Each second of film contains 24 individual frames. A foot-long piece of 35mm film has 15 frames in it. Using feet and frames with edge numbers made complicated editing much more feasible. This was the first time code, and it was used while editing film on machines similar to the one shown in Figure 3.2.

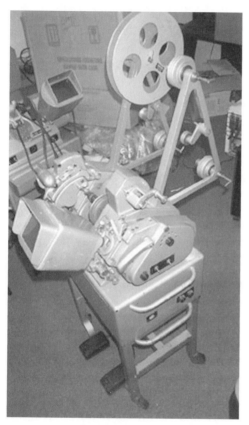

Figure 3.2 A Moviola machine that is still used to edit film and magnetic audio film together using the system of feet and frames for counting.

NTSC versus PAL

With the advent of television and then videotape recording, new editing systems developed that allowed video to be edited from multiple-source tapes onto a final master tape. Manufacturers of different videotape systems developed their own versions of editing systems that used proprietary time codes that were unusable by other systems. The lack of an industry-wide standard became a big problem because no one manufacturer's system could use another's time code information. In 1969, the Society of Motion Picture and Television Engineers developed a new time code standard that allowed all editing systems to speak the same language. However, there are still two different standards in video. The first is the NTSC video standard, which is used in America and Japan, for the most part. The second is the European video standard, called PAL (Phase Alternate Line) or EBU (European Broadcast Union).

The frame rate of television in the United States was based on the carrier frequency of electrical current coming out of the AC outlet. This was a convenient source of a stable time reference that video systems could use. Each frame of a NTSC video signal contains two fields, and each field contains half of the horizontal lines that comprise the video image—one field has all the even lines, and the other contains the odd lines. As the AC line frequency is 60Hz, engineers used that cycle to trigger each field of video. Black and white television had a resulting frame rate of 30 frames per second (60 cycles/2 fields per frame = 30 frames per second). With the advent of color TV, the frame rate had to be lowered by .1%, resulting in the 29.97 frame rate commonly used today. Obviously, video no longer uses the 60Hz AC line frequency to trigger video fields. Now, quartz clocks that can run at other speeds are used for more accuracy and dependability.

In Europe however, the reference frequency used in electrical systems is 50Hz. So the PAL/EBU system derives 25 frames per second from the 50 fields per second that the AC line frequency generates.

Color versus Black and White

When color video was developed, broadcasters wanted to keep the current black and white transmission system intact. Nobody wanted to force consumers to buy new televisions in order to see the new color broadcasts. Engineers finally came up with a system that allowed color TV to be backwards compatible with existing black and white televisions. Due to the frequencies involved, a slight adjustment had to be made to the frame rate in order for the new color system to work with both color and black and white televisions with predictable results. The frame rate was slowed down by .1%, resulting in a rate of 29.97 frames per second. This small adjustment allowed the new color TV broadcasts to be viewed on the older black and white TVs. All NTSC video systems in use today have a frame rate of 29.97fps. Audio-only productions typically use the old 30 frames per second code simply because it follows the real-time clock and can be easily divided into seconds for quick adjustments.

Although the new frame rate solved the problem of black and white compatibility, it created a new problem for video editors. As the new frame rate was a little slower than 30fps, it would not display the correct time in relation to the clock on the wall after a minute or so. This drift would increase as time went on. After an hour of real-time, 29.97 SMPTE reads: 00:59:56:12, a difference of over three seconds. For relatively short program material, such as commercials, this was not a problem. However, for anything longer than one minute, the time code drift is significant. This is where drop-frame time code comes to the rescue. Drop-frame SMPTE skips some frame numbers in order to achieve accurate real-time display. The actual video frames themselves are not lost. The time code merely skips certain frame numbers along the way, so that it can display the current real-time more precisely.

Time Code Calculators   A good way to understand how different types of SMPTE time code relate to one other is to use a time code calculator. Many freeware versions are available on the Web for both Mac and PC. Download one and start converting different types of SMPTE, starting with simple increments of time, such as one hour. You'll quickly see how each frame rate and frame count relates to another. Having one of these calculators around can be very handy when you're in the trenches, working.

Parameters of Time Code

SMPTE has only two parameters that affect the format. The first is the frame rate, which is how fast the time code is going. The second is the frame count, which determines which frame numbers are skipped in order to stay aligned with the real-time clock.

Now that you're armed with a basic understanding of SMPTE and how it works, I will describe each SMPTE format, what it is used for, and any quirks or problems associated with it.

Frame Rates

The different frame rates used in SMPTE time code correlate to the different number of still images used per second to create moving visual media. Here's a list of all major SMPTE frame rates, not including special versions used in transfers. Those will be covered later.

- **NTSC B&W Video 30fps:** 30fps is used only in music or audio-only applications. It will not line up with traditional video signals, because the standard definition video signals use either 29.97fps for NTSC or 25fps for PAL/EBU. 30fps does relate to pulled-up sample rates, which will be discussed later in this chapter. Also, straight HD video can be captured at 30fps.

- **NTSC Color Video 29.97fps:** This is and has been the standard frame rate for NTSC color video since its creation. Make sure you know whether you are using the drop-frame or non-drop-frame version of this frame rate.

- **PAL/EBU Video 25fps:** This frame rate is used in Europe and countries in which the PAL/EBU television system is used. Be careful not to confuse it with the film rate of 24fps.

- **Film 24fps:** Film is often shot at 24 frames per second, but may also be shot at 29.97fps or 30fps, depending upon production needs. Film may be transferred to video for use in a product whose final format is video or only for the purposes of editing, in which case a film cutter would return to the actual film to create the final version. Film-to-video transfers use different SMPTE frame rates in different situations. We will talk more about this later in the chapter.

- **24p HD Video 23.976fps:** DTV or hi-definition television cameras (HD for short) implement a frame rate of 23.976 called 24p. This is to help them look more like film than traditional video cameras. The rate is slightly slower than actual film in order to facilitate easier transfer to NTSC video at 29.97fps. Although it's possible for some HD cameras to shoot at a true 24 fps, 24p most often refers to a frame rate of 23.976 fps.

- **HD Video 50fps:** HD video for Europe and other PAL/SECAM regions. Conforms to twice the normal PAL frame rate of 25fps. This makes for easy conversion between the two.

- **HD Video 59.94fps:** HD video can be recorded at this high-speed frame rate. It is easily converted into NTSC standard definition since it is a multiple of 29.97fps.

- **HD Video 60fps:** This is currently the highest standard frame rate used. Some HD cameras always record at this frame rate and use internal conversions to create other frame rates from this data.

Frame Count

Recall that drop-frame time code skips certain frame numbers in order to maintain accurate real time in its display. The actual frames are not skipped, just their numbers. The frame count of SMPTE is determined by whether and how frame numbers are skipped. Drop-frame only applies to 29.97 SMPTE as all the other frame rates follow the clock exactly. It is common in software to see 30fps have a drop-frame and non-drop frame counts. This is somewhat of a misuse of the term (see the following sidebar).

Drop Frame

In order to lose those extra 18 frames in every 10 minutes, drop-frame must skip two frames every minute for nine minutes and none in the 10th minute, for a total of 18 frames in 10 minutes. This cycle repeats every 10 minutes. As there are 1,800 frames of video in 10 minutes at 30 frames per second, the 18 frame *numbers* that are skipped (remember, no video frames are skipped, just their numbers) correlate to the .1% speed change to color video at 29.97 frames per second. Now, the 29.97fps drop-frame time code number you see at the end of one real-time hour reads 01:00:00;00 on the time code display. (See Figure 3.3.)

Beware of 30 Drop-Frame Time Code   Many manufacturers, including Digidesign, label one time code format as 30fps drop-frame. This is not a real format. The term is commonly misused as a name for 29.97 drop-frame. If you think about it, 30fps does not need to drop frame numbers in order to be in sync with the real time clock. There would be no normal use for 30 drop frame time code. In Pro Tools, the time code options include both 29.97 drop-frame and 30 drop-frame. The 30 drop-frame is a true 30fps with skipped frame numbers. In relation to the real-time clock, this format runs faster and after one hour of real-time reads 01:00:03;18. This format is very misleading and should be used only when correcting errors in existing time code or when loading production audio from a film shoot shot at 30fps drop-frame, to be later pulled down to 29.97fps. Beware, and double check your time code format!

The Semicolons in Time Code Readouts   Whenever you see a SMPTE time code number that has a semicolon separating the seconds from the frame numbers, you are looking at drop-frame time code. Sometimes, all separators for drop-frame are semicolons. But beware—just because there are no semicolons in the display doesn't mean it is *not* drop-frame code.

Non-Drop Frame

Non-drop frame time code is simply time code that does not skip any frame numbers (see Figure 3.4). Some video post-production houses use 29.97 non-drop frame as the in-house time code format; usually these houses work more with short duration projects, such as commercials. With times less than 60 seconds, the difference between drop-frame and

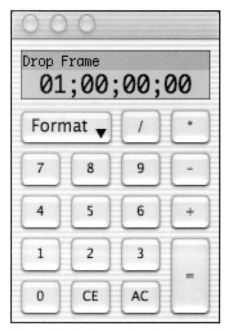

Figure 3.3   A time code calculator displaying SMPTE in drop-frame format. Notice the semicolons.

non-drop frame is not significant. Some video editors prefer to use non-drop frame SMPTE all of the time, so that every frame has a consecutive number. This can help make time code calculations easier.

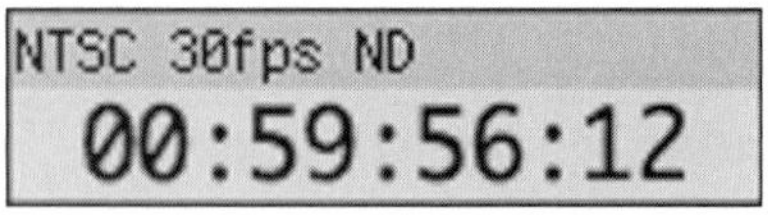

```
NTSC 30fps ND
 00:59:56:12
```

Figure 3.4   The same calculator after converting one hour to 30fps non-drop frame. No semicolons.

Current Usages and Practices

Typically, most AV projects use 29.97 drop-frame time code as a standard. Some commercial post houses will use 29.97 non-drop frame because most of the work done there is not much longer than a minute. Music-only sessions tend to use 30fps, because it has a convenient relationship to real-time. Film uses 24fps but is often transferred to video, resulting in 29.97fps non-drop. HD cameras may use 29.97fps, 24, or even a special 23.976 rate (often referred to as 24p) for direct transfer to NTSC videotape on location or later in post. The choices are many, and the confusion runs high.

Knowing what time code you're using and why you're using it is imperative when using Pro Tools. Pro Tools has the ability to change time code formats within software, which can be helpful but can also lead to mistakes and more confusion. Once you have established a time code standard for a project, everything else is more straightforward.

When using the wrong SMPTE frame rate or frame count, you will notice, over time, that the audio will gradually slip either ahead or behind the video. It might take a minute to notice this drift, but it will eventually become apparent. Pay attention to the lip sync. It is not as simple as going to the end of your Pro Tools session and playing to see how bad the sync is by the end. When Pro Tools syncs up to a videotape, the SMPTE coming from the videotape machine will give Pro Tools a frame number to start on. Pro Tools will be in sync at that frame, no matter where it is, and then begin to slip from that point on. The only accurate way of determining if the sync is slipping is to watch from the beginning for at least a minute or so. With shorter program material, determining slippage is more difficult.

In any event, as I said, it is imperative that you know what the correct frame rate and count are for your current project. Try to clear up any confusion as early as possible in order to avoid a big mess later on.

To Drop or Not to Drop?

To drop or not to drop? There should only be one factor that determines whether you choose drop or non-drop: how you want your time code to relate to the real-time clock. Another factor arises, though, when there is a mistake you must correct for in some other aspect of the production. Any preference for non-drop code facilitates the ease of calculating offsets and figuring shorter lengths. However, with so many time code calculators available, the ability to count frames quickly seems a little moot.

Many video editors want to see each frame number without any skips. It can be disconcerting for a video editor to create a 10-frame video transition that starts at 00;08;59;24 but ends on 00;09;00;06. Do the math. As there are semicolons separators, you know that these are drop-frame time code numbers, which skip two frame numbers every minute except the 10th. Counting 10 frames from 00;08;59;24 but skipping frame number ;00 and ;01, you will end up at 00;09;00;06. In non-drop frame, the 10th frame would be 00:09:00:04. All modern software and equipment running in drop-frame mode will adjust for skipped frame numbers and create transitions and other edits with the correct length and position. Don't be afraid of drop-frame SMPTE. Download a time code calculator and mess around in drop-frame mode. You will get the hang of it quickly.

Frame Rate versus Frame Count   Once again, let me mention that 30fps drop-frame (DF) code is a misleading term that is not part of the SMPTE specification. It is used when transferring production audio recorded for a film shoot that will be transferred to video. The frame rate will then be slowed to the standard 29.97fps DF. Remember to keep the frame *rate* and frame *count* separate in your head. 29.97fps SMPTE still has 30 frames of video in each second of SMPTE time. However, each second of SMPTE time is slightly longer than a real honest second on the clock. 30fps SMPTE keeps right up with the real-time clock and does not need to skip any numbers. If it did so, it would display time that was running faster than real-time. Wouldn't that be extra confusing? Still, you'll find the 30fps drop-frame setting in Pro Tools. The purpose of including it is to allow you to correct for certain film transfers with 30fps drop-frame time code on production audio tapes.

2-3 Pull-Down

When film is transferred to videotape, is must be converted from a frame rate of 24fps to the color video standard of 29.97fps. These two numbers do not have a nice, neat mathematical relationship that would make it easy to transfer frames of film to frames of video. The solution to this problem is called *2-3 pull-down*. The following subsections explain how 2-3 pull-down works for film and audio transfers.

Film Transfers

Each frame of film is like a 35mm picture. It contains one image out of a series that together will make up a movie when played back at 24fps. Recall that a video frame is actually two "fields," each containing half of the total image. One field has the odd horizontal lines in the picture, and the other has the even lines. For every frame of video you see, two fields have been displayed that together make up the complete video frame. Fields move at 59.94fps, so that the actual frame rate is half that, or 29.97fps.

The machine that transfers film to video is called a *telecine* machine (see Figure 3.5). It copies successive frames of film to certain fields of video in a 2-3-2-3 relationship. The first frame of film goes to the first two fields of video. The second frame of film goes onto three fields, field one and two of the second video frame and field one of the third frame. The next film frame goes to the second field of video frame three and the first field of frame four. This goes on in the 2-3-2-3 pattern for the duration of the film transfer. This way, the film has the same basic running time on video at 29.97fps as it had originally at 24fps—but there is a slight difference. To make this process work, the film is slowed by a very small amount (.1%) to roughly 23.97fps. Hence the term *pull-down*. The frame rate is pulled down to match the video rate of 29.97 using the two field, three field transfer technique. "But what does this mean for audio?" you ask.

Figure 3.5 A modern-day telecine machine from Cintel. It is used to transfer film frames to videotape, one by one, using the 2-3 pull-down process.

Telecine Transfers: 2-3 or 3-2   Telecine transfers typically start with two then three fields of video per frame of film. Telecine machines are capable of beginning with three video fields then two, but this is atypical. You will often hear the transfer process incorrectly called 3-2 pull-down. Unless specified prior to the film transfer, the process will begin with two fields of video for the first frame of film, three fields for the second frame of film, and so on.

Pull-Down Audio Sample Rates. Let's say that during a film shoot at 24fps, the production audio is recorded directly to a DAT machine at 48kHz with time code running at 30fps. When it comes time to transfer the film to video, the audio will be transferred to the same videotape. Because the film speed must be slowed down slightly to match the video frame rate, so too must the audio. The sample rate will slow from 48kHz to 47.952kHz (also called 48kHz pull-down), and as a result, the time code recorded at

30fps will magically wind up at 29.97fps. Amazing, isn't it? This way, the audio time code will line up exactly with the video time code while transferring. The downside is that a sample rate of 47.952kHz cannot be transferred digitally without going through a sample rate converter (see Figure 3.6). Most film transfer facilities will *not* do this. They will make an analog copy of the audio from the DAT or field recorder to the VTR.

Sometimes the audio is not transferred during the film transfer—there might be problems with the production tapes, or perhaps the transfer facility does not have the capability. Either way, there will be times when you have to retrieve production audio from the original DAT tapes used on the shoot. If you try to transfer takes directly into Pro Tools without accounting for the speed difference made during film transfer, your audio will be out of sync with the transferred video. There are several ways to compensate for this speed difference. Some of these methods require additional hardware, such as Digidesign's Sync IO, USD, or a third-party synchronizer. But you can compensate for speed difference without hardware using only the Pro Tools software, including Pro Tools LE. More on that in Chapter 5, "Recording to Picture."

The basic method for transferring audio from a film shoot to video transfers of that film involves slowing (pulling down) the source tape by .1% using a hardware synchronizer or work clock generator and then recording the audio into Pro Tools using either analog connections or a real-time sample rate converter such as the one found on the HD 192 IO interface. The analog connection has the disadvantage of being a generation loss. The sample rate converter is a better option but is only available in the 192 IO interface or in an outboard sample rate converter such as the Z-Systems z-8.8a, shown in Figure 3.6.

Figure 3.6 The Z-Systems z-8.8a router and sample rate converter. It can take incoming digital audio at one sample rate and convert it to another in real-time. It also functions as a very handy digital router for my studio.

Pull-Up Sample Rates. Some portable DAT machines have the ability to record faster than the standard sample rate of 48kHz. Recording at 48.048kHz (called 48kHz pull-up) during filming has the advantage of transferring digitally later during a film transfer. When 48.048kHz is pulled down for the film transfer, it winds up back at 48kHz. This way it can be digitally recorded onto the VTR along with the film. The time code frame rate still is recorded at 30fps, so it will pull down to 29.97 when played back at the normal 48kHz sample rate.

This scenario holds true for projects that are shot on film but that will remain in video format throughout the rest of production and delivery (such as the made-for-TV movie that never shows in theaters). If the project will eventually be shown in theaters on film, a slightly different approach might be necessary. Audio that will eventually be used for a film release will have to do one of two things: It must either go through the reverse process of 2-3 pull-down (see Figure 3.7) to return to the film rate of 24fps (to reverse the 2-3 pull-down process, it is necessary to "pull-up" the sample rate of the finished audio to match up with the original film speed of 24fps), or it must be edited using 24fps as a reference and never change speed.

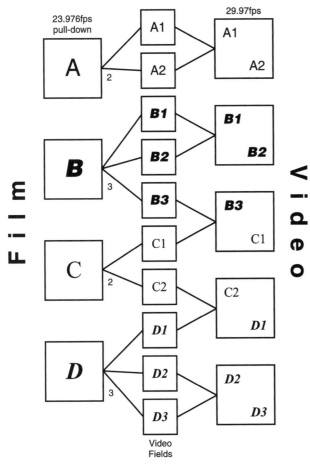

Figure 3.7   2-3 pull-down block diagram.

24p HD Video

HDTV is bringing a whole new technology to video. HD cameras, such as the one shown in Figure 3.8, are able to record in a format known as *24p* (24fps progressive scan) that allows video shot with HD cameras to look more like film than traditional video cameras using interlaced images at 29.97fps. In order to transfer these HD images to regular video, you go through the 2-3 pull-down process. This can be done after the shoot, although some cameras can use a special frame rate of 23.976fps to record initially. Recording at 23.976fps allows a hardware unit to translate the HD image into a NTSC video image running at 29.97 in real-time. Directors can record simultaneously to HD video and regular NTSC video (external deck), allowing them to view the shots on less expensive NTSC equipment.

The Panasonic VariCam uses a technique of recording the video data at a fixed rate of 59.94fps. The output of the camera can then be mathematically manipulated to achieve any desired frame rate, whether 24, 23.976, 29.97, or even 50fps. This simplifies the recording technology while offering the flexibility of multiple output frame rates.

Figure 3.8 A Panasonic AJ-HDC27 Variable Frame Rate 16:9 HD Cinema Camera (VariCam) capable of recording at 23.976fps, among many other frame rates.

The optical mechanism in the camera can run at an independent frame rate from the recording portion in order to achieve certain visual effects, such as motion blur or slow motion.

Cameras such as the Panasonic VariCam or the Red One can record multiple tracks of either 16 or 24 bit 48kHz audio directly while running at 23.976fps. This eliminates the transfer process later and speeds up production. If the production audio was recorded while the camera was running at 24fps, the same pull-down conversion used in film transfers must be done in order for the audio to be in sync at NTSC speed.

SMPTE Time Code Scenarios

Now that you have the technical background, let's examine potential project scenarios and see how the audio and time code would be handled. With the advent of HDTV, acquisition and delivery formats have expanded, creating many varied possibilities.

NTSC Video to NTSC Video

The simplest situation is a project shot on NTSC video that is destined to be seen only on broadcast TV or on VHS tapes and DVDs. In this scenario, the time code will run at 29.97 throughout the project. The choice to use drop-frame or not depends upon the requirements of the delivery format or the working practices of the video post facility and editor.

When shooting video, there are two choices for time code. The first is time-of-day code, which simply means that at the start of the day, the SMPTE generator is set for the time of the day and will run constantly until shooting is over, displaying the hours of the day. Time-of-day would be drop-frame time code if the production team decides that it should follow the real-time clock. Reality television would be a candidate for drop-frame time code. The advantage here is that the time of day at which each take was recorded is conveniently stored on tape in the SMPTE time. For any given day, there is also a unique SMPTE time for every take filmed. This can help eliminate confusion during post-production.

The second choice is called *runtime SMPTE*. In this situation, SMPTE runs only when the camera is running. When filming stops, so does the SMPTE. Typically, whoever changes the tapes in the video camera will also change the starting hour of the time code to reflect the tape number currently being used, making it easy to identify each tape just by looking at the time code's hour number. This technique is most helpful on shoots that last less than one day. If shooting runs into more days, the chance of creating a tape with the same hour number increases, leading to more possible confusion later if you don't clearly label each tape.

During post-production, video is simply transferred into a video editor workstation without any time code or frame rate changes. Audio will remain at 48kHz and use the same time code as video. Layback and delivery are just as easy. The only choice is whether to use drop-frame or not. If the program material exceeds a minute in length and is destined for broadcast, the final master should use 29.97 drop-frame in order to keep the time code in sync with the clock on the wall, giving an accurate indication of how long the material runs.

Okay, that was simple. Let's look at a more complicated process.

Film to NTSC Video

Many projects are shot on film for the look but edited on video for ease and then are delivered to the public on video, whether on television or on videotape and DVD. Although the visual process is standard, there are a couple of different ways to handle the audio.

Film cameras typically run at 24fps when filming scenes in which the audio is also being recorded. When 24fps is used for film, audio time code is recorded at 30fps. Film cameras are capable of filming at 30fps and 29.97fps while audio is being recorded as well. In these situations, audio time code will be 30 and 29.97, respectively. Usually, 24fps is the frame rate for the film camera, and 30fps is the rate for the audio deck.

Why have two frame rates (24 and 30) running at the same time? Because once the film has been slowed down during the 2-3 pull-down process, the audio will be slowed by the same amount, resulting in the NTSC standard rate of 29.97fps. Here's where the choice comes in. In order to slow the film down, the audio must slow down as well. Otherwise, the audio will not be in sync with the transferred video. The only way to do that with a digital recording is to slow the sample rate down. If 48kHz was used while filming on the set, it will have to be slowed down to 47.952 during the film transfer in order to remain in sync with the transferred film on video. This results in an analog transfer or D/A-A/D conversion to the videotape copy. The other choice is to record using a "pulled-up" sample rate of 48.048kHz while filming, so that during transfer the sample rate will slow down to 48kHz, making a digital transfer of the audio possible. In either case, the videotape of the film transfer will have audio that is in sync with the film footage, uses 29.97fps SMPTE, and has a 48kHz sample rate with digital video formats.

The rest of this scenario plays out just like the video-to-video version, in which the only choice is whether or not to use drop-frame SMPTE during post-production and final delivery.

Film to Film

When a project starts on film and ends on film (such as a feature film in theaters), the choices for time code increase. Because the final format will be film running at 24fps, there is no need to record audio during the shoot at 48.048kHz (called 48kHz pull-up), as eventually the 2-3 pull-down process will have to be reversed back to 24fps for the final film release. Reversing the pull-down would result in a non-standard sample rate (48.048kHz) for the final mix. Typically, film will be transferred to video for editing, effects, and computer manipulation. Then, once the film is in final form, it will be transferred back to a film print for presentation in theaters.

There are two ways to deal with the pull-down issue. First, you could follow the example in the previous section of a film-to-video project including the 2-3 pull-down process during transfer to video. In this case, the process would include a final step to reverse the transfer process when going back to a film master. This final step involves "pulling-up" the sample rate of the final mix in order to match the original speed of the film. In this scenario, another sample rate conversion must take place in order to create a 48kHz digital master. If the production audio was recorded at 48kHz and transferred to video using a 2-3 pull-down process, large portions of audio have undergone *two* digital to analog to digital conversions by the time the final mix is done. This is not a preferred method, although it will work and can be of high quality.

The second and preferred method is to transfer production audio directly into Pro Tools and then pull down the operating sample rate of Pro Tools during post-production in order to match the timing of the reference videotapes. Because the film editor will most likely be editing on video, the film will be slowed down due to the 2-3 pull-down process. You can pull down the Pro Tools audio word clock while syncing with edited videos of the film. When it comes time to print the final mix, Pro Tools can be run at the normal sample rate of 48kHz and will be in sync with the original speed of the film. This way, no additional D/A-A/D conversion is necessary during the final mix, allowing the full quality to be maintained. It is a little more confusing to work this way, but the results will be superior due to the fact that no analog transfers were made.

In addition, Pro Tools is capable of *pulling up* a QuickTime file as an alternative to audio pull-down. In Pro Tools LE systems with the DV toolkit installed, this option can be used as a cost-effective alternative because it does not require the use of an external work clock source to pull the audio clock down to film speed. QuickTime will pull the visual image up to video speed, allowing you to edit audio seamlessly at 48kHz. The QuickTime file must be at the correct film speed of 24fps for this to work.

Importing Music While in Pull-Down Mode   Be careful when importing score music or any other audio that has been created in sync using videotape transfers of film material. If the composer or other audio editor created this material without using the pull-down mode, you will have to convert the sample rate or do an analog transfer to match your pull-down condition. Also, incidental music used by the director during the video edit will have to be conformed to pull-down in order to maintain sync in the final mix.

24p HD to Video

Starting a project in 24p HD video and finishing in regular NTSC video is very similar to a film-to-video project, with some exceptions. When using 24p HD as a source for NTSC video, the video will always be shot at the pull-down frame rate of 23.976fps. This allows an immediate transfer to NTSC video without any special equipment. Audio can be recorded either directly to the HD camera at 48kHz or to an external DAT machine at 48kHz using 29.97 SMPTE, as the video frame rate is already pulled down. Audio can be transferred directly to video without any speed changes. This means that you can capture production audio digitally into Pro Tools without any fuss.

Once all of the audio is in Pro Tools, you can proceed exactly as if you were working on a film-to-video project working at 48kHz and laying back directly to a VTR using 29.97 SMPTE. One of the great advantages of certain HD video cameras is the ability to resolve 24fps to other SMPTE frame rates. For instance, you can play back 24p video at 23.976fps and still output 29.97 SMPTE. This is simply not possible with film, because the telecine process is first required to resolve to 29.97.

True 24fps HD to Film (or 24p HD)

Many movies these days are being shot on HD and then projected from film in theaters. In this scenario, 24fps HD would be the original format, and film would be the master format. For audio, the time code scenario is similar to a straight film-to-film project. You would start by using 24fps on the camera. If audio were recorded to another deck besides the camera, it would be at 48kHz using 30fps SMPTE time code. The audio would have to be pulled down in order to maintain sync with transferred footage onto video. You could complete post-production in Pro Tools using pull-down mode. When the final mix was completed, returning to 48kHz would bring the audio back up to the original 24fps speed. You can also use the video pull up technique in this scenario.

Without using pull-down sample rates (or video pull-up) during editing, each transfer from 24fps to 29.97fps video and back again would require either a sample rate conversion or analog transfer for the audio. This is the less desirable path, of course, but in some situations might be the only way to go. The reality of budgets and digital logistics must be taken into consideration, and Pro Tools has the flexibility to work under many constraints.

Film to 24p HD

As film captures the light so well, many movie-makers will still find film to be the way to shoot. HD affords the ability to endlessly edit and create all sorts of effects and CGI (computer generated images), all while remaining in a high-quality digital medium. It only makes sense that many projects will begin on film and end up on HD in their final form. This can be treated like a film-to-film project and use the 24fps rate throughout. No audio should need to be pulled down unless you are working with an NTSC reference videotape. QuickTime movies can retain the 24fps rate and allow you to work at the correct film speed for the entire editorial process. However, if you are using external viewing equipment such as a projector or other NTSC device, pull-down will have to be used during post to work at 29.97fps.

HD to Just About Anything

With digital video, the frame rate is adjustable, and the resolution is variable. Once an HD project is completed, there are ways of converting it into various other frame rates and resolutions, depending on the destination market. Japan likes 1080i more than progressive scan (720p) material that is preferred in the U.S., for instance. With HD, the preference depends on the needs of the production itself. This is part of the decision-making process that goes on during pre-production.

HDTV is a data specification. The video frame rate and audio sample rate can be changed. That is a great part of the system. Different resolutions are supported within HDTV. Broadcast formats can change and will do so at some point in time. Keeping up with the technology will help you stay ahead in the industry.

Here are the current HDTV broadcast standards:

- **1080 60i:** 60 half frames interlaced at 59.94 frames per second. Used by NBC, CBS, PBS, and HBO. Also used in Japan.

- **720p:** 30 full frames running at 29.97 frames per second progressive scan. Used by FOX and ABC.

- **1080 50i:** 50 half frames per second, interlaced. Used in Europe and in other PAL/ SECAM regions.

As you can see, there are a lot of options for handling time code and sample rates. You must have a concrete idea of where the project will end up in order to create the highest quality mix at the proper speed and sample rate for any of the media discussed in the previous sections.

HDTV Standards   Because the HDTV broadcast is a data stream, the format of the video in that stream can be in a variety of frame rates and resolutions. Networks may change their standards at any time, so any information provided here about network broadcast formats could change at any time. Be sure to have the most current information before deciding on HD formats.

Audio for HD could end up at 24fps, 23.976fps, 29.97fps, or even 25fps in the case of PAL. Your mixes should be running at 48kHz relative to these frame rates. Basically, any of the previous scenarios could apply to a project ending on HD.

SMPTE time code can be a confusing subject, but as you gain experience working with different video formats, you will be more comfortable dealing with the various time code formats. Now that you have a basic understanding of how SMPTE and synchronization works, let's get Pro Tools set up to work with video.

4 Getting Started with Pro Tools and Video

Now that you have a strong background in the technology you'll be using, it's time to configure Pro Tools for working in audio post-production. If you have an HD or LE system with the DV toolkit installed, you are at a distinct advantage because it includes an SMPTE time code ruler to help *spot* audio regions to time code, among many other features. But it is not necessary to have an SMPTE ruler, and Pro Tools LE systems without the DV toolkit are also capable of working with time code and video via MIDI time code (MTC) and QuickTime with certain limitations. Using MTC does require some workarounds and perhaps a dedicated synchronizer to achieve higher precision sync. These workarounds are explored in this chapter.

What Is Spotting? The term *spotting* or *to spot* audio to time code refers to the process of viewing a film or video and deciding at what time code values certain sounds will be heard. Putting the actual sounds at the correct time code locations is also known as *spotting*. The term most likely comes from the practice of searching for, or spotting, on-screen elements that will require additional sound in post-production. It's rather like a fancy game of "I Spy" for professionals.

Hooking Up Your Equipment

Because you are reading this book I assume you have a working knowledge of Pro Tools and are able to perform basic recording, editing, and mixing functions. I will not go into setting up the normal audio hardware that came with your system. If you have not already set up your basic Pro Tools system, please refer to the user guides and tutorials provided with the system. If you would like more detailed information than the literature that comes with Pro Tools, you can refer to your manual and to the companion book in this series—*Pro Tools Power!* by Colin MacQueen and Steve Albanese—where you will find detailed information on the operation of your Pro Tools system. *Pro Tools for Film, Video, and Multimedia* covers the operations related to video and post-production specifically.

That said, some special hardware requirements must be met in order to work with video. A synchronization device must be plugged in and configured. Video monitors must be hooked up and provided with images to display. If other tape decks such as VTRs, DATs, or MDMs are involved, you must connect and configure a 9-pin machine control or MIDI Machine Control (MMC). In addition, you must set up and configure any DV video equipment or specialized video hardware such as Avid Mojo.

After your equipment is set up, you must test the whole system for sync accuracy. To do that, you will need some video material that has audio with it—preferably something with lip sync dialogue for checking sync. Any video monitors or projection systems that you plan to use in the studio should be ready. Any third-party synchronizers or special hookups to a video machine room should be present and functioning. If you are working in a larger facility that has other video and audio studios connected together, it is a good idea to be in touch with the technical personnel in charge of maintaining and configuring the machine room and other systems. These people can be a valuable source of help and information.

You'll also need to make sure that any digital connections are clocked properly and any audio connections to video equipment are working well. You should plan a synchronization layout for your setup. Take a moment and make a list of all of the gear you want to work with and identify the pieces that will need to run in sync with Pro Tools. Consider all sources of audio that you will be using, which could include DAT, Nagra, three-quarter inch, or Betacam VTRs, DV, MDM, studio microphones, CDs, mobile hard drives such as Firewire devices, and even cassettes. Having all these elements readily available to you while you work can help speed up your workflow, thus allowing you more time to be creative.

Typical Equipment Setups

Although there are many possible ways to set up a Pro Tools workstation, certain situations might lend themselves to a particular setup. The next subsections examine several studio scenarios.

Audio Suite within a Multi-Room Facility

The most complicated and involved setup would be an audio suite within a larger, multi-room facility such as a video post-production house. In this situation, audio from your edit suite must stay in sync with other equipment in the facility in order to be available to the machine room where the VTRs and routers reside. Typically, a facility like this will have a house sync generator, such as the Tektronix shown in Figure 4.1, that sends out signals to all tape machines and processors—including the edit suites—and keeps each piece running in sync with the others. The synchronization of all the

Figure 4.1 The Tektronix SPG-422 Component Digital Master Sync Generator. This unit is capable of generating stable clock signals for analog and digital video systems as well as for digital audio systems. It can generate NTSC and PAL/EBU signals simultaneously.

equipment allows everyone in the facility to access any tape machine or any processor in any room in the entire facility, which in turn allows for flexibility and compatibility among all of the studios.

You need to derive your digital clock source from the house sync generator. This can be done in several ways. Some house sync generators have a dedicated audio word clock output that can be used to drive many digital audio devices, including Pro Tools audio interfaces. Typically, this word clock will run at the video standard of 48kHz. Pro Tools HD hardware is capable of using the word clock as a clock source, but Pro Tools legacy hardware (the 888s, 1622s, and so on) cannot use this type of signal directly. A Universal Slave Driver or other similar device must be used to convert the incoming word clock into Digidesign's 256× Superclock. It is also possible to use another device that will lock to a 1× word clock, such as the Yamaha 02R digital mixer, and then slave Pro Tools to the digital audio outputs of that device. Chaining several digital devices together like this can lead to increased jitter in the resulting audio signal and should be avoided if possible.

Video black burst is a signal used to synchronize multiple video tape decks. It is usually based on the 29.97Hz rate of video frames in NTSC video (or 25fps PAL standard). The Pro Tools Sync I/O and Universal Slave Driver can use this signal to derive word clock and keep the Pro Tools audio clock synchronized with other video devices and equipment in the machine room. The Sync I/O and Universal Slave Driver can reference the video black burst signal and generate both the standard word clock and the older Superclock used in Digidesign legacy hardware.

Most multi-room facilities use an audio-video router to connect each room to the central machine room. These routers can connect various types of signals to and from every room. These signals include analog video, analog audio, analog SMPTE time code, serial digital interface (SDI) video, AES digital audio, 9-pin machine control, and more. If AES digital audio is supported by the router and used in the machine room, an AES digital audio signal can function as a sync source. As long as the digital audio signal is resolved or synced to the house clock, everything should work fine.

The Dubbing Stage   The *dubbing stage* is a large room built to emulate an actual movie theater outfitted with equipment used to create the final mix of a film. The acoustics are controlled and standardized so that what you hear in the dubbing stage is what the audience will hear when they see the movie in theaters. Because the number of audio tracks it takes to make a modern film can reach well into the hundreds, it can take several engineers to mix the film. Also, there may be editing stations in the room used to perform last-minute changes to various elements used in the mix. There could be as many as five or six full-blown Pro Tools rigs running at the same time to accomplish this task. Having all these systems running together in perfect sync is one of the most complex setups imaginable. The use of a house sync generator to drive the film or video playback and all Pro Tools systems using distributed word clock or other signals will be absolutely necessary. Even though this is a single-room facility, the synchronization needs are as complex as those needed for a multi-room facility.

Single-Room Audio Studio

In a single-room audio studio, synchronization is simpler. If you are *not* synchronizing to a VTR, sync is much easier. Simply use internal sync in Pro Tools for your reference. If you need to pull down your audio clock for film or HD work, you'll need a Digidesign Sync I/O, Universal Slave Driver (USD), or some third-party synchronizer to generate pull-down word clock speeds.

If you *are* synchronizing to a VTR, the Sync I/O or other synchronizer will be necessary to resolve Pro Tools to the VTR's video output, or you'll need to use a black burst signal as a reference by both Pro Tools and the VTR. If the video sync signal is not somehow connected between the VTR and Pro Tools, unpredictable sync will result.

Home or Project Studio

In a home or project studio on a limited budget, sync will most likely take the form of using QuickTime movies for video reference. This way, no extra hardware is needed to sync Pro Tools with video. The computer itself acts as the synchronizer by playing the movie files internally. The only disadvantage to this is that the computer will use resources to play a QuickTime movie that could otherwise be used for audio processing. You might not be able to play as many tracks with as many plug-ins while viewing Quick-Time movies.

Audio Clock Source

The audio clock source is perhaps the most important element in any digital audio system. This clock determines how fast and *accurate* the sample rate of digital audio is. The quality of any digital audio signal is in no small part determined by the quality of the clock driving it. In the case of audio for video, it is also the method used to control the speed of audio during playback in order to maintain sync with video.

Digital audio clocks are found in several forms. The most commonly used form is found in the digital audio signal itself. Any AES, S/PDIF, Toslink, ADAT, TDIF, MADI or other digital audio signal contains, embedded within it, a clock source determining the sample rate of that signal. Any time you connect one digital output to another input, the clock information from the source can be used by the destination device to synchronize the two. This principle can be used to synchronize Pro Tools with video equipment as well.

Another typical source for audio clock is word clock, which is a square wave signal oscillating at the sample rate's frequency, 48kHz for instance. This signal can be connected via BNC coaxial cables to many digital audio devices, ensuring that they will all be running at the same sample rate. Pro Tools legacy interfaces use a proprietary work clock signal, called Slave Clock or Superclock, that is 256 times the sample rate of the current session. Standard 1× work clock will not work with older Digidesign hardware (888s, ADAT Bridges, and 001s). The HD series of hardware will accept 1× word clock and 256× Superclock as sync sources.

Digidesign's Sync HD and Sync I/O

Digidesign's Sync HD (shown in Figure 4.2) and Sync I/O are both capable of resolving many types of audio and video clock sources. For instance, they can be connected to a black burst video sync source and derive word clock or Superclock that will sync Pro Tools hardware to the black burst signal—and thereby all video equipment using the

Figure 4.2 The Sync HD flagship synchronizer for Pro Tools HD.

same black burst reference. The following is a list of all sources that the Sync HD and Sync I/O can use to resolve the audio clock:

- **Video black burst:** A standard NTSC video signal that is entirely black in color.

- **Normal NTSC video signal:** Any video source such as the output of a VTR.

- **Tri-Level Sync:** HD video sync signal up to 1080p 60fps.

- **Word clock:** The standard digital audio clock signal.

- **LTC:** Longitudinal time code in SMPTE format; regular, analog SMPTE.

- **AES digital audio:** The clock information contained in every AES digital signal.

- **Bi-phase:** Used with mechanical, mag, and film machines.

- **Tach:** A variation of bi-phase.

- **Pilot tone:** AC line frequency (60Hz or 50Hz) used on film locations to sync cameras with audio tape deck. This is not used very much today.

Both the Sync HD and Sync I/O have a time code inserter capable of reading VITC through a video signal and then "burning" the time code visually into a window on the video image. This is called a *time code burn-in* and can be very helpful when spotting audio to video.

Third-Party Synchronizers

There are many third-party synchronizers available today that can resolve the audio clock to a number of sync references. Although they aren't as integrated with Pro Tools as the Sync HD and Sync I/O, many of these units are capable of doing the same things. The Rosendahl Nanosync HD shown in Figure 4.3 can resolve different video standards together along with all the various audio sample rates to a single internal or external master clock source. The Nanosync HD also accepts HD tri-level sync signals (1080i/p and 720p), which are becoming standard as HD video becomes more popular.

Figure 4.3 The Rosendahl Nanosync HD master clock generator/resolver.

SMPTE Time Code Reader, MIDI Interface

As discussed in the Chapter 3, "Synchronization and SMPTE Time Code," positional information is necessary to synchronize two systems. SMPTE time code, whether LTC, VITC, or Sony 9-pin, provides positional information, but needs to be converted into a format Pro Tools can use. You need a time code reader to do the conversion. The Sync HD and Sync I/O interface will read incoming SMPTE from any source and relay it to Pro Tools for positional references. Most MIDI interfaces are capable of at least reading LTC and MTC and relaying this to Pro Tools. The only difference is that the Sync HD and Sync I/O can also provide a clock source for resolving the speed of your system to any fluctuations in the incoming SMPTE. MTC by itself is not capable of continuously resolving the speed of Pro Tools. Thus, over time, the sync may slip. MTC, when used in conjunction with a word clock signal that is resolved to a master clock source, can keep Pro Tools in sync with external devices over longer periods of time—theoretically forever.

LTC versus VITC Time Code   Longitudinal Time Code (LTC) is an analog signal recorded on to a track of its own. You can listen to LTC just like any other audio signal. Vertical Interval Time Code (VITC), however, is not a signal you can listen to. It is recorded along with a standard NTSC video signal on a VTR in between video fields. In order to use VITC, you must have a Sync I/O or Universal Slave Driver. These devices can extract the VITC signal from the video output of a VTR.

In all situations, a SMPTE time code reader is essential when working with external hardware. If you plan on working only with QuickTime movies internally with Pro Tools, you don't need a synchronizer, because Pro Tools itself handles synchronization internally. Capturing and creating QuickTime movies is another story, and I will address this later in the chapter.

9-Pin Machine Control

The Machine Control option for Pro Tools is almost essential for post-production work. This option allows you to use the industry standard 9-pin remote protocol to control many types of video and audio tape decks from the transport controls in Pro Tools. When paired with the proper synchronizer, the Machine Control option allows for seamless synchronization control when locking Pro Tools to a tape machine or hard disk recorder.

In large film dubbing studios, a central transport control located at the mixing station might be used to control several Pro Tools systems, along with HD video playback systems and other equipment. Consoles such as the Harrison MPC4-D and Euphonix System 5 have built-in machine control systems that use the 9-pin protocol. Record arming buttons on the console can even place Pro Tools tracks in record-ready mode.

Once you have connected the 9-pin cable to your VTR, you'll be able to operate all transport controls of the 9-pin deck along with track arming abilities. When using Machine Control while locked to Pro Tools, the 9-pin machine will automatically locate to the cursor position in your session. You will also be able to automate laybacks just by selecting the area of the timeline that you would like to record onto the remote deck, arming some tracks, and pressing the Record button.

Machine Control can be used to load in production audio for use with an edit decision list (EDL) exported from a video- or film-editing workstation. This process requires additional software, such as Virtual Katy (VK Premium Tools), that can import industry-standard EDLs such as CMX and Sony 9000 and then create an edited version of the audio file that correlates to the video and audio edits in the EDL. I'll go into more detail about conforming EDLs in Chapter 5, "Recording to Picture."

The basic function of 9-pin machine control is keeping a tape machine in sync with Pro Tools while editing and mixing audio. The tape machine provides synchronized video images to look at while you're working on the related audio. 9-pin control allows Pro Tools to direct the tape machine to rewind, fast-forward, locate to specific SMPTE locations, enter play or record mode, and arm certain tracks for recording. The tape machine can relay time code information back to Pro Tools in the form of serial time code over the 9-pin cable.

9-Pin Connections and Settings

If you have a Sync HD in your setup, you have two 9-pin ports available on the back of the unit. If not, you need a supported serial connection to your CPU in order to connect the 9-pin cable provided with the Machine Control software package. For most operations, the DigiSerial port on HD Core and Mix Core cards can be used. Currently, the only supported third-party serial device for Apple CPUs is the Keyspan USA-28x USB-to-serial converter. The Keyspan offers the greatest compatibility with various 9-pin devices as tested by Digidesign.

9-Pin Control   You may experience difficulty using the 9-pin ports on the Sync HD and Sync I/O. There are issues in getting them to work right. The Keyspan adapter is the recommended device to use for 9-pin control.

Connect the 9-pin cable to the tape machine's 9-pin port. If you're in a multi-room facility with Machine Control routing, you might have to connect to a 9-pin router input. Doing so will allow you to control any 9-pin–capable deck in the machine room.

Once connected, Machine Control needs to be enabled and configured. Follow these steps:

1.   Select Peripherals from the Setups menu. The Peripherals setup window will open, as shown in Figure 4.4.

2.   Click the Machine Control tab.

3.   Check the box to enable the 9-pin serial connection.

4.   You can now select the port to which you have connected the 9-pin device.

Once the port is selected, leave Machine Type set to Sony 9-Pin unless your particular tape machine needs another type. The node type BVW-75 will work in most situations. The node type is the protocol that the device is using with the 9-pin connection. The Sony video tape decks are a common standard used in the industry. The BVW-75 is a Sony model video deck with a common protocol. If your deck is older or unique in some other way, another setting might be better. Look in the Node pop-up menu for your device name and experiment until you get the best results.

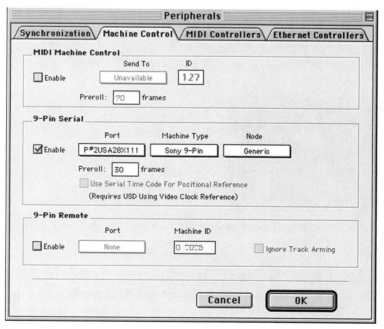

Figure 4.4 The Peripherals setup window, Machine Control tab. Here you can configure the 9-pin machine control connections.

Set the Deck to Remote Operation   It is necessary to put any 9-pin device into Remote mode in order for Pro Tools to control it. If the device is set to Local mode, all 9-pin commands will be ignored.

9-Pin Operation

There are three basic ways to use the 9-pin machine control. The next subsections discuss those methods.

Remote Control Only—No Sync. The first way to use the 9-pin machine control is to simply control the deck remotely via the Pro Tools transport controls. This method can be used to cue a tape machine and view video independent of the audio in Pro Tools. It is most useful in a multi-room facility in which the physical deck is not in the same room as you are. Being able to control the deck remotely is a big help in such a case.

In order to enable remote control only, you must select Machine from the Transport submenu found on the transport control, as seen in Figure 4.5. Once you have done so, the transport controls (Play, Stop, FF, and so on) will control the 9-pin deck only. When you click the Play button or enable play by pressing the spacebar, the 9-pin device will start playing, but Pro Tools will remain stopped. Fast-forward, rewind, stop, and slow and fast-play commands should work with most decks. You can even type in a time code number, press Return, and have the deck locate to that position. Try them all and see what your deck is capable of doing via 9-pin control.

Figure 4.5   The Transport submenu. This selects what device the transport controls in Pro Tools connect to.

Pro Tools as Transport Master and SMPTE Slave. The second way to use the 9-pin machine control employs Pro Tools as the transport master but makes the deck the SMPTE master, and Pro Tools will slave to the incoming master time code. This mode is the one you will use the most. When using this mode, it seems as though Pro Tools is the master and the video deck is slaving to it, because the operation is so quick and responsive, and you are using the normal Pro Tools transport commands (spacebar, Selector tool, and so on). Of course, this is not the case. It is an easy mistake to make, but it is one that will make it harder to troubleshoot later if there are any problems locking up the two. Here's how Pro Tools can be the transport master but the SMPTE slave:

1. Set the transport to Pro Tools in the Transport submenu on the Transport window, as seen in Figure 4.6.

2. Click on the Sync icon on the Transport window (Cmd+Shift+J). The button will start flashing. This indicates that Pro Tools is waiting for incoming time code to lock to. You will also see the message "waiting for sync" flashing in the lower-left corner of the Edit window, as shown in Figure 4.6.

3. Now when you enable Play, the tape deck will locate to a point equal to the cursor position in the Pro Tools Edit (the same as the Start time) window minus the amount of pre-roll set in the 9-pin setup window. If you have a pre-roll amount enabled in the Transport window, this amount will be included in the position of the remote deck.

4. You will see a moving vertical line in the Edit window that represents the position of the 9-pin device as it locates to the proper pre-roll position. Both the Fast-Forward and Rewind buttons flash during this phase.

5. Next, the video deck will enter Play, and Pro Tools will flash the Play button, indicating that it is waiting for valid time code and the starting frame number to begin synchronized playback.

6. Once the original cursor position in Pro Tools has been reached, the Play button will stop flashing and illuminate steadily, indicating that synchronized playback has begun.

Congratulations, you're in sync! Locating to a new start position is as simple as clicking somewhere in the Edit window and pressing Play.

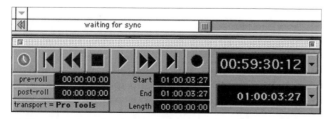

Figure 4.6 Pro Tools in transport-master/time code-slave mode. Notice the "waiting for sync" message in the Edit window.

Remote Deck as Transport and SMPTE Master. The third mode of machine control is used for laying back to the tape machine or recording your final mix onto tape. In this mode, the tape deck is the transport master and time code master. Pro Tools merely slaves to the incoming time code. The unique aspect of this mode is the ability it affords you to automatically punch in and out on the remote deck. Here's how remote punch-in and punch-out work with the remote deck as transport master and Pro Tools as SMPTE slave.

1. Select Machine in the Transport submenu.

2. Click the Sync icon in the Transport window (Cmd+Shift+J). This mode behaves very much like the previous mode except when you enable Record.

3. Recording will occur only on the remote deck and not in Pro Tools. You must first configure the record-enabled tracks and the Edit mode on the remote deck. This is done in the Machine Track Arm window, which is shown in Figure 4.7. Depending on the type of deck you're controlling, there will be anywhere from two to eight Record buttons corresponding to the tracks on the remote deck. Usually, the first two Record buttons are the first two audio channels on the deck.

Arm with Caution   Be careful when arming tracks on a remote deck! Sometimes, the video track can be inadvertently record-enabled, and then you run the chance of erasing someone else's work. Make sure you experiment on a work tape first to determine how the record-enable buttons operate your particular machine. Try a practice layback on the work tape to see how Pro Tools and the deck behave during the operation. Pro Tools also offers an Edit Preview mode that allows you to practice your auto-edit without actually recording, only monitoring the input. The track arming window allows you to choose the Edit Preview mode.

---

4. Next set the record mode of the remote deck. The choices are Auto Edit and Punch In/Out. In Auto Edit mode, the deck will enter Record at a specific time code number and stop recording at another time code number. Recording will occur only on the record-enabled track(s). In Punch In/Out mode, you can manually punch in and out on the remote deck.

5. In Assemble mode, all tracks, including time code, will enter Record immediately after the transport starts to play. Assemble mode is not often used for audio layback because it involves the video and time code tracks as well. Insert is what you want to use 99.9% of the time. In Insert mode, only the tracks you

record enable will be recorded on. This prevents accidental erasure of the video and time code tracks. You should always use Insert mode unless you're in some very unique situation. Pro Tools systems with Avid Mojo options could possibly use the Assemble mode to layback audio and video, but it is stated that the video output of the Mojo system is not broadcast quality and should only be used as a reference.

6.   Determine your punch-in and punch-out times and enter them into the Pro Tools Edit window, or select the corresponding area on the timeline using Grid mode set to one frame. This will determine exactly when the remote deck will enter and leave Record.

7.   Make sure you are in Auto Edit and Insert mode. Press the Record and then Play buttons on the transport and watch the cursor move to a cue point ahead of the Record in-point and begin playing.

8.   Pro Tools will sync to incoming time code, and when the in-point is reached, the remote deck will go into Record on the tracks that were enabled and continue until you press Stop or the end point is reached.

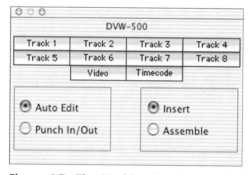

Figure 4.7 The Machine Track Arm window. Here, you can record-enable tracks on the 9-pin remote tape deck and choose a record mode, including Edit Preview for rehearsing insert edits.

9-Pin Remote Deck Emulation

On the Machine Control tab of the Peripherals window, there is another checkbox for 9-pin remote, as shown in Figure 4.8. Checking this box allows Pro Tools to be controlled by another device via 9-pin connections. For example, you might use this option if you were working on a large film mix in which the master controller used 9-pin to operate all the tape decks and other devices—such as Pro Tools—together. Many large-format film-mixing consoles have 9-pin control built into their work surfaces. This mode is rarely used outside of the dubbing stage, and if you're mixing entirely inside of Pro Tools, it should not be needed at all. You can enable the 9-pin remote by selecting it as the transport in the Transport submenu. Once Pro Tools has been placed online, the master controller will be able to operate the transport, record-enable various tracks, and punch-in and punch-out of Record.

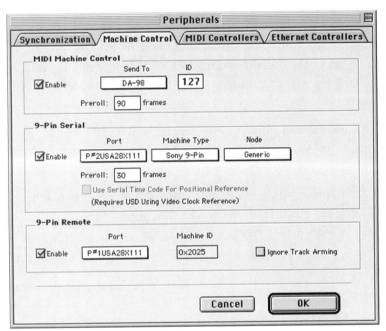

Figure 4.8 The Machine Control tab of the Peripherals window. The 9-pin Remote option is checked, allowing another device to control Pro Tools via a 9-pin connection.

MIDI Machine Control (MMC)

MIDI Machine Control (MMC) is a protocol that uses MIDI connections to allow remote control of certain tape decks and other MIDI software. It is supported in equipment such as the Tascam MMR-8, Digital Performer, Nuendo, and a host of other audio software. It is similar to 9-pin remote in that you can control transport and record-enable functions on the remote unit. The only connections necessary are MIDI cables to and from your Pro Tools MIDI interface and the remote device. MMC does not provide sample-accurate sync. It is merely a form of transport control with track arming capabilities similar to 9-pin control. The remote unit or software must be resolved to the same audio clock as Pro Tools and receive time code in some form for sample accurate sync using MMC. MMC is coupled with MTC over the same MIDI connection for positional information.

MMC Connections and Settings

You configure MMC in the same place as 9-pin control. You must define what MIDI ports the MMC device is connected to. The device should be connected both ways, as MMC requires information to travel back and forth between the master and slave for best operation. If you only have a connection to the MMC device, MMC will still work in a limited fashion. You must assign an ID number to MMC devices in order to use them—as it is possible to connect many MMC devices together in one system, each one needs to be identified separately. The slave device ID needs to be set the same in both Pro Tools and the MMC device's setup.

MMC Operation

MMC operation is very similar to 9-pin operation once it has been configured. In fact, you can use the previous examples of 9-pin operation and substitute "MMC" for "Machine" and MMC will operate the same. The one noticeable difference in operation will be that non-linear MMC devices such as sequencers will locate instantly to any SMPTE number. Also, Pro Tools does not allow arming of record tracks through MMC; you must manually record-enable them. Virtual VTR is an example of a non-linear device that can be used as a MMC slave. It will seamlessly follow every move you make in Pro Tools.

It is possible to run both a 9-pin device and a MMC device in sync together. All machine control modes operate the same way. The mode depends on which devices are "online" as determined by the Online submenu of the Transport window. If there is a check beside the device name, it will be synchronized to the system when the Sync icon is on or flashing, as shown in Figure 4.9. Typically, MMC is used for audio devices such as sequencers or multi-track decks such as the Tascam DA-88 or Sony PCM-800. These decks can be used to mix down multi-channel mixes such as 5.1 surround.

Figure 4.9   Here, the Transport submenu has been set so that both 9-pin and MMC transports will be locked together along with Pro Tools.

Video Playback Monitors

In some situations, seeing the movie image on the computer monitor will be sufficient. Whenever you're recording something in which the performer needs to see the picture (like in ADR recording), you'll need a second monitor in the studio. In the case of an orchestral scoring session, a large projection system might be necessary. In any of these situations, a secondary video feed for the studio must be hooked up. If you're slaving Pro Tools to a dedicated VTR, a simple *mult* (multiple or Y-connection or through a video distribution amplifier) of the video output of the deck can be used to send a composite signal to a TV monitor in the studio. It is also nice to have a separate monitor and speakers for your clients to watch where they are sitting. This can help keep them from lurking over your shoulder.

Integrated Avid Video Options

There are now several options for dedicated Avid video solutions integrated into Pro Tools.

- AV option XL for Windows XP

- Avid Mojo SDI

- Avid Mojo

All of these options include a dedicated video capture device that handles video playback and output for Pro Tools. Those who work all day, everyday, on complex video projects can benefit from enhanced compatibility with Avid video projects, lowered strain on the host CPU, and a high-quality dedicated video output. The video device reduces the load on the CPU by handling all of the video compression and decompression that otherwise would be done by the host processor. This way, you're free to use more RTAS plug-ins and run higher track numbers in your sessions without overloading the CPU. The video output on the card can be used to feed any number of monitors for you, the client, and talent in the studio.

Avid Mojo and Avid Mojo SDI are systems that include Avid video features that let you import OMF, AAF, and MXF projects containing video files directly in Pro Tools. These projects can include video edits in the timeline along with the edited audio. Capturing video directly to the Pro Tools video track is also supported, eliminating extra steps involved if you need to digitize video from tape.

Third-Party Video Cards

Various third-party video cards can also be used to output high-quality video from Pro Tools. A multi-head computer video card such as the Raedon 9800 can be used to feed a computer monitor and a dedicated NTSC video monitor. QuickTime video can be directed to the NTSC video output, and hardware acceleration from the video card will lessen the strain on the CPU. An adapter can be placed on the card's second output that will convert it to a standard NTSC composite signal connection.

Firewire and DV Decoders

A more cost-effective method of outputting NTSC video for monitoring utilizes "pro-sumer" DV video decoders to handle video output. The DV codec has long been a popular pro-sumer-level video format, and entry-level hardware is not expensive. Most video-editing facilities support this format and will be able to give you dubs on one of several sub-formats of DV with time code.

MiniDV tapes can be played by consumer camcorders, such as the Sony TVR-17, and support hi-quality digital video, 16 bit/48kHz stereo audio, and SMPTE time code. By using video software such as iMovie or Final Cut Pro, you can capture these movies through a Firewire connection and create QuickTime movies that Pro Tools can use. Many—but not all—MiniDV camcorders allow time code-synchronized control through the Firewire connection.

Not All DV Equipment Is Created Equal   The DV video format has evolved into several different tape formats. MiniDV is essentially a consumer format. Sony's DVCAM is designed for more professional applications. Panasonic DVCPRO is an alternative professional format. The data stream for all three of these formats is essentially the same, with certain modifications to increase the record time on tapes or to improve linear editing capabilities. Equipment made to the MiniDV spec might not always contain professional features needed in the studio. Not all MiniDV camcorders support time code and would not be usable in this situation. Be sure to have the latest information before purchasing a consumer-level camera or deck.

When Pro Tools is playing back the DV movie, it can be sent back out through the Firewire connection to the camcorder to be decoded by the camera. Connect a monitor to the camera's output, and voila, you have full-screen video playback in sync with audio. The camcorder acts like a dedicated video card in the computer. It will reduce the CPU usage, thus allowing more horsepower for audio. For a modest investment of $1,000 or so, you can have a digital video tape deck capable of decoding the Firewire output of QuickTime movies played by Pro Tools. That's a lot of bang for the buck! There are also standalone decoders, such as the Canopus ADVC-100 and DVCAM

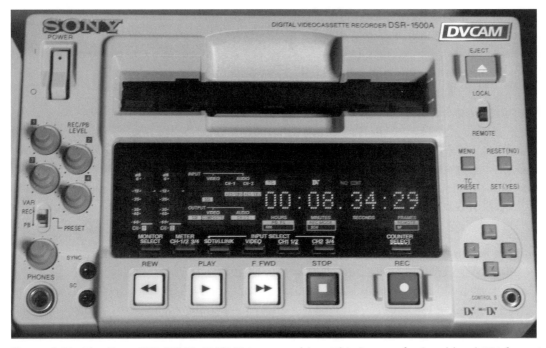

Figure 4.10 The Sony DSR-1500A DVCAM tape machine. This is a professional-level DV format video tape deck capable of converting DV movies via Firewire into full-screen video output suitable for normal video monitors.

VTRs, that will stand more abuse than will delicate consumer camcorders. One such decoder is shown in Figure 4.10.

Caveats About DV Decoding   The DV camcorder requires some time to process the DV stream from the computer. It will be necessary to compensate for this induced delay, and Pro Tools has an option for doing so. Under the Movie menu, choose Set Movie Sync Offset. Here you can enter a value in quarter frames to offset the playback of the DV stream in order to compensate for processing delays in the decoder. You'll have to load some audio from the video clip into Pro Tools for reference. View the video along with the audio to determine how much of an offset is needed. Some experimentation will be required to get it just right, but once it is set up for a particular DV device, it will not need changing until another device is used. You may also use a device such as the Syncheck (www.syncheck.com), which will give you a very accurate measurement of the sync between audio and video.

Virtual VTR Software

If CPU usage is a big concern, and you have another Macintosh computer available in the studio, you can use a software solution that keeps all of the video processing on another computer. Gallery Software (http://www.virtualvtr.com) has a little app called Virtual VTR, seen in Figure 4.11. It can play QuickTime movies while slaved to MTC—you can copy your movie file to another computer, assign a SMPTE start time, feed it some MTC, and watch it sync right up. Virtual VTR can also act as a 9-pin slave machine similar to a VTR and be controlled by a master controller such as Soundmaster's ION/ATOM multi-machine synchronizer. Dubbing stages can use systems like the ION/ATOM to control multiple Pro Tools systems, Virtual VTR, and other equipment right from the console's controls—this makes all the different systems act like one giant tape machine for the operator.

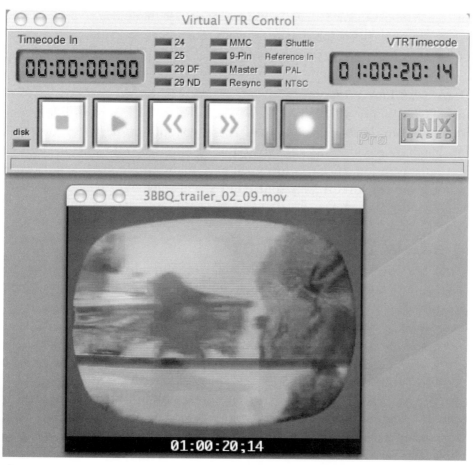

Figure 4.11 The Movie window and status bar in Virtual VTR.

Even if you're using Virtual VTR on another computer, you'll still need some way of outputting the video signal in order to connect video monitors and projection systems. If you're using DV files, the Firewire connection to a camcorder or other decoder is possible. (You'll have to calibrate an offset in Virtual VTR to compensate for processing delays in the camera.) High-quality digital video cards from Aja, BlackMagic, and Pinnacle can give Virtual VTR video resolution up to full uncompressed HD with professional I/O, such as component and SDI options. With the proper video card, Virtual VTR is capable of frame-edge accurate sync to your Pro Tools session using a common video sync reference or black burst. All types of QuickTime media are supported, from lo-res compressed files to full HD resolution video for playback on large screens or projector systems.

Time Code Burn-In   Another useful feature of Virtual VTR is the ability to create a time code burn-in window for any QuickTime movie. See the section on time code burn-ins at the end of this chapter for more details.

Dedicated Hard Disk Video Recorders

Another video playback option is a standalone video recorder that is hard-disk based, such as the Doremi V1 or the Rosendahl Bonsai. These types of recorders feature instant random-access playback of video and audio, variable compression ratios, 9-pin control, and frame-accurate operation. Such recorders will have to digitize source video in order to use it, requiring another VTR to play source tapes. This type of system is expensive but can provide a more professional degree of functionality and dependability.

Creating a New Video Session

Once all of your equipment has been connected and configured for video, it is time to create a new video Pro Tools session. Close any current session you might have open, unless you are already working with one that needs to be viewed with picture. Choose File > Create Session > New Session in order to open the New Session dialog box, shown in Figure 4.12.

Choosing Sample Rate and Bit Depth

The sample rate of almost any film, video, or multimedia audio should be 48kHz. If you're working in hi-resolution sample rates, 96kHz would be appropriate. This way, any further conversion back to 48kHz later will be relatively painless. 44.1kHz is not a standard sample rate for video. However, there might be certain situations in which 44.1kHz would be the better choice for computer-based multimedia work—certain

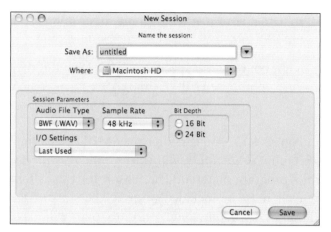

Figure 4.12   The New Session dialog box in Pro Tools 7. It includes choices for file type, sample rate, bit depth, and I/O configuration.

media creation applications might prefer a 44.1kHz source file for audio. Be sure to discuss this with the content creators during pre-production.

The bit depth choice is more complicated. You must weigh factors of speed and efficiency against audio quality and dynamics as they relate to the current project. For instance, if you were starting a film project that was very serene, and you wanted the quietest noise floor possible, 24 bit is the way to go. In fact, I would suggest that 24 bit is always the preferred bit depth. In cases in which you are working with OMF files from an Avid workstation, the source media could be 16 bit (although the current Avid systems support 24 bit audio). When converting 16 bit OMFI into Pro Tools sessions, it will take more disk space once converted to 24 bit files. The newer AAF format supports 24 bit media and is preferred.

Choosing Frame Rate and Frame Count

The choice of frame rate and frame count depends on the nature of your current project. Once again, choice of frame rate should be determined in pre-production. Typically, a NTSC video session will use 29.97fps SMPTE with or without a drop-frame count. If the video is in PAL/EBU format, a frame rate of 25fps will be used. Film and 24p HD sessions can use 29.97 as well, but it might need to be pulled down in order to match the speed change of the 2-3 transfer process. In some cases, a frame rate of 24fps will be used for projects that will end up on film in their final format.

HD video can often use higher frame rates of 50 to 60fps. When these higher frame rates are used, it is possible to use their lower multiples in Pro Tools. For example, a 60fps HD video can run in Pro Tools at 30fps. 59.94fps is commonly used for HD running at

NTSC speed and can use 29.97fps in Pro Tools. You just want to use an even multiple of these higher frame rates.

Small-duration Internet media projects might not require a specific SMPTE format if they will not be using any tape format. Flash files do not use SMPTE time code as a reference.

Choosing Session Start Times

In the Session Setup window shown in Figure 4.13, you can alter the SMPTE start time of the current session. Pro Tools defaults to 00:00:00:00. Most videos will use 01:00:00:00 as a standard start time for program material. The reason for this is that certain test tones and countdown pre-rolls must be included prior to the start of the program. If a start time of 00:00:00:00 is used, anything prior to that will have SMPTE times in the high numbers—23:59:55:15, for example. When the actual program starts, SMPTE will pass through the "midnight hour" and go from 23:59:59:29 to 00:00:00:00. This transition has unpredictable results with many SMPTE readers and VTRs. The use of 01:00:00:00 as a start time eliminates this unpredictability. However, it is not a good idea to set the Pro Tools session start time at 01:00:00:00, because you need to allow for some space before the program starts to allow for test tones and sync beeps, such as the standard 2-beep tone. This requires that the Pro Tools session start time be earlier than one hour. The actual material itself should start at one hour.

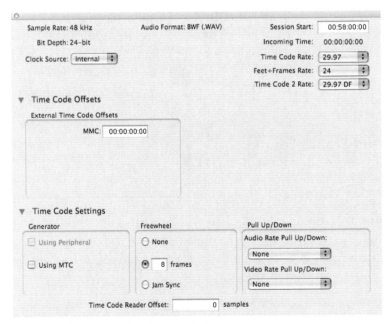

Figure 4.13 The Session Setup window. Here you can change the SMPTE start time of the current Pro Tools session, among other things.

The 2-Beep SYNC Tone and How to Create One   The 2-beep is a standard way of synching audio tapes to video or film reels. A short (one-frame duration) 1kHz tone beeps exactly two seconds before the program material begins. These beeps can be used later to line up the audio with film or video. It is very easy to create a 2-beep tone in Pro Tools using the Audiosuite plug-in called Signal Generator. Set your grid value to :01 frame, and then create a new mono audio track. Select a one-frame piece on that track starting at 00:59:58:00, and then open the Signal Generator plug-in and set the frequency to 1000Hz (1kHz) and the level to −20db. Press the Process button, and you now have a one-frame beep two seconds before the start of the program. Now someone else can use the sound of that beep to line up the first video frame that has the "2" countdown number in it, and your audio should run in sync with that video, assuming the clock (speed) reference is the same for both.

Two minutes before 1 hour, or 00:58:00;00, will work in most situations. This allows plenty of time to include calibration tones, 2-beeps, and *slates* (small recordings made of the engineer talking and giving information about the upcoming program), and pre-roll for tape decks. The typical procedure for video post-production facility is to start tape at 00:58:00;00, run color bars and a 1kHz reference tone from 00:58:30;00 to 00:59:30;00, and then begin a 10-second countdown at 00:59:50;00 to the program start at one hour.

It is possible to change the session start time in the Session Setup window later if you need to. When doing so, a dialog box will appear that asks you if you would like to maintain time code or maintain relative positions, as shown in Figure 4.14. If you just want to increase the amount of time before the program starts, choose the Maintain Time Code option. Choosing the Maintain Relative Position option will not create any more time before the first audio region. Instead, it will simply change the SMPTE start times of all regions in the session so that they remain in their same positions relative to the start of the session.

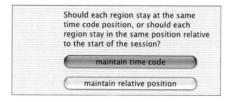

Figure 4.14   The change session start time dialog box in Pro Tools.

The other reason for placing some time before your program in Pro Tools is to allow for the lockup time of external tape machines. No mechanical tape deck can sync up instantly; neither can Pro Tools, for that matter. Some pre-roll is needed to stabilize any synchronized system. This pre-roll should take place while no audio is playing. Pro Tools will not output any audio until stable sync has been established. Anywhere from two to ten seconds might be needed for pre-roll. There is an option for machine control that will allow you to define a pre-roll value in frames. Once this value is set for a particular tape machine, it should not need to be changed.

Importing Video Files

Bringing video material into Pro Tools is very simple. Making sure that the video material is of the proper format and type for your needs might not be that simple. If Quick-Time movies are provided for you in data format on DVDs, CD-ROMs, or hard drives, importing them directly can be quick and painless. If you are provided with videotape and cannot sync to the VTR directly, you'll have to digitize the footage yourself and create a compatible QuickTime movie. Even if you *can* sync directly to this VTR, you may still want to digitize the footage in order to take advantage of the non-linear aspect of QuickTime movies in Pro Tools. With VTRs, you must wind the tape to different locations in your session. This takes time. QuickTime movies locate instantly to any position in your session and remain in frame-accurate sync with your session no matter what type of editing you're doing. Wherever your cursor is, the QuickTime movie will instantly locate to that position. The VTR can only locate as fast as its transport mechanism will allow.

Keep in mind that the larger-size QuickTime movies (720 × 480) can use more system resources. This may limit the number of RTAS plug-ins and audio tracks you can use. All new Macs can view DV movies through the Firewire port natively and do not tax the CPU that much. The DV codec does not require a large amount of CPU time to process since each frame of video is compressed individually. However, the file sizes are quite large and may require a dedicated hard drive for video files only.

DV movies look great and are easy to digitize with iMovie, Final Cut Pro, or Virtual VTR. Pro Tools in OSX will direct the DV stream out through a Firewire connection to which you can hook up your DV camera. Certain cameras are able to pass the DV information directly to their video output connector for use with a full-size monitor. This is a great because you can view hi-resolution video on a full-size monitor, and you can even connect multiple monitors if needed. The movie will instantly locate to any position and will be frame accurate. What more could you want?

Importing Avid video media requires the addition of one of the Avid video hardware products such as Avid Mojo. Avid Mojo hardware reduces the load on the host CPU for normal QuickTime playback as well as Avid media playback. Certain Avid media can be played back by Virtual VTR as well.

Opening QuickTime Movies

Once a properly formatted QuickTime movie has been created, importing it into Pro Tools is relatively easy. Select File>Import>Video. A dialog box will open that allows you to find the correct QuickTime file. Once you have selected a file and pressed the Open button, you are offered importing options that include the destination for the file (track or region list), the location in the timeline, as well as several other options such as audio importing, as seen in Figure 4.15.

A new track will be created in Pro Tools with the same name as the QuickTime file. The track defaults to the Key Frames mode, in which frames of video are displayed in the timeline for easy location reference. The use of this mode is processor intensive; to conserve CPU resources, you can switch to Block mode. The movie track behaves similarly to an audio track and can be moved around by the grabber and placed using Grid or Spot mode. It is not possible to trim or edit the movie file in LE systems without the DV toolkit option installed.

Figure 4.15 The Video Import Options dialog box.

Once you have opened the QuickTime movie, press Play and have a look. If you start Play before the movie start time, you will see the first frame frozen on-screen until the movie start time has been reached. Similarly, when the end of the QuickTime movie arrives, the last frame will be frozen while Pro Tools continues to play. Often the first and last frames are black, so this may not be noticeable, but when there is an image present you might wonder if the movie is "online" or not.

Once you have imported a QuickTime movie, it is possible to disable video playback temporarily without deleting the video track. Taking the movie offline can be helpful when working on very small areas of audio because it frees up the system to work a little faster. Depending on your CPU, this could be very important—especially on native LE systems. You can also hide the video track just like any other track in Pro Tools, helping to keep the clutter down. Hiding the video track in the Edit window does not disable video playback features but does free up some system resources. There are two ways to change the online status of a video track:

1. Click the O button on the active video track to toggle its status.

2. Use the key command Cmd+Shift+J to toggle the active video track status.

Playing the Main Video Track   Although there can be multiple video tracks in one session on HD and DV toolkit systems, only one video track at a time may be online and played back. This is referred to as the main video track. It is denoted by the small QuickTime icon next to the track name. When this icon is blue, that video track is the main video track.

Capturing DV Video from Tape

With the Avid Mojo option, you may capture video right into Pro Tools just like recording audio. The video track can be placed in record and off you go. Using a Sync I/O and machine control options, this process can be sample accurate and locked to time code. The Mojo options make working with video much easier on a day-to-day basis, but for those who do not have that option, there are other ways to get video from tape into Pro Tools.

If you must capture DV video yourself without an Avid Mojo option, you'll need a separate application (such as iMovie, Final Cut Pro, Adobe Premiere, or Virtual VTR) and a DV playback device such as a MiniDV camcorder with a Firewire connection (Sony calls it iLink).

Time Code Burn-In Windows   A visual representation of the SMPTE time in the video itself can be quite useful. A visual representation can be generated by certain devices that will take an incoming SMPTE time code source and display the numbers within a video signal, typically at the bottom of the screen in a black area called a *burn-in window*. QuickTime is capable of displaying time code in this fashion. Using the Virtual VTR application is the only way I have enabled this feature in QuickTime. Simply open any movie file in Virtual VTR and under the Playback menu select Reset Time Code Reference, and a dialog box will open that allows you to set the starting frame number, the frame rate, and the position of the time code display, as shown in Figure 4.16. Once you have enabled this time code window, it will be seen whenever that movie is played, regardless of the application used—Virtual VTR, QuickTime Player, or Pro Tools.

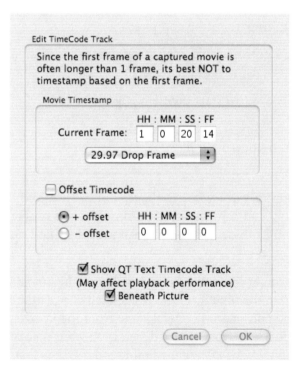

Figure 4.16   Virtual VTR software non-linear video player. This application can play back Quick-Time movies synchronized to MTC or 9-pin control. It also has the added capability to create time code burn in Windows directly in QuickTime.

Capturing DV Video with iMovie

iMovie is consumer-level video-editing software for Macintosh. It supports the DV codec as its native format for video. The iMovie interface is simple and lacks many pro features such as time code support. iMovie is capable of digitizing DV video and editing clips with frame accuracy. Without the time code support, though, it will be necessary to have some other time information within the video itself. This could take the form of a time code burn-in window or a "5, 4, 3, 2 . . ." countdown with a 2-beep. Either of these will allow you to place the DV file at the correct time in Pro Tools.

Following are the steps to take in order to digitize DV video with iMovie:

1. Locate the video you want to digitize on tape.

2. Launch iMovie.

3. Create a new Movie project by choosing File > New Project. The new project will open up with the capture clips mode ready.

4. Connect your playback device via Firewire to the computer.

5. Play the source material either using iMovie's controls or manually on your playback device.

6. Click the Import button when you want to start digitizing, as shown in Figure 4.17.

7. Click the Import button again when you would like to stop digitizing.

Once you have digitized the video you want to work with, you'll see it as a slide in the first clip window. While in the Clip Editor, you can trim the clip down to the proper starting and ending frames by dragging on the tabs found in the timeline of the Clip Edit window, as shown in Figure 4.18.

Next, drag the clip from its window in the upper-left down to the timeline at the bottom of the iMovie window. This places the clip in the timeline. Once the edited clip is in the timeline, choose Export from the File menu and select To QuickTime from the iMovie: Export dialog box, as shown in Figure 4.19. The format choice depends on what type of file you want to work with. To use the hi-quality of DV, select Full Quality DV as your format for export. You will then be allowed to name the file and perform the export. Now you have a QuickTime DV file that can be imported by Pro Tools and synchronized with your audio session.

Figure 4.17   The iMovie clip capture window. Here, you can digitize DV video from a Firewire playback device and export the clip for use in Pro Tools.

Determining the First Frame   When using iMovie to digitize video, it is not possible to be frame accurate when digitizing. You must have a time code burn-in or some sort of timing information such as a 2-beep or visual countdown to determine what is the first frame of program material. You can trim the digitized video in iMovie so that the *first* frame of the QuickTime movie is the correct one. My advice is to capture more video than you think you'll need, in order to allow for proper trimming once it is digitized. The exported movie should start at a known frame number so that aligning it in Pro Tools is simple.

Capturing DV Video with Final Cut Pro

Final Cut Pro is professional-level video editing software capable of digitizing DV video from Firewire sources such as consumer and professional MiniDV camcorders with an IEEE 1394 (Firewire or iLink) interface. It is possible to frame-accurately digitize video using DV's built-in time code, as long as your playback device supports time-code addressing (most MiniDV camcorders do). Digitizing in Final Cut Pro is a bit complicated because of its enhanced accuracy.

Figure 4.18 The clip editing tabs in iMovie. Use the two lower tabs below the start and end of the yellow section to define the start and end points of your movie clip. The start point should be a frame that can be easily identified for proper placement in your Pro Tools session.

Following is a step-by-step method for capturing video using Final Cut Pro:

1. First connect your Firewire playback device to the computer and turn it to playback or VCR mode.

2. Launch Final Cut Pro.

3. Make sure your audio/video settings are correct. Select File > Audio/Video Settings, as shown in Figure 4.20. The Sequence and Capture presets should both be set to DV NTSC 48kHz (at least for NTSC standard video, not PAL/EBU). The device control should be set to Firewire NTSC. These are typically the default settings. The External Video setting does not apply for capturing.

Figure 4.19   The iMovie: Export dialog box. Here you can determine the file type of an exported movie file from iMovie.

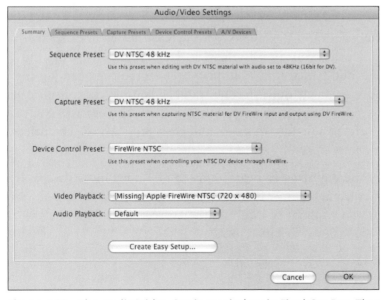

Figure 4.20   The Audio/Video Settings window in Final Cut Pro. These settings are correct for digitizing DV video from a consumer camcorder or other Firewire, DV playback device in NTSC format.

4. Once the camera is connected and Final Cut is configured, select File > Log and Capture. The Log and Capture window will open as seen in Figure 4.21.

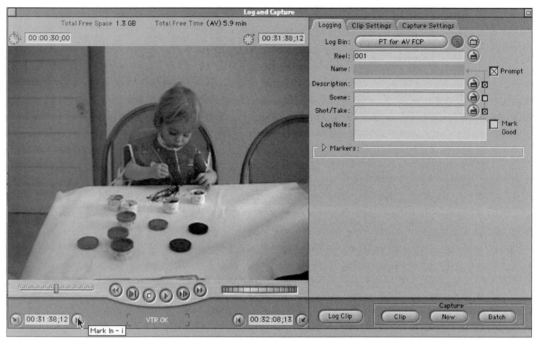

Figure 4.21   The Log and Capture window in Final Cut Pro.

5. In this window, remote control the connected playback device in order to locate the segment of video you want to digitize. The left slider shuttles the device both forwards and backwards, and the wheel on the right can jog the device in very small increments down to one frame. The time code display in the upper right tells you where on the tape you are currently located. You can type a specific time code value into this box and then press Enter. The device will locate to that tape position.

6. Set a start point for the digitizing to begin. This can be done in two ways. If you know the correct frame number to start digitizing on, you may type it into the lower-left time code window or locate to the correct position and click the Mark In button, as shown in Figure 4.22.

Figure 4.22   The Mark In button in the Log and Capture window of Final Cut Pro.

7. Once you have set an In point, an Out point must be set in order to capture the video. Either type a specific time code number into the time code value by the Mark Out button or locate the playback device to that point and press the Mark Out button in the Log and Capture window, as shown in Figure 4.23.

Figure 4.23 The Mark Out button in Final Cut Pro.

8. Now that you have defined both an In and an Out point, press the Capture Clip button in the far lower-right of the Log and Capture window, as shown in Figure 4.24. This will begin the digitizing process.

9. You'll be prompted to name the clip; go ahead and do so. Remember the name in order to find it in the browser later.

10. The playback device will cue to a point ahead of the In point in order to pre-roll the tape. Playback will begin, and when the In point is reached, Final Cut Pro will digitize the video clip and store it on your hard drive. When the Out point is reached, digitizing will stop. The process is frame accurate, and no video outside of the defined points will be recorded.

Figure 4.24 The Capture Clip button in Final Cut Pro's Log and Capture window.

11. Once your clip has been digitized, you can place it in the timeline to prepare for exporting. Look in the browser window for the clip name you just digitized. If this is a new Final Cut project, it should be one of two items listed in the project Browser window. The other item will be the blank sequence (Sequence 1) you will use next.

12. Drag the clip from the browser window to the blank sequence timeline, where you will see three tracks appear with the clip in them, as shown in Figure 4.25. The tracks are video (V1), audio left (A1), and audio right (A2). Make sure you drag the clip to the very start of the timeline. You may play the clip here to double-check that everything is okay before exporting.

Figure 4.25 Drag your clip into the timeline and play it to make sure it works. Make sure to drag the clip to the very start of the timeline so that the exported file will begin correctly.

13. Now that the clip is in the timeline, you can export it as a QuickTime movie file. Choose File, Export, QuickTime. The Save dialog box opens, offering you choices for exporting, as shown in Figure 4.26.

14. Choose the DV Stream option for the format, name the file appropriately, and export the movie. Now you have a QuickTime DV movie that can be imported into Pro Tools.

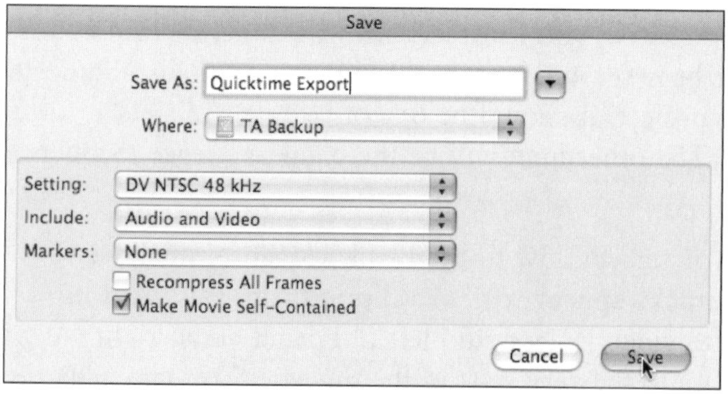

Figure 4.26 The Save dialog box in Final Cut Pro. Here you can select the format and settings for the exported movie file.

Virtual VTR   Virtual VTR is also capable of capturing video in many different formats, including DV. If there is time code present in either the DV stream or via MTC, Virtual VTR will automatically timestamp the newly created file so that Pro Tools may place it at the right start time in the session. If you use Virtual VTR for playback as well, the second VVTR computer can capture video while another session is taking place on the Pro Tools system, minimizing downtime in a busy studio.

Multiple Video Tracks and Regions (HD and DV Toolkit Only)

It is possible to have more than one video track on Pro Tools HD systems and even LE systems with the DV toolkit. With these systems, there can also be multiple movie clips on each track. Only one video track can be active at a time, and so each video track has a special icon to designate the active track, as seen in Figure 4.27. Only the active track's movie clips can be seen in the Video window or via external monitors.

Video regions may be edited in much the same way as audio regions, including cut, copy, paste, and trim operations. Video regions may be grouped with audio and MIDI regions across multiple tracks. Video regions cannot have fades or crossfades and cannot be processed by time-stretching or compression.

The limitations of multiple video tracks and regions are as follows:

- Only one video track can be active at a time.

- Systems with Avid hardware can mix QuickTime and Avid media in the same session but not on the same video track.

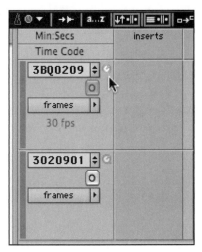

Figure 4.27 When more that one video track is created in Pro Tools, the small QuickTime icon determines which track is active. By clicking this icon on a video track, that track becomes active.

- Once the video engine rate (same as the video frame rate) of the session has been set by importing the first video file, all other video files imported into the session must have the same frame rate.

- Heavy usage of RTAS plug-ins can affect video performance due to CPU usage.

The use of multiple video regions on one track can really be helpful. One example is in the advertising world where one 30-second TV spot can have multiple variations in the ending voiceover. This could be for various locations, differing regions, or even different phone numbers. For example, suppose you have a commercial for contact lenses that's going to air in five different markets across the country. Each location may have a different phone number for ordering. This may be displayed on-screen and spoken by the voiceover at the end of the spot. It could also be the same video with only the voiceover changing at the end.

In either case, the Pro Tools session could contain five different video regions, one for each market, or it could have a single video region that is duplicated five times, one for each market. Once the base spot has been created, all of the audio tracks can be copied to new locations to make various versions for each market. If the only thing that changes is the voiceover, once the base spot has been copied, the ending voiceover may be deleted and re-recorded with the proper phone number or store locations. This will keep all the various permutations of the spot within one Pro Tools session and consistent from one version to another if mix automation is copied as well.

When working on a long-form project such as a feature film, the use of two movie tracks can be useful. For example, one movie track could contain a lower-resolution version of the movie with a time code burn-in window for quick spotting and editing. The second video track could contain the HD full-resolution movie with no time code window for full screen or projector viewing. In order to change movies, you only need to click the active button on each track to make that movie version viewable. Using the lower-res version can increase the response time of the Pro Tools session while performing intensive editing.

You may also have multiple video playlists on each video track as an alternative to multiple tracks. All these features add versatility to any video post-production workflow.

Changing Movie Offsets

When you first import a movie file, the start time of the movie defaults to the beginning of your session. As discussed earlier, it is not a good idea to have your program material begin right at the start of the session; it's better to have it start a minute or two later in order to allow for pre-roll, test tones, and sync beeps to occur before. If your movie file starts at the very first frame of the program (typical), you'll need to change the movie start time to be the same as your audio program. With HD and LE DV toolkit systems, this can be done several ways. The first is using *Grid* mode. The second is using *Spot* mode.

Here's how to change movie start times in Pro Tools using Grid mode (for more information on Grid mode, refer to Chapter 6, "Editing to Picture"):

1. Set the Grid value to 1 frame.

2. Enter Absolute Grid mode (F4 or Grid Mode button). Be sure not to use Relative Grid!

3. Using the grabber tool, select the movie in the Edit window.

4. Drag the movie until the left edge lines up with the correct start time (usually 01:00:00:00), as shown in Figure 4.28.

5. Let go of the movie region. The start time has now been modified.

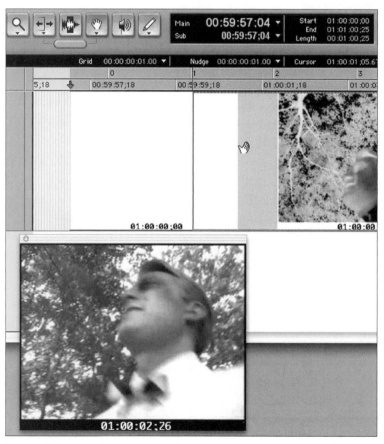

Figure 4.28 Moving a movie file to a new start time in Grid mode.

Here's how to change movie start times using Spot mode (for more information on Spot mode, refer to Chapter 6):

1. Enter Spot mode (F3).

2. Using the grabber, select the movie in the Edit window.

3. The Spot dialog box will open, as shown in Figure 4.29. Select the time code for the time scale (or minutes and seconds in LE without the DV toolkit).

4. Enter the new start time and press the OK button. Voila! Your movie will start at the new time.

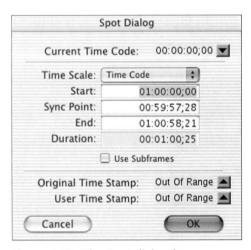

Figure 4.29 The Spot dialog box.

Time Code and LE Systems: You Can Still Do it!   Even though Pro Tools LE without the DV toolkit does not include time code rulers, you can still work with time code and QuickTime movies relatively easily. Once you understand synchronization concepts, having the time code ruler will no longer be essential. The minutes and seconds ruler will work as a substitute for a time code ruler. If you take one second and divide it by your frame rate, you'll get a measure of how long one frame is in milliseconds. At 29.97fps, a frame is about 33ms (or 1,602 samples at 48kHz) long. With this in mind, you can roughly calculate where frames will fall.

Any time I use the time code ruler in this book, simply substitute the minutes and seconds ruler. Granted, this method is not accurate to frame boundaries, but then again, audio timing is more precise than visual timing anyhow. Adjustments smaller than a frame are necessary for good audio timing. In addition, once a QuickTime movie is loaded, you can find frame boundaries by nudging the cursor around until the movie changes one frame. (You'll find more on nudging in Chapter 6.) A time code burn-in window can also substitute for an SMPTE ruler in Pro Tools. Use Virtual VTR or QT Sync to "turn on" the time code window in QuickTime and use that as your time code ruler.

Checking Sync

Now that you have a QuickTime movie imported into Pro Tools and starting at the correct time, you should check to see that it is playing correctly and in sync. The easiest way to do that is to watch someone talking in the video to see if the lips are moving in sync with the words. When you first import a QuickTime file, you can also import any audio from within it at the same time.

Importing Audio from QuickTime Movies

If the QuickTime movie has an audio stream in it, Pro Tools can import this when you import the video. The Video Import Options dialog box shown in Figure 4.30 has a checkbox for importing the audio from the file. If you choose the New Track destination, the audio file will be placed in the timeline at the same position as the video file. You may then watch the video with its associated audio file in sync within Pro Tools. The video and audio should be in sync just as they were in the QuickTime movie itself.

Understand that just viewing a video and listening to its related audio is not a foolproof way of determining sync. It is known as "eyeballing it." The only accurate way to determine whether sync is correct is to have a time code burn included with your video (discussed next) or a 2-beep that can be used to align the audio and video. Having both would be ideal.

Examining Lip Sync

Determining if your video and audio are playing in correct sync without a time code burn-in is easiest when watching people talk on-screen. We are so used to watching people talk everyday that a sense of what looks in sync and what does not is very natural. It might take some time to develop a very accurate measure of lip sync, but practice makes perfect. Try offsetting dialogue from its video frame by frame until you notice the change. Try it in both directions to get a feel for what bad sync looks like, whether it's early or late. With practice, you will quickly be able to tell if dialogue is properly in sync with the video.

Figure 4.30 The Video Import Options dialog box allows you to import audio from the selected video along with the video itself. Pro Tools can then place both the video and audio regions in the timeline together.

After encountering and correcting bad sync, you should try to determine what has caused the error. Just making the correction without knowing why the error occurred can lead to major troubles later. It might simply be an error you have made while importing or placing the QuickTime file, or it could have resulted from bad or incorrect time code on the source tape. Some frames might have been dropped during the capture process, creating flawed movie files. Perhaps the video editor that gave you the Quick-Time file included some black frames before the true first frame of video, causing the dialogue to be some frames earlier than the video. Communication between you and the video editor is crucial for these reasons.

Time Code Burn-In Window

A time code burn-in window is a display of SMPTE within the video image. This allows the viewer to see at what frame number the current video frame is. A time code burn-in window can be very helpful when spotting audio using a cue sheet. A time code burn-in also helps to accurately check the sync of video and audio in Pro Tools. When a Quick-Time movie with a time code burn-in is loaded into Pro Tools, you can easily see if the frame numbers in the burn-in are aligned with the time code ruler in the Edit window, as shown in Figure 4.31.

It is also possible to create a time code burn-in window from an external video source (such as a synchronized VTR) using the Sync I/O. This option creates the window in real

Figure 4.31   Here, you can see a time code burn-in in the QuickTime Movie window of Pro Tools. Notice how the frame number in the movie window matches the one in the time code display of the Transport and the Big Counter.

time, and the image is not recorded onto the video. This can be nice when you want to watch the video without any time code window present. Simply turn the window off, and you'll have a clean image to watch. Refer to the Sync I/O's documentation for further information.

If you notice a discrepancy between the time code numbers of the burn-in window and those in the Pro Tools time code ruler, the movie file is not at the correct offset, or there is a frame rate problem. Check to see whether the burn-in window has any semicolons in it, as that will denote drop-frame time code. Make sure Pro Tools is set to the same frame rate and frame count as the QuickTime movie. Consult with the video editor to find out what frame rate was used originally.

Make Sure You're in Sync   It is imperative that your reference video is properly synchronized within or with Pro Tools before continuing to work on any post-production project. The following chapter deals with importing audio files from other workstations that all need to reference the same time code values to ensure the intent of the creators of the material remains intact. If your reference video file is not at the absolute correct time code value, all subsequent work you do on the project will come into question later when things don't quite sync up for layback. This can lead to costly errors in the production schedule and fingers pointing in your direction. The time code burn-in is the only bulletproof assurance you have that you are properly synchronized to the video.

You are now set up, configured, and ready to begin work on a video project. The next chapter is all about recording and getting all the necessary audio into Pro Tools and ready for editing.

5 Recording to Picture

Now that Pro Tools is set up and ready to go, it's time to start recording and importing audio for a new project. The audio data that you'll be using in this project can come from several different sources. A large portion of this data will come from the video editor; this will include audio that was recorded during filming and edited together with the video. The video editor might have also included some music files (temp score) and maybe even some basic sound effects of files that you will import as well. You might have to record audio from a videotape or even DAT tapes, and music may come in the form of a CD or on DAT. You will also record material live in the studio. All this material will eventually be synchronized with the video given to you by the video editor as a reference.

Appendix B Flow Chart Help   Appendix B contains a flow chart of where different sources of audio and video might come from and how they are incorporated into one Pro Tools session in order to combine them into one complete soundtrack.

There are basically two types of live recording that you'll need to do. One is synchronous recording of material that was originally recorded during filming, along with replacement or augmentation of that material. This includes ADR, foley, and sound effects that are tied to the picture. The second type of recording is additive material that is not necessarily recorded live with picture, such as voiceovers and music. Because more difficulty lies in accurately recording and assembling synchronous material, I'll spend more time discussing it in this chapter.

Using Audio from the Set (Production Audio)

Audio recorded while filming can come to you in many forms. A video editor may give you an OMFI file or an EDL that refers to the original source tapes. An edited version could come on videotape or in a QuickTime movie. There are so many sets of circumstances that can occur in the production of a film or video that you must be prepared to handle just about anything. Let's start with the oldest and most basic way of transferring audio clips from the video editor to Pro Tools, the EDL.

EDLs

An EDL, or Edit Decision List, is a list of time code values and tape names, in the form of a text file generated by the video editing system, that can be interpreted and used to collect various audio or video segments and place them in a certain order, thereby creating an edited work. Analysis of this text file will tell you where to get each piece of audio and where to put it in time relative to the picture. Analysis can be performed by computers as well as by people, which is helpful when problems arise. There are three basic standards for EDLs in wide use today: the Sony 9000 EDL, CMX style EDLs, and the Grass Valley Group version, or GVG. Each one is slightly different but contains the same basic information. The CMX 3600 is the most widely used EDL format, and I'll use it as an example to further explain how EDLs work and how you can use them with Pro Tools.

CMX 3600 EDL

Figure 5.1 shows a small CMX EDL generated from Final Cut Pro. In this example, three audio files are edited together over a 20-second portion of the video. The first audio clip is from a tape called R1103, the second from R0101, and the third is from R0207. The two time code numbers on the left determine where on R1103, for instance, the first audio file comes from. The next two time code numbers are the start and end points in the timeline where the audio file will be placed within Pro Tools. Other indicators determine what *type* of edit occurs—crossfade, cut, and so on. The types of edits done in video editing are more complex than those with audio; these indicators can usually be ignored for the most part with audio. For example, multiple video cuts may occur during the span of one audio file as the camera angles change. The video editor should remove all video edits from an EDL before giving it to you, keeping it simple. The example in Figure 5.1 is a very simple EDL containing audio edits only.

```
TITLE: PT FOR AV CMX EDL
FCM: DROP FRAME

001  R1103    AA    C        00:21:29:19 00:21:35:21 01:00:00:00 01:00:06:02
* FROM CLIP NAME:   PRE SET A1

002  R0101    NONE  C        00:00:44:06 00:00:49:08 01:00:06:02 01:00:11:04
* FROM CLIP NAME:   URBAN 1
AUD  3     4

003  R0207    AA    C        00:11:10:02 00:11:19:05 01:00:11:10 01:00:20:13
* FROM CLIP NAME:   OFFSTAGE B
```

Figure 5.1 An excerpt from a CMX 3600 EDL generated by Final Cut Pro.

Each edit is noted by a three-digit number on the left. The next alphanumeric string to the right is the reel name or number. The reel name can be any combination of eight letters and numbers; it tells you what tape the source material is from. It could be a videotape, an audio file from a location recorder, or even a DAT tape. The first edit, 001, is from reel, or tape (they are typically referred to as reels, regardless of the type of media), R1103. The next item is the edit type, in this case AA. This indicates a stereo audio edit, which is the most typical type. Most video editors will not get into very tricky, single-track audio edits if the project is moving on to a sound editor. It is your job to perform the trickier editing and mixing of audio, anyhow. Next comes the transition indicator. The C simply means a straight cut. You might find a dissolve here, which would mean an audio crossfade occurs. A dissolve is noted by a D followed by a three-digit number indicating the length of the crossfade in frames.

Next come the time code numbers. They are paired as start and end times for each clip's source and destination locations. The first two SMPTE numbers are the start and end times of the clip on the source tape. The next two SMPTE numbers are the start and end times within the project where this clip is located. Stated another way, the first pair determines where the clip comes from on the tape, and the second pair determines where the clip goes in the Pro Tools session.

The text following the asterisk is used for comments and descriptions only. It does not affect how the edit occurs. In this example the clip name is given; having the clip name can be helpful when you're trying to discern what an edit is for.

Following is a breakdown of the first edit:

- Edit 001 is a stereo edit. AA

- The type of edit is a cut only, no crossfade. C

- The reel where the source audio can be found is R1103.

- The source material starts at 00:21:29;19 and ends at 00:21:35;21.

- This audio clip will be placed on the first two tracks, starting at 01:00:00;00 and ending at 01:00:06;02 in the timeline.

- The clip name for information purposes only is PRE SET A1.

The second edit (002) comes from reel R0101 but has an edit type of NONE, because this audio clip will go on adjacent tracks. Because no edit will occur on the main two tracks, the edit type is NONE. Notice the phrase AUD 3 4 underneath the edit. This determines on which tracks the audio clip will be placed—in this case Tracks 3 and 4.

The reasons for placing audio on Tracks 3 and 4 could be many. The audio from edit 002 could overlap the audio on Tracks 1 and 2. Different processing or levels could be needed on this clip. In this example, the audio does not overlap. Let's imagine that it's a music clip and would need to be at a different level and EQ setting than the dialogue material on Tracks 1 and 2, so the video editor chose to place the audio on Tracks 3 and 4.

Conforming EDLs

The first step in starting work on any video or film project is conforming all of the audio that the video editor has used in the final video edit. Although it is possible to import all of that media using data formats such as OMF and AAF files (which will be discussed later in this chapter), the media received from the video workstation might be compromised in some way or could be incomplete. For example, during the film transfer, the production audio could have been transferred via analog connections resulting in a generation loss. Or the video editor might only have been able to use two channels of audio, but the production sound engineer recorded with four or six tracks on the set, providing many more options for the post-production phase. In both cases you will need to get the original source tapes or files and conform them to the video EDL to maintain the highest quality in your workflow.

Manual EDL Conforming from Source Tapes

When using EDLs you get from a video editor, you might be capturing audio from video or DAT tapes. Each tape should be labeled correctly, with the reel name and time code information on it. Communication is the key here. I have seen made-up names for tapes in EDLs that don't correlate with the tape label, leading to major confusion. Video editors might not realize that you'll have to use their EDL to capture audio, so you'll need to make that clear in pre-production.

In order to use an EDL to capture audio into Pro Tools manually, you must first synchronize the source tape deck with Pro Tools. Next, you'll need to locate the source deck to a position before the first time code number in the EDL's line for this edit. You should be far enough ahead of the start time to include pre-roll and handle amounts needed (see the following note). Set your start point at the beginning of the handle, before the actual source start time. Set your end point at the EDL's end time plus your handle amount, as shown in Figure 5.2. Now you can arm your tracks and put Pro Tools in Record. Make sure you have set your preferences to Record Online at Insertion/Selection and not at Time Code (or ADAT) Lock, as shown in Figure 5.3. Otherwise, Pro Tools will start recording as soon as it sees enough valid time code and will ignore your start and end times.

Figure 5.2 Setting up Pro Tools to capture an audio clip, including handles, while locked to tape. Here, I am capturing the first clip from the example EDL. The track name is the reel number, and the locate points are two seconds beyond the start and end times of the clip, in order to allow for handles and editing later.

Handles   When digitizing audio, it is a good idea to capture more than the EDL specifies in order to facilitate creative editing later on. The extra bits of audio you capture on either side of an edit are called *handles*. These handles allow you to adjust edits once they have been created in Pro Tools. If a word is slightly cut off in an edit, you will be able to "open up" the region to allow the whole word to be heard. Fine-tuning edits in this way is a big part of the audio editor's job. Typically, handles are two to five seconds in length. That is, the audio clip you capture will start two seconds before the EDL's source start time and end two seconds after the source end time. If two clips in the EDL are very close to one another on the source tape, you can simply digitize the combined section that contains both clips. This can save time during digitizing and also provide you with more handle options while editing.

With hard drive space becoming more economical everyday, another method for capturing audio from tape is to simply capture all the audio on every single tape that is part of the production. In addition to conforming EDLs, this will give you instant access to alternative takes of dialogue, room tone, and other sounds that may come in handy later on in the process. Plus, recording a whole tape is less demanding on the users than grabbing little bits here and there on each tape. Just load a tape, start recording, and go grab some coffee!

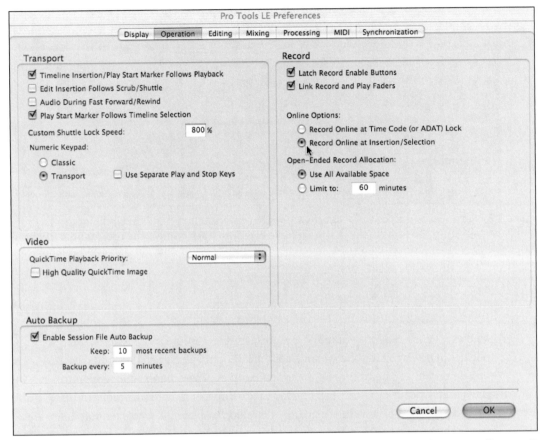

Figure 5.3 Choose Preferences > Operations > Online Record Options. When recording audio from time-coded sources, use the Record Online at Insert/Selection option in order to capture regions with specific time code values.

It is a good idea to capture all of your clips at once before placing them in order. When all the clips have been captured, you can save the session under a different name before you begin moving them all around to their destination locations—doing so allows you to return to the original session in order to find a missing clip or fix an edit. You can also use multiple tracks to capture clips and then edit on other tracks. Create a track for each source tape in your project, naming it appropriately so the files will have their reel name included. Then create tracks for your destination edits. Multiple playlists could serve the same function as well. Use one playlist for capturing each reel and others for EDL placement. Try to stay as organized as possible, because mistakes are easy to make in this process.

Once you have captured the clip, you can trim it and then place it at the correct time according to the EDL. With Grid mode on and a grid value of 1 frame, use the Trimmer tool to trim away the handles, leaving only the audio clip specified in the EDL, as shown in Figure 5.4. Next, drag the region to the appropriate destination track. Switch to Spot mode and click on the region. The Spot dialog box will open, allowing you to enter the start time of the clip as defined by the third time code number in the EDL. In this case, edit 001 has a destination start time at 01:00:00;00, as shown in Figure 5.5. This makes sense, as it is the first audio clip in this mini EDL.

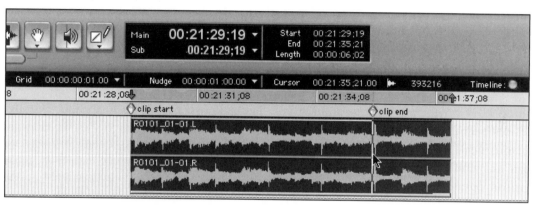

Figure 5.4 Trimming an audio clip to the correct EDL source start and end times. Use Grid mode and set the grid value to one frame.

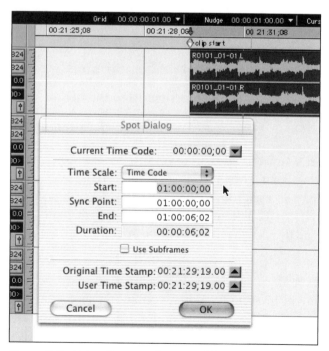

Figure 5.5 Using Spot mode to position a region according to the EDL's destination times.

Alternatively, you can use a source/destination model and copy audio from one location (source) and paste it to the destination, thereby preserving the original audio file in its source location for use later. This method is preferred for long form projects where it is very possible that you will have to reconform the audio to a changed EDL or refer back to the original files for alternate takes. This method works better when you have chosen to record each tape in its entirety or have loaded files from a digital location recorder.

For this method, it's best to have each source file on its own track or playlist to avoid problems with overlapping time code. If a film or video shoot occurs over more than one day, there will be source tapes that have the same time code values on them because there are only 24 hours possible for SMPTE time code.

This method takes advantage of the Selector tool. Follow these steps for each line in the EDL:

1. Find the source track for the EDL step. Either bring up its associated playlist or select its track.

2. Make sure that the Main counter is set to time code.

3. With the Selector tool active, click anywhere in the source track and enter the start and end source times from the EDL into the edit selection values at the top of the Edit window.

4. Copy the audio (Cmd+C or Ctrl+C).

5. Select the destination track or click anywhere in the destination track.

6. In the Edit start value, type in the destination start time from the EDL.

7. Paste the audio from the Clipboard (Cmd+V or Ctrl+V).

If the edit involves anything other than a straight cut (C), it will be necessary to create a fade or crossfade of some duration at that point. Usually, this step requires some judgment on your part as an editor. It can be done at a later time after the EDL is conformed and you are fine-tuning. If the edit is marked "AUD 3-4," it probably overlaps other audio on the main tracks. As you conform, you can decide which track each edit will go on, building your session as you see fit. You might choose to place each character's dialogue on separate tracks, for example. This could also happen in a later step if you choose.

This process can be repeated for each edit in an EDL. When you are finished, you will have a replica of the audio edit contained in the video workstation from which the EDL was generated. EDLs can have a variety of edit types in them. It's often useful to capture both tracks (two tracks in most cases, but there could be more) from the source material, as doing so allows for more choices when editing and mixing the project later on. Production sound mixers will typically record two sources, one on each track (L and R or channels 1 and 2), to allow for flexibility during post-production. Usually, there will be a boom mic or shotgun mic on one track and a combination of wireless body mics and other mic types and placements on the other track. Although certain decisions about which track or combination of tracks will be made during the video edit, you should keep your options open. It's part of your job to determine which mic or track sounds the best in a particular situation.

This entire process described here is known as "conforming" an EDL to picture. It is also referred to as "loading and spotting audio to picture." In the process, you are gathering audio files and arranging them so that they conform to the edits prescribed in the EDL. The result should be an edited audio track that is in sync with the related video.

Following is a step-by-step synopsis of conforming an EDL to picture. This synopsis is intended to provide you with a quick reference guide while you are conforming EDLs.

1. Examine the first edit in your EDL to determine what source tape and time code values are used.

2. Insert the proper tape or reel into your 9-pin deck.

3. Locate the deck to a position that is ahead of the EDL's source start time.

4. Using Grid mode set to one frame, select an area in the Pro Tools timeline that corresponds to the start and end times of the EDL source clip plus handle times.

5. Record this clip onto the proper track(s) while in sync with the VTR or other source deck.

6. Trim the region to the exact start and end times of the EDL clip.

7. Move this clip to the proper destination track or playlist.

8. In Spot mode, set the start time of this clip to the EDL's destination start time.

9. Repeat this process for every clip in the EDL.

Automated EDL Conforming (Virtual Katy)

For any project over a minute or so in length, conforming EDLs can become a lengthy and arduous task. Software tools are available to automate this process. These tools are capable of reading different formats of EDL files and automating the process of recording source audio, including handles, trimming to the proper length, and placing (spotting) the regions at the correct SMPTE position and on the right track(s). If you'll be working with any long-form material over two or three minutes in length, an investment in this type of software will pay off. There are currently two main packages that automate the conforming process in Pro Tools: Virtual Katy (www.virtualkaty.com) and Titan (www.syncrhoarts.com).

Virtual Katy was developed by John McKay while working on the *Lord of the Rings* trilogy. The production itself involved many changes during the post process. This was due to the many demands of extensive CGI used in the film and the deadlines required. One of the sound assistants, Katy Wood, was charged with constantly updating Pro Tools sessions with newly conformed audio from the latest film edit. Her job entailed much of the tedious manual conforming discussed here. Over the course of making those films, a system was developed and then coded into software that would automate the process, saving valuable weeks of time spent simply conforming audio. This time can be spent on more creative pursuits, such as sound design, mixing, and so on. This evolved into the Virtual Katy software.

Virtual Katy examines an EDL file and then, using the source/destination model, conforms source audio tracks into edited tracks as defined by the EDL. To begin, you must load in all the source material either from tape or from files created by a digital location recorder on separate tracks in Pro Tools, each track corresponding to a "sound roll" number or source reel. You can then load in the EDL to Virtual Katy, and it will display the source reels and events in the EDL, as shown in Figure 5.6.

The EDL is used to create an edit list. This is called a "change plan" in Virtual Katy. Once a change plan has been created, Virtual Katy can send commands directly to Pro Tools to cut and paste the various portions of audio from the source tracks to their destination times on the same track. You specify an "offset hour" as a starting location for the EDL so as not to overlap any source material. In this way, Virtual Katy's actions are completely non destructive to the original audio in Pro Tools.

Once the audio has been conformed, it must be "spotted" to its correct start time to be in sync with the video or film (01:00:00;00 in most cases). On longer form material such as a feature film, you might be conforming sections of the film separately and then combining them later to create the complete master. Films are broken down into reels due to the fact that only so much film can physically fit on the actual reels themselves. Usually this works out to be 20 minutes of film per reel. Reel designations also provide a convenient method for breaking a film down into smaller parts to make it easier to deal with. Even in a feature-length film made in HD video, the production might still break the film down into "reels" or sections of the piece.

Virtual Katy is an exceptionally deep and complex program that is capable of many other types of conforming involving changes to existing material. This comes into

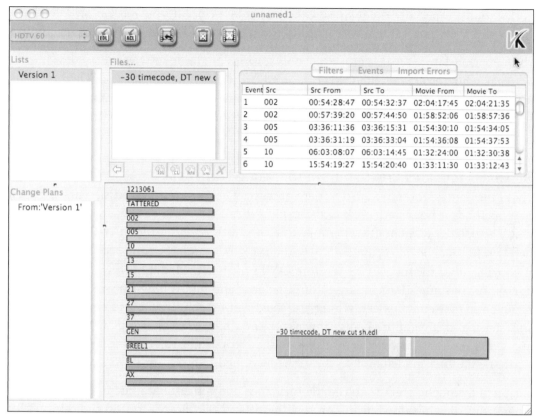

Figure 5.6   Virtual Katy after importing an EDL file.

play when a film or video is altered after you have started working on it and have completed some amount of editing and perhaps mixing. When the changes come in, you need to reconform to the changes in the edit without losing all the work you have done. This process is covered in Chapter 6.

Importing OMFI Files

OMFI, or Open Media Framework Interchange, files are data files that can contain audio, video, and EDL information all in one document. This standard was created by Avid and is used throughout the audio and video industries to transfer projects from one workstation to another.

You will need the DigiTranslator option in order to use OMFI files. DigiTranslator will examine the OMFI file and then create a Pro Tools session with all of the audio files, fade files, and a session document. During this process you can change the audio file format, bit depth, and sampling frequency for the new session. Some video workstations, especially older ones, can run at 44.1kHz. If you receive an OMFI file that is 44.1kHz, you can convert it to the standard of 48kHz during the translation.

Although translating OMFIs into Pro Tools sessions might be relatively easy, it is important that whoever creates the OMFI knows how it is going to be used. When creating OMFI files for audio post-production, there are guidelines to follow that will ensure that the transfer works properly. In the next sections, I'll discuss the guidelines, and then I'll walk you through translating an OMFI file into a Pro Tools session.

Guidelines for OMFI Creation from the Video Workstation

OMFI files can be formatted in a variety of ways. The most dramatic difference between these methods is how media is handled within the OMFI. It is possible to embed all the media associated with an OMFI composition inside the OMFI file. It is also possible to merely reference the original media files and not go through the time-consuming process of copying all of the media files into the OMFI file itself. Media files, whether audio or video, can consume a large quantity of disk space and take a long time to copy. Having a single file that contains everything you need can be convenient and eliminate confusion. In the case of Pro Tools, my experience has been that the OMFI file with embedded media works better and has fewer errors than referencing external media. So, that's the first guideline: Use the embedded media option in most situations.

The second guideline relates to the file format of audio files contained in the OMFI file. When using the embedded media option, there are three choices for the audio format of the embedded files. The first is AIFF-C, which stores audio in the AIFF format. The second is the SDII format; this used to be the native file format of Pro Tools and of the Avid video editing systems on Macintosh computers. SDII files have been phased out of use by both Avid and Digidesign. The third is WAV, or Broadcast WAV, which is a cross-platform standard. The Avid Symphony uses the WAV file type natively. It is also possible for editors to use multiple file formats and sample rates within one video project. With all of these possibilities, it is probably prudent to use the AIFF-C embedded media format, as this will cause the fewest hassles. Converting all audio into this cross-platform AIFF file eliminates any sample-rate discrepancies or different file types in the OMFI. You will have the option to convert these files into either WAV or AIFF when you convert this file into a Pro Tools session.

The third guideline pertains to miscellaneous information that might be contained in the OMFI file. Video editors should be able to export only the audio files of a project without including video files. Also, the sequence they export should be consolidated so that only relevant audio files are copied to the OMFI. Consolidation is a process that occurs inside the video workstations, wherein the unused bits of audio and video are removed from the video project prior to conversion to OMFI. If the sequence is not consolidated, every audio file the editor currently has in bins associated with this project can be included in the OMFI, even if they are not used in the sequence. It's kind of silly to get a 1.5 gig OMFI file for a 30-second spot that really only uses 200MB of data. Figure 5.7 shows the export screen from the latest version of Avid Media Composer set up for a consolidated and embedded AIFC OMFI export.

DigiTranslator Conflicts   DigiTranslator cannot convert a consolidated OMF or AAF file that contains embedded video. It causes a crash when doing so. Ask the video editor to remove any video files and EDL information from any OMF or AAF file.

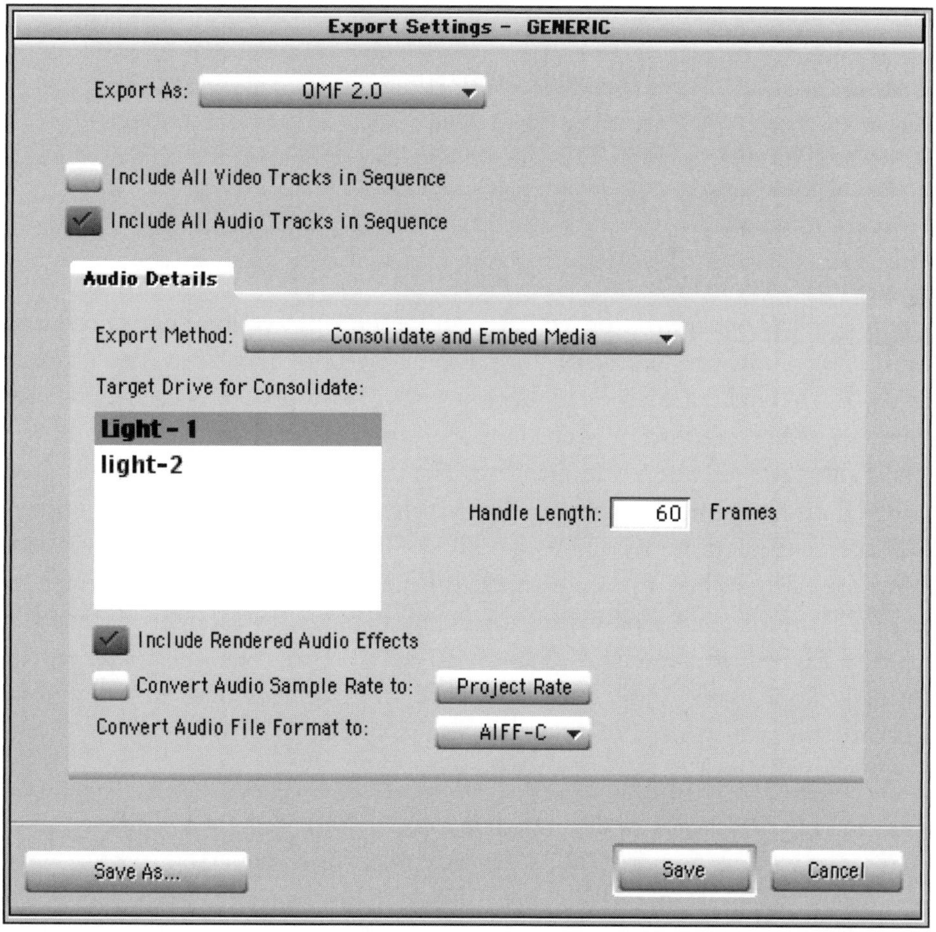

Figure 5.7 The export screen from Avid Media Composer. It is set up for creating a consolidated and embedded OMFI file with AIFC audio files and no video files.

In the case of a long-form project that will go through several revisions while you are working on it, referenced media might be a better idea. When referencing media, the OMFI file does not contain any audio files. It contains references to audio files that are located somewhere else. This type of OMFI file is similar to the EDL file mentioned earlier in this chapter. This OMFI only describes where certain audio files should be placed within the timeline. The actual audio files themselves need to be available in order for the OMFI to use them. In this case, any reference to the audio file must be copied from the video workstation to the Pro Tools computer. In some cases, it is possible to copy all of the digitized audio from the video workstation to the Pro Tools computer. This way, no matter what the new edit coming from the picture editor is, you should have the relevant audio media already on your system. These smaller, EDL-only OMFI files can be sent via email, making it convenient to work over long distances.

More About OMFI   Further information on OMFI can be found at Avid's Website (www.avid.com). PDF documents found there describe in detail the methods for transferring OMFI files between video and audio workstations.

Using DigiTranslator with OMFI and AAF Files

Prior to version 5.3.1, DigiTranslator was a standalone application that translated OMFI files into Pro Tools sessions. You didn't even need to have Pro Tools open. Since Pro Tools 5.3.1, DigiTranslator has been a part of the program itself and now supports the newer AAF standard as well. It is still an add-on that must be paid for separately, but it functions within the application. The current version of DigiTranslator functions within the File menu. It is accessed any time you open a session or import audio into the current session. By choosing File > Open Session, you can select OMFI/AAF files directly. When opening an OMFI/AAF file, Pro Tools will refer to the embedded media if any exists or search for external media to reference. Once the OMFI/AAF has been opened, saving it causes a new Pro Tools session document to be written to disk along with Audio Files and Fade Files folders that are created in the same directory into which the Pro Tools session is saved.

Referring to Embedded Media   When referring to embedded media in an OMFI file, you'll need to keep the initial OMFI file on your audio drive, preferably in the same directory as the Pro Tools session that refers to it. Removing the OMFI file is like deleting the Audio Files folder in a normal Pro Tools session folder. Any additional recording done into a session created from an OMFI file will be placed into a new Audio Files folder in the directory where the current Pro Tools session is located. In order to embed the new audio into an OMFI file, it will be necessary to export from Pro Tools a new OMFI file with embedded media.

You can choose from many options in the Import Session Data dialog box (see Figure 5.8), which is accessed by choosing File > Import > Session Data. You may choose to refer to the source media, which will use the audio data directly from the OMFI/AAF file. You will

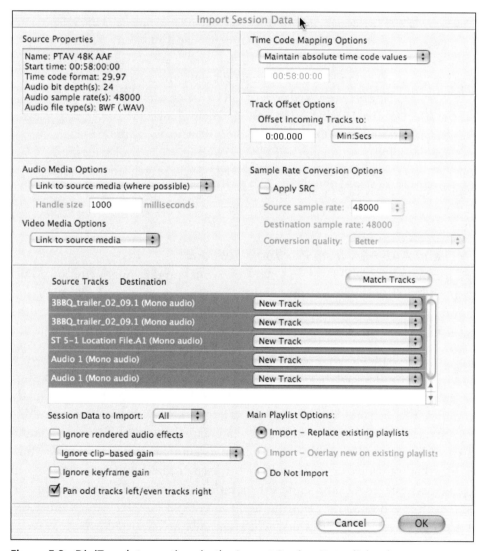

Figure 5.8 DigiTranslator options in the Import Session Data dialog box.

need to keep the OMFI/AAF on your audio drive as part of the session. If you choose Copy from Source Media from the Audio Media Options pull-down menu, new audio files will be created from the OMFI data and placed in the Audio Files folder of the currently open session. You can then delete the OMFI/AAF file, as it has unneeded duplicate media within it and may be using up valuable disk space. Be careful when deleting any major media files from your system, though—be absolutely sure that you do not need them before doing so!

AAF Files   Avid and Digidesign, along with other leading multimedia manufacturers, have come together to create a new EDL, multimedia interchange format that addresses the shortcomings of OMF. To that end, the AAF standard has emerged as a cross-platform EDL/media format supported by a variety of applications. When working between Avid or Final Cut Pro video editing systems and Pro Tools, AAF files should provide the best workflow. Functionally, AAF files work in much the same way as OMF, with a better level of cross-platform usability and extended audio file support with BWF 24 bit files. Many of the same options exist when importing and exporting AAF files. These subsections on Digi-Translator equally apply to AAF and OMF files.

Creating OMFI and AAF Files from Pro Tools Sessions

In some cases, picture editors will need an OMFI file from you that might contain ADR, foley, or other audio. They might use this file to fine-tune their edits or add material. The OMFI allows them more control of the audio during this process. They can turn the music down, just listen to the ADR, or trim fades and edits as necessary.

Avid systems are not capable of recognizing edits that have boundaries between SMPTE frames. This means that if you have edits that fall between the exact start and end of a frame, the OMFI translation must resolve this edit so that it falls exactly on a frame. Think of Grid mode. The translation to OMFI will truncate any edits that do not begin or end exactly on a frame and will create little audio files that contain the portions of audio that fall between the frames plus enough silence to create a full-frame audio file. The portions of audio left in between frame boundaries pop up in Avid as "sample accurate edits" and can be frustrating to editors. DigiTranslator can crop your edits to frame boundaries, but the result might not be what you want. Keep this in mind if you are creating sessions that will eventually be imported back into Avid. Also, Avid will not recognize any handles in the OMFI file, so don't bother supplying them.

Staying Current As with any computer technology, audio and video tools change rapidly. Avid's Media Composer receives regular updates, and features will change with each update. Make sure you stay current with all the latest features. Any limitations discussed in this book may have changed by the time you read it. Use the Internet to find the latest information on any software product you are working with.

In order to export an OMFI file from a Pro Tools session, you must first select all the tracks you want to include in the OMFI. Being able to export only a few select tracks to an OMFI is a handy feature that allows you to have a large session with many tracks but export only the tracks that might be needed, such as ADR or foley tracks. Many video workstations cannot handle the high track counts that are possible in Pro Tools. You might have to submix several of your tracks in order to export an OMFI that can actually be used by the video workstation. On the other hand, Final Cut Pro 6 has extensive audio features, including support for up to 24 tracks of 24 bit/96kHz audio files. This ability allows you to export many tracks from Pro Tools via OMF back into Final Cut for the video editors to use.

Once you have selected the desired tracks in Pro Tools, choose File > Export Selected Track as New AAF/OMF. The dialog box shown in Figure 5.9 will open. Choose the Enforce Avid Compatibility option if you're planning to export to an Avid workstation. The Quantize Edits to Frame Boundaries option will be checked and grayed out. You may want to choose the 16 bit option if you are exporting to an older Avid system that does not support 24 bit files. Choose Embedded OMFI as the audio format to place all audio media within the OMF file itself. The sample rate should be determined by the needs of your project—Avid can use both 44.1kHz and 48kHz sample rates.

In certain circumstances, it can be beneficial to use referenced media instead of embedded media—usually in facilities that have video and audio studios together and that may share drives and media easily. If you use referenced media, it is possible to send back an OMFI that is very small, as it does not have to contain any media files. This assumes that no new media files have been created that are part of the current project. As long as the media used for the OMFIs reside on both computers, exchanging OMFI files without embedded media will work.

Avid and Digidesign along with other leading multimedia manufacturers, have come together to create a new EDL, multimedia interchange format that addresses the shortcomings of OMF. To that end, the AAF standard has emerged as a cross-platform EDL/Media format supported by a variety of applications. When working between Avid or

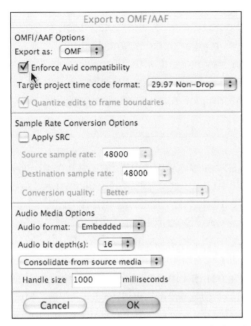

Figure 5.9   The Export to OMF/AAF dialog box. DigiTranslator's options are set to encode an OMFI file for use in an Avid system.

Final Cut Pro video editing systems and Pro Tools, AAF files should provide the best workflow. Functionally, AAF files work in much the same way as OMF with a better level of cross-platform usability and extended audio file support with BWF 24 bit files. Much of the same options exist when importing and exporting AAF files. The previous section on OMF files applies for AAF files equally.

Recording from Production DAT Tapes

You will often need to record audio from the original source tapes or production audio tapes. Doing so can be necessary when you need to conform EDLs from source tapes, record wild takes of dialogue, or gather ambience recorded on location. Usually, production audio comes in the form of DAT tapes. The picture editor has a copy of any production audio that was synchronized to picture, usually from videotape copies or film transfers. The videotape could be straight out of the camera that shot the footage or it could be a copy made prior to editing, and that copy could have been made using an analog transfer process or a digital one. Without being privy to every step the audio has been through during all the transfer, digitizing, and OMFI creation, you cannot guarantee the quality of the audio you receive from a picture editing workstation. Some software will convert the audio in both bit depth and sample rate when it is imported. Video laybacks may use an analog signal path. The point is: If you want the highest quality, you must go to the source—in this case, the original recordings made during filming. Using source tapes will require some sort of EDL conforming and/or speed correction, depending on the format of the film or video.

DATs from a 24fps Shoot (Film or HD)

In the case of a film shot at 24fps and transferred to video using 2-3 pull-down, you will need to change the playback speed of the production audio to match the speed change caused by the film transfer to NTSC video. If you are working at 48kHz pulled down (47.952kHz) in Pro Tools, a direct digital transfer will be possible. You might have to temporarily switch to normal 48kHz operation while transferring, but switching back to pull down will make the speed adjustment correctly.

If you're working with videotape transfers of the film and are not operating with a pulled down sample rate, you will need to make an analog transfer or use a sample rate converter while digitally transferring the original audio. In this case, you need to be able to slow the speed of the playback DAT machine.

What's a SimulDAT?   SimulDATs are DAT tapes made during the film transfer process. They will sync directly to the transferred footage on videotape. For a film-to-video project SimulDATs are ideal, as you can use direct digital transfers into Pro Tools without altering the speed. This can be helpful for those without a hi-end time code DAT machine capable of varispeed and can be discussed during pre-production. You'll need to know if the film transfer facility supports SimulDATs.

The most common method of altering the playback speed to match a film transfer is to reference the DAT machine that has 30fps SMPTE on it to a video signal running at 29.97fps (if the machine is able to reference video as a sync source). As the DAT is using the reference video signal to determine its playback speed, it is expecting to receive 30 frames/60 fields at its video sync port. Instead, it sees 29.97 frames/59.94 fields per second—which is .1% slower than 30fps—resulting in the slowing down of the audio. The DAT will play at 47.952kHz and cannot be digitally transferred into Pro Tools running at 48kHz. You should record either using analog connections or using a sample rate converter that will convert the incoming 47.952kHz to 48kHz on-the-fly.

For the budget-minded, there is another way to alter the playback speed. As DAT machines that reference video sync signals are rather expensive, you may also transfer files directly into a 48kHz session digitally with any DAT machine and then use the Pro Tools Import Audio window to convert the sample rate of the files to adjust their playback speed. This technique is very simple to do but requires careful thought and accurate information regarding the sample rate used during the actual recording.

Once you have recorded all the source tapes into Pro Tools at 48kHz, you will need to re-import those files into a new session. It is advisable to keep this session in a separate directory so as not to inadvertently erase the original files. The Import Audio dialog box has a pull-down menu for the "source sample rate" in the lower-right area. When Apply SRC is checked, this menu lets you determine the ratio of sample rate conversion to apply to imported audio files regardless of their original sample rate. In this case, the file's original sample rate is 48kHz.

Because you want to slow the audio file down to match the −0.1% speed change caused by the telecine transfer, select 47.952kHz as the source sample rate as shown in Figure 5.10. The idea is that you are tricking Pro Tools into thinking these files were already pulled down and forcing Pro Tools to convert the sample from the slower speed. Pro Tools will then sample rate convert the files, thereby adjusting the speed to match the pull-down in the video. Always make sure to use Tweak Head for the highest quality sample rate conversion process.

Frame Rates and Pull-Down   When using this work around, make sure to set the Pro Tools SMPTE frame rate to 30fps while recording from DAT. Doing so assures accurate time information from Pro Tools. When you have finished sample rate converting all the "tricked" audio to pull-down, switch the Pro Tools session frame rate to 29.97 to reflect the −.1% speed change that has occurred.

If the production sound mixer recorded audio at 40.048kHz during the shoot, you will not need to use a pull-down to work with that original material from DAT. By playing those tapes at 48kHz, the pull-down is already achieved. This method works best when the delivery medium is for NTSC broadcast at 29.97fps, 48kHz. Proper documentation by the production sound mixer is very important in this regard. With short clips, you might not notice the drift of a non-pulled down audio. After 30 seconds, non-pulled audio can drift up to a frame out of sync. After 10 seconds the drift is about a third of a frame. Doing some careful sync tests between the video editing workstation, the production audio source files or tapes and Pro Tools can help eliminate problems of this nature.

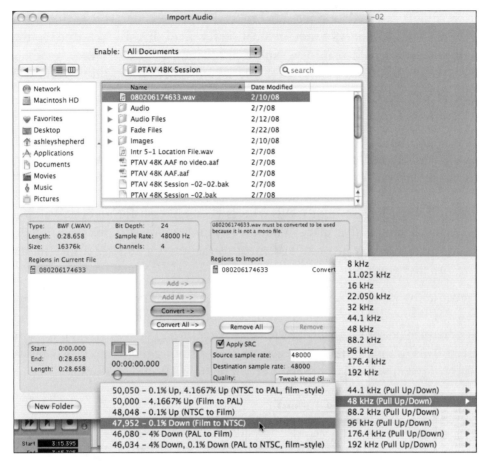

Figure 5.10 The Pro Tools Import Audio dialog box allows you to apply sample rate conversion based on any possible source sample rate from the submenu choices, including all variations of pull up/down rates.

DATs or Videotape from a 29.97fps Shoot (Video, HD, or Film)

Recordings made on a shoot where the camera was operated at 29.97fps should require no speed conversion to match the NTSC videotape. Digital transfers should be possible without any sample rate conversion. Make sure you know whether the SMPTE format is drop-frame or non-drop frame—that could make a real difference.

Digital Field Recorders

The emergent new standard in location recording has become the digital field recorder. Professional machines of this type are able to record multiple channels of audio at high-resolution sample rates while referenced to SMPTE time code. This is similar to actually having a small Pro Tools system on location for recording. In fact, prior to the widespread use of digital field recorders, some production companies did just that. Episodes of *Survivor* used a Pro Tools DIGI 001 system to record multiple tracks of location audio during the shoot.

Nowadays, digital field recorder technology has matured, and with several manufacturers offering high-end multi-channel field recorders in small, durable packages (Fostex, Sound Devices, and Edirol), their use is widespread. Most production sound mixers are using this technology in feature films and television episodics today. *Pearl Harbor* was recorded using a DEVA recorder, and 99 percent of the dialogue in the film is from the original recording and not ADR. This is no small task for an effects/action film in which so much action takes place in noisy environments—such conditions would normally require ADR. This is just one testament to the quality and versatility that a digital field recorder can bring to any production.

The DEVA recorder by Zaxcom, pictured in Figure 5.11, is the first professionally used hard disk recorder for production audio. It records directly to an internal hard disk, and the audio files can then be copied to an external drive such as a DVD-RAM. As it records to the Broadcast WAV standard, it is not necessary to record this audio into Pro Tools. It may be transferred directly via Firewire hard drives or from DVD data discs.

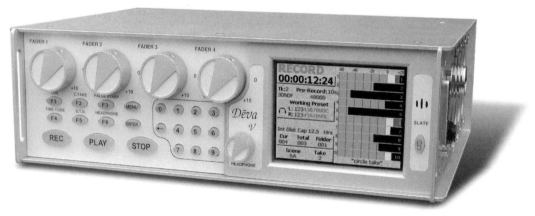

Figure 5.11 Zaxcom's DEVA, a hard disk recorder used for production audio.

One of the advantages of digital field recorders is the capacity to record more than two channels of audio, in some cases up to 10 tracks on one machine. Multiple field recorders can be jam-synced together for an unlimited number of tracks in a location environment. This allows the production sound mixer to use more discreet microphones and record them on separate tracks. These tracks can later be loaded into Pro Tools for you to use in the final mix.

When using a large number of discrete tracks on location, it is common practice for the production sound mixer to create a mono or stereo track that is a composite mix of all the recorded tracks, called the "production sound mix." This can be used by the video editor as a reference audio track without having to deal with each separate track that was recorded. This allows the video editor to get on to editing without having to worry about creating a decent audio mix to listen to from many discrete microphones.

The issue becomes how to gain access to all the audio tracks during the sound edit in Pro Tools. There are a couple of workflow methods you can use to accomplish this, and Pro Tools provides some unique tools to help.

Digital Field Recorder Workflow

When using a digital field recorder on a large film project, proper pre-production is essential to gaining all the benefits of the field recording device. If the production sound mixer and the camera assistant on the shoot are not using the same naming scheme for reels, shots, sound rolls, and time code, re-syncing field recordings to the final edit might become impossible or at least extremely time consuming.

Field recorders such as the Sound Devices 744T embed metadata into each sound file that contains critical information regarding the time code at which the recording began, the name of the scene/take, the number of audio channels recorded, and more. Because these field recorders are software based, their operating systems are being updated constantly. The metadata capabilities they have will change as time goes on. Be sure to evaluate the latest version of software for each field recorder that you will use. The best method is to perform a sync test prior to the start of production to ensure your workflow will not have any problems.

The following list shows all the various types of metadata that Pro Tools will recognize and display in the Digibase browsers:

- Duration
- File comment
- Date modified
- Date created
- Number of channels

- Format

- Sample rate

- Bit depth

- Original timestamp

- User timestamp

- Tape

- TC rate (or FPS)

- Channel names

- Scene

- Take

- Shoot date

- Sound roll

- Sound roll TC

- Sound roll TC rate (FPS)

- User bits

- Tape ID

- Project

- Circled (keeper take)

- Clip name

---

iXML Metadata   There is a lot of information that you can add to each sound file. The basic information that you can add to the BWF portion of the file includes the sample rate, timestamp, a description, and a few others. Much of the remaining data is coded into what is known as the iXML header portion of the file. Many more fields of information are available in iXML, but the problem is that there is no one standard that has been set for the industry to use. Certain conventions have been adopted by some manufacturers in order to get some functionality out of iXML, but they do not always translate between various applications and devices. This presents one more case in point for the

testing of any workflow methods prior to starting production. Make some
recordings with the actual field recorder that will be used and then take them
to the telecine operator (in the case of a film shoot) or directly into Pro Tools and
see just what metadata will translate.

The key metadata that concern the conforming of multi-channel audio files to the guide
track of a film are as follows:

- Shoot date (also the file creation date)

- Tape ID

- Sound roll

- Alternate channel tape ID

- Alternate channel sound roll

- Scene

- Take

- SMPTE/timestamp

The camera assistant, script supervisor and production sound mixer must log the same
exact name for each tape used during a shoot. Pro Tools can identify the metadata and
match it with the same information found in the AAF/OMF file or an EDL generated by
the video editing workstation and then use that to match multi-channel audio files to the
mono or stereo guide track (production sound mix) found in the session. In other words,
each edited region of the production sound mix that was imported via AAF/OMF can be
associated with an audio file from a multi-channel field recorder that contains matching
metadata.

This whole process can be as simple as importing the original files from the field
recorder into Pro Tools, and if all metadata has been preserved during the video editing
process, the newly added regions will automatically be combined with their "relatives"
found in the edited production sound mix track. It can also get very complicated if all
the issues have not been worked out during pre-production meetings and tests. For
example, the very notion of having a "tape" ID or sound roll number is quickly becoming outdated because many newer cameras do not use tape media, and digital field
recorders do not create "rolls" of tape anymore. In the age of file-based workflows,
you must develop naming schemes and ways of identifying various video and audio files.

Cinema Audio Society   Have you ever noticed the letters C. A. S. after a person's name in the credits of a movie? This refers to membership in the Cinema Audio Society. This professional group is composed of audio engineers and associates involved in the making of films and television soundtracks. Their goal is to provide communication between the various disciplines involved in making film sound, from production sound mixers to the final re-recording mix engineers. To that end they hold seminars and meetings to discuss various issues that arise. There have been several such meetings on the very subject of using digital field recorders in modern production workflows. These seminars have been videotaped and are available to the general public for viewing at their Website: http://www .cinemaaudiosociety.org/. Please visit this site for more information.

Multi-Channel Takes

Once all channels of a multi-channel field recording have been "married" together in Pro Tools, you can then access each channel from the various edited regions in the session. You may exchange a region of a multi-channel file with another correlating channel from the same recording. This allows you to explore all the various microphones that were recorded on location and pick the most appropriate mic for a particular edit. For example, the production sound mix could have been made from a mix of the boom mic and several lavalier body mics from each principal actor in the scene. The resulting edit would cut between each character's lines from various perspectives in the room. Depending on the perspective, you may choose which mic sounds the most appropriate for the shot.

In order to access these matching channels, you must first select a region with the Grabber tool or a portion of a region with the Selector tool. Using the Selector tool, you Ctrl-click (in Windows) or Command-click (on the Mac) on the selection and choose the matches from the pop-up menu, as seen in Figure 5.12. If there are matches available for that selection, they will be listed here. Simply choose the channel you want to try, and Pro Tools will replace the audio in your selection with the alternate channel. Now you can hear the dialogue from another perspective instantly.

In addition to matching other channels within one field recorder, audio files from a second field recorder can be accessed in the same way if certain criteria are met. They must have overlapping timestamps for the selection you have, and one of the following conditions must be met:

■ Both the scene and take fields match exactly

■ The shoot dates of both files must be the same

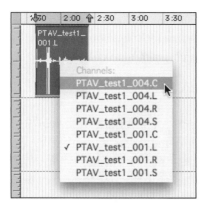

Figure 5.12   The Matches or Alternate Channels contextual menu is used to select alternate channels from a multi-channel field recording.

- The tape names or IDs match exactly

- The sound roll names match exactly

- The alternate channel sound roll names match exactly

- The alternate channel tape names or IDs match exactly

Once those criteria are met, the Matches contextual menu will contain channels from both multi-channel audio files. Figure 5.12 shows the Matches contextual menu, where two different four-channel audio files have matching criteria and are available as alternate channels of the same recording (from take 004 and 001). That offers eight total alternate channels from two separate field recordings—all available from a simple contextual menu. This is an elegant solution for dialogue editing in post. Don't like the sound of that mic? Try an alternate channel in one mouse move.

Multiple Field Recorders   With the success of reality television and an increase in 24-hour multi-camera shoots with a cast of 10–20 people, the needs of production sound have grown exponentially. In reality TV shows such as *Big Brother,* characters can move between various camera locations and interact with other characters in other locations on the set without any warning, causing all the production sound teams to scramble in order to record each body microphone to the right camera for that moment. Changing radio frequencies of receivers for each camera obviously can result in lost dialogue in the heat of the moment. What producers have resorted to is using a central duplicate multi-channel recorder that picks up all the body mics from every character 24 hours a day. With this backup recording, the audio post-production team can always get any missing dialogue lines from this central recorder. Using the metadata technique outlined previously can save many hours of editing time by providing alternate channels across multiple field recordings instantly.

It is possible to trick an audio file into becoming a match for alternate takes in Pro Tools. The audio file must already have an overlapping time code with the region that exists in Pro Tools. It is not possible to edit the timestamp of an audio file once it has been recorded. Some iXML editors will allow you to edit the user's timestamp, but this will not affect the matching takes function in Pro Tools. The original timestamp must overlap somewhere within the audio files for this to work.

The Digibase browsers in Pro Tools allow you to edit some of the metadata within an audio file. You would need to manually edit the scene and take numbers to match or perhaps edit the sound roll names to match before importing those files into the Pro Tools session, as seen in Figure 5.13. Once they have been imported, those channels will be available as alternates to the region already in the session that matches the time code and secondary metadata that you have edited.

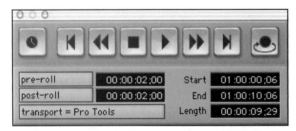

Figure 5.13   Editing the scene and take numbers in the Digibase browser.

Recording Dialogue and Narration

The most important parts of nearly all film and video productions are the dialogue and narration that occur throughout. A great deal of effort goes into making the dialogue clear and accurate. Smooth dialogue audio helps draw the viewer into the production. In many cases, dialogue recorded on the set might be unusable due to environmental factors. As we've learned, it is possible to replace certain dialogue segments in the studio using ADR (Automated Dialogue Replacement). Animation dialogue, voiceovers, and narration are also recorded in the studio. This section is devoted to recording dialogue, in its many forms, in the post-production studio.

Replacing Existing Dialogue (ADR)

Imagine that you are a production sound mixer on a film about a WWII submarine crew. The set is a re-creation of a WWII sub that can be moved and turned by large hydraulics and electric motors in order to simulate the rocking of a submarine under fire from depth charges. The hydraulics and motors are constantly making a racket, and it seems that every time the main character says a line, one of these motors makes a horrible sound that can be heard everywhere, including through the body mic and boom mic—rendering the recording useless. The machines have to be in operation, as the boat needs to move during these scenes. What are you going to do? ADR, the process of replacing these lines with new ones recorded in an audio studio by the same actor, is the answer. Any recorded dialogue that contains too much environmental sound or is flawed in other ways must be replaced in post-production using ADR.

As ADR may be done weeks or months after a specific scene was filmed, the talent will need to practice their lines while watching and hearing themselves in the original scene. Getting it just right can be difficult. A common practice is to "loop" one line at a time, repeating it and recording each pass while the talent reads the line while watching himself or herself on a monitor. This process, known as *dialogue looping,* helps the actor get into the moment and relive the scene in order to get a recording that closely matches the original filmed performance.

Using Loop Record Mode

Pro Tools has a special record mode called *loop record* that can help with ADR. Select Loop Record from the Operations menu or press Option+L to enable loop recording. A loop figure will appear around the Record button in the transport window, as shown in Figure 5.14. Using Grid mode, select an area about five seconds in length for a test recording. Record-enable a track and start recording. You will see that the area will first record as normal, but then Pro Tools will cycle back to the start point and record over the same area again and again until you stop. If you have a QuickTime movie loaded, it too will cycle in sync with Pro Tools, allowing the talent to see themselves again for each take.

Note that the pre-roll and post-roll settings are not taken into account when loop recording. In other words, if you set up a pre- and post-roll amount to give the talent time to prepare before saying the line, Pro Tools will start out with the pre-roll amount, but as soon as the end point is reached, it will immediately return to the start point without pre-roll and continue recording, completely ignoring the post-roll amount and only pre-rolling for that first cycle.

It is common practice to create countdown beeps for the talent. Three beep tones allow the talent to prepare and accurately time the start of the line. Set up in and out points

Figure 5.14 Loop recording. The arrowed circle around the Record button indicates that you are in Loop Record mode.

that include the countdown beeps and some breathing room after the line, as shown in Figure 5.15. Granted, this method uses a little more disk space than needed, but it gets the job done nicely. It is sometimes necessary to copy the original line to a spot before the countdown beeps so that the talent has a reference. Some actors like to have the original line playing in one ear as they re-read it. You should be prepared for just about anything.

Creating Countdown Beeps   Creating beeps is pretty simple. In Grid mode, select an area of one frame. Open the Audiosuite plug-in Signal Generator. Set it up for a 1kHz sine tone at −20db or so. Press Process. Now you have a tone beep. You can Option+drag this new region to a place one second later. Repeat. Now you have three beep tones at one-second intervals. You can select all three tones plus another second worth of time after the last tone and consolidate selection (Command+Option+3) to create one region with three countdown beeps in it. If you line up the end of the region with the start of the line to be re-read, you will have a perfect countdown for the talent.

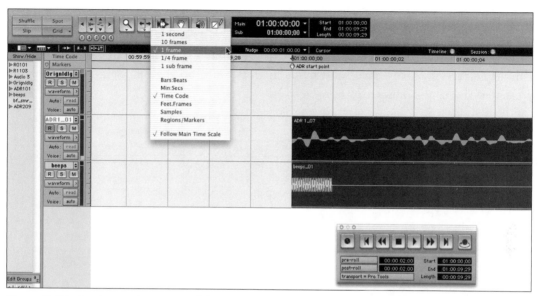

Figure 5.15 Setting up loop record for ADR. Notice the in and out points include the countdown beeps before and a short space after the line that is being replaced on the track above. This gives some pre and post-roll for the talent to catch a breath and prepare.

Loop recording does not create multiple files, one for each time it loops. Instead, Pro Tools records one continuous file that has regions in it that correspond to each cycle of the loop recording. The last region is usually shorter than all the rest because you must press Stop *before* the end point or Pro Tools will go back and start a new region. Each time you record, a new file will be created with a unique name. Each pass of the loop during that recording will have a corresponding region that is also uniquely named according to the conventions. You will be able to keep track of each take and each pass in those takes using the naming convention.

As only the last pass of the loop recording is left "on top" in the track, you need to be able to drag other takes from the Audio Regions List window into the track for auditioning and editing, and you need to be able to do this with sample accuracy. The region needs to be placed exactly where it was recorded initially or it will be out of sync with the picture. A simple way to achieve accuracy is to set up your in and out points using Grid mode with the grid value set to one frame. This way, every region created during the loop recording will start on a specific frame number. Dragging regions from the list into the Edit window this way is easy and somewhat foolproof. Using markers at the start of an ADR line can also help speed up editing and auditioning of takes.

Loop recorded regions will also be listed as alternates in the contextual menu. Click anywhere within the region with the Selector tool and right-click or Ctrl-click (Windows), Command-click (Mac) to see the list of available alternates for the region. If multiple record passes have been made at this point, all regions will be available as alternates, as seen in Figure 5.16.

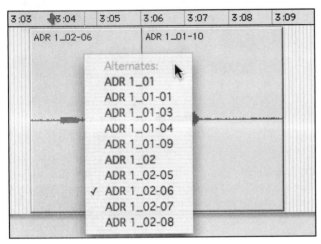

Figure 5.16 Alternate takes from two record passes using Loop Record mode as seen in the contextual menu.

It is always possible to re-sync a region to its original record location by using Spot mode. In Figure 5.17 you can see the Spot dialog box and in the lower portion, the original timestamp number. This timestamp is created when the file is originally recorded. By clicking the up arrow next to the timestamp number, you can place the original timestamp in the region's start time slot. After you click OK, the region will move to its originally recorded location.

File Management and Pro Tools' Naming Conventions

Looping dialogue can create many audio files that need to be organized in order for you to make sense of them all. You must also understand the naming convention in Pro Tools to keep track of ADR takes. Pro Tools names audio files and their associated regions starting with the name of the track they are recorded into. For instance, say you're about to start an ADR session, and you create a track called ADR 1 for the first line you want to loop. You could use the character's name and a scene number or anything else you like, as long as you know what it means. Pro Tools will name the first file recorded into that track ADR 1_01. The next time you record onto that track, the

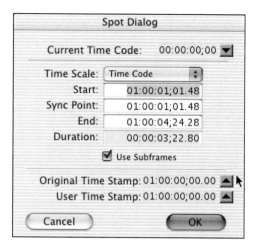

Figure 5.17 The Spot dialog box being used to place a region at its original recording time by using the timestamp at the bottom of the window. Pressing the arrow button next to the Original Time Stamp SMPTE number will load that number into the start value for the region.

file will be named ADR 1_02, and so on. If you change the name of the track to ADR 2, the next time you record onto that track, the filename will be ADR 2_01, and so on.

Let's say you record four cycles of the five-second loop of ADR 1. In the Audio Regions List, you will now find the bold name ADR 1_01 for the entire file and then a series of regions named ADR 1_01-1, ADR 1_01-2, and so on, one for each pass of the loop recording. Figure 5.18 shows the Audio Regions List after recording several takes, each with four passes of the line. You can see all the region names created by just these two takes.

As long as you take reasonable notes while recording, it should be a snap to recall the favorite take and pass the director noted while recording. If the director wants to hear the third pass of take 4, you should be able to right-click on the region, choose that take from the Alternates list, press Play, and listen. Having the region list sorted by creation date, as shown in Figure 5.19, will keep your most recent takes at the top of the region list, making it easier to find them when you need them.

Undoing Record Does not Do What You Think   "Undoing" after recording does not get rid of the audio file you have recorded. The audio file will be removed from the region list, but it is still on disk and will remain there until you redo the recording (which will keep the file intact) or until you record again, in which case that file will be erased and recorded again, keeping the naming convention intact.

The only way to undo a recording in progress is to press Command+Period while the transport is still moving, either in record or during post-roll. This will end the recording and leave no audio file on disk. The take number will not increment. It will be as though nothing had happened.

It used to be that Pro Tools would keep incrementing the take number even if you removed the last take in the region list. You could use the remove regions command (Command+Shift+B) to remove and delete regions and files from disk, but the take number would still increase. This problem has been addressed, and the naming convention will work correctly and respond to Undo commands, and keep your file structure sane. ADR can create a huge number of audio files, and dealing with them can be a bear. With a proper naming convention in place and the Alternates contextual menu, it is possible to keep your ADR session well organized so as to speed up the process of recording and then choosing the best takes.

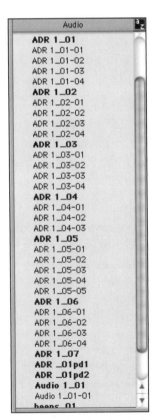

Figure 5.18 The Audio Regions List after several takes of ADR 1 in Loop Record mode. Each take has four passes, each with its own region name below the filename in bold.

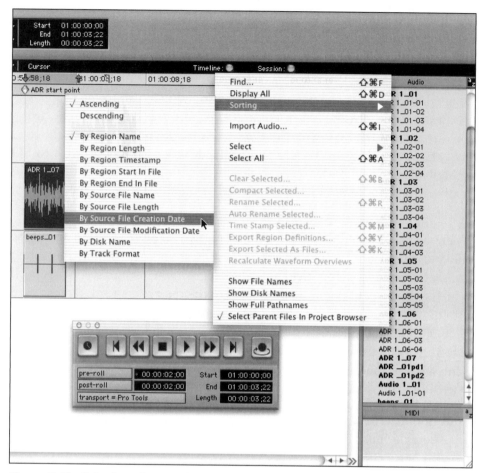

Figure 5.19 Selecting the Sort by Source File Creation Date option will keep the most recent recordings at the top of the region list.

From a workflow point of view, there are many other ways to do ADR. For instance, you could use playlists to keep track of different takes or even different characters' ADR lines. Depending on how you like to work, different situations will require different work models. The method above should get you started, and along the way you will find what works best for you.

Third-party solutions that are specifically designed for ADR work do exist. Gallery Software's ADR Studio is designed to integrate into Pro Tools and help automate the process of ADR. ADR Studio also handles much of the paperwork and note taking involved in an ADR session, allowing you to compile and sort though the recordings. Control of record or "on air" lights, air handling fans, or any other sort of contrivance you can imagine can be automated by ADR Studio. For a full-time ADR studio, this type of software is a must.

Recording Technique

When recording ADR, you want the new dialogue to sound identical to the original so that smooth transitions are possible when editing ADR into the original tracks. If the sounds are too disparate, ADR lines will stand out like sore thumbs later on in the mix. It then becomes the job of the re-recording mix engineer (which could be you!) to EQ and alter the ADR lines to match the original production audio. Your recording technique can greatly reduce the amount of work needed at the mix to match the sound of ADR lines.

To make the new dialogue sound identical to the original, you need to know what type of microphone and mic placement were used during the shoot. The production sound log sheets should give you a clue. It is nice to be able to go on the set and see for yourself how the mics are being done. In the ADR studio, try to re-create the mic placement used on the set. Use the same microphone, if possible. The recording room should be rather large (>5000 cu ft) and uncolored by early reflections. This can help when you need to place the mic farther away from the talent. Try to get the talent in the same positions as they were in the shoot—standing or sitting can affect the sound of their voices dramatically. Try to avoid having a solid table in front of the talent unless there is one in the scene you're working on. Tables, music stands, and any other obstruction in close proximity to the person reading can affect the sound quality. Music stands with light frames and holes in them work better for holding scripts rather than large, heavy stands or tables. Try putting a piece of carpet on the stand to reduce reflections into the mic. Figure 5.20 shows a typical ADR setup.

Recording Voiceovers and Narration

Voiceovers and narration are usually recorded in the studio. Certain exceptions exist wherein the talent's voice is from another scene and is being superimposed in the current scene to function as narration, but 99.99 percent of the time, voiceovers are recorded in a controlled studio environment.

Voiceovers usually have a warm and close-up quality, which separates them from the more natural-sounding dialogue on-screen. To achieve this sound, a rather dead recording room is used, along with a large diaphragm-condenser microphone. The talent is normally quite close to the mic in order to take advantage of the mic's proximity effect, which will increase the low-end response and warm up the voice. Be careful not to get

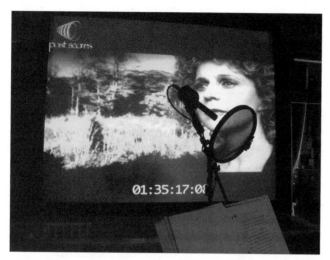

Figure 5.20 A typical ADR setup using the standard Sennheiser MKH 416B shotgun mic to mimic the mic situation used on the set. Notice the music stand with a light frame to avoid sonic coloration.

too close and boomy, as clarity is very important for a voiceover. Good voiceover talent will know how to control the mic and their diction, including plosives like "B's" and "P's." Still, because the talent is so close to the mic, it is a good idea to use a pop filter to lessen any wind noise and plosives.

Plosives, POP Filters, and Mic Placement   *Plosives* are sounds that occur during normal speech that result in a small amount of wind exiting the mouth. The letters P, B, T, F, and sometimes S can cause this to happen. This wind can interact with the microphone diaphragm, causing undesirable low-frequency sounds. Positioning of the mic outside the path of the wind coming from someone's mouth can help minimize these artifacts. A common technique is the use of a pop filter to prevent the wind from getting to the microphone. Professional announcers and narrators will have good technique for minimizing the plosives in their speech. For inexperienced talent, a pop filter or creative mic placement can be used to great effect in minimizing these unwanted sounds.

There is no special workflow when recording voiceovers. Just create a track and start recording, with a stopwatch handy. You might need to put a piece of music underneath while recording if that is how it will be heard in the end; the music can help the talent time their reading accurately and create a pace for the narration. Timing each take of a voiceover is important especially in short TV commercials, where time is money and the client has certain key points that must be emphasized.

Backup Recorder During Sessions   It is a good idea to have another recorder running while recording someone in the studio. Talent is usually paid by the hour, and if you were to lose some recording due to a disk failure or some other unforeseen event, having a backup can be a lifesaver. It is common to have a DAT machine running in the background during a session. This way, if the perfect take happens but your computer fails to capture it, the DAT will have a copy that you can load in later. This can save studio time and keep a project on schedule. A secondary DAW can function as a backup recorder—DAT machines are becoming scarce.

A Note About Animation Dialogue

Animation is always a special case. Traditionally, no animation takes place until the dialogue has been recorded. This means that the dialogue recorded in the studio is really the beginning of production for animated projects. Recording dialogue for animation requires a multiple microphone setup. This allows several actresses and actors to be in the same room, or at least to be able to see one another and react to each other's lines. This is necessary for the dialogue to have a natural flow, to sound "real."

Animation dialogue sessions are often videotaped in order to give the animators visual clues for facial expressions and mouth movements. With cameras involved, time code becomes necessary, as each video clip must reference the same SMPTE as the audio recording. The animation team needs to be coordinated with audio for the process to run smoothly. If you are involved in a mixed media project that includes film or video and animation, the audio complexities are magnified. Time code could be just about anything, from true 24fps film up to 60fps HD video. Careful planning and communication will help minimize the trouble.

For animation dialogue, it is best to have a large room with high ceilings, fairly dead walls, and a low reverberation time for recording. With multiple characters recording at the same time, acoustic separation without a loss of visual contact is a factor. A large room that can accommodate all of the actors can be a plus in this regard. Also, a large room makes the recording more neutral by reducing early reflections. As the animated characters may be in any situation—outside or inside—a neutral recording can be manipulated to emulate many different spaces. If there is too much room sound in the dialogue, it will be difficult if not impossible to make the dialogue sound like it took place outside. Small isolation booths might sound dead, but usually their small dimensions result in low frequency modes (100–400Hz) that do not sound natural. If you are stuck with a small recording room, effective bass trapping will be needed to achieve desired results.

Creating Rough Tracks for Video Editing

When you have finished recording the dialogue, you might end up with many tracks of production audio, ADR, and narration. It is then possible to create a "rough" dialogue track that other editors, both for picture and sound, can use to help their process along. You can use this rough dialogue track to help in recording foley. The picture editor can use the rough track to help fine-tune the visual edit. The dialogue track is the basis for the whole soundtrack of a film or TV show.

In order to provide a complete dialogue track that is usable for everyone, you must export a mixdown file. In the case of a film or other long-form project, the complete film or video might be broken up into several parts to make it more manageable. Normally, these are called *reels,* and each reel might be 20 minutes in length—this way, each session does not reach an unreasonable size. A two-hour session with 64+ tracks and a gazillion edits is not likely to be very stable on any system. Breaking it down into six 20-minute reels makes the process much more manageable.

In order to create this mixdown file, select the whole project timeline or reel as shown in Figure 5.21 and choose Bounce to Disk from the File menu. The Bounce dialog box, shown in Figure 5.22, will open. If you are sharing files with other editors, publishing the file as an OMFI would be a good choice. The OMFI file will ensure proper sync when imported to another workstation. Otherwise, creating a stereo AIFF file at 48kHz/ 16 bit resolution will be usable by most anyone. Make sure that the SMPTE start time is specified to any editor who will use the file. The timestamp Pro Tools creates might not be recognizable by other applications.

Beware Timing Delays   When processing audio using TDM and RTAS plug-ins, timing delays are generated that affect the start time of bounced audio files. Enable Automatic Delay Compensation in order to avoid this effect of processing delays. Although the delays themselves might be very small, their cumulative effect could potentially create an offset of a frame or more after several generations. Delay compensation is covered in Chapter 8.

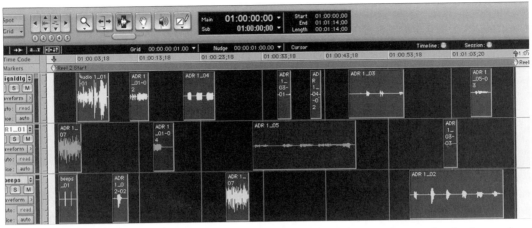

Figure 5.21 Selecting the whole project or reel. The use of markers at the very beginning and end of a file can make this easy to do.

You could store these files in a folder called Rough Tracks or Rough Dialogue Tracks. That way, the file will not be confused with more completely mixed dialogue tracks. This will also give others working on the project a way to identify rough tracks from other mixes. Complex naming schemes can be created to help determine what a certain file is for in a large project. Experience and experimentation will help you come up with a naming scheme that works for you. The organization needed for a large project such as a film is complex and paramount to getting the job done well and on time.

Using Markers to Select the Whole Project Timeline   Create a marker at the exact start time of the program material in your reel. This marker could simply be called "start." Also create a marker called "end" at the exact end point of the reel. Use Grid mode with a value of one frame to place the cursor before creating a marker so that the marker will be at the exact SMPTE time you specify. Once both markers are created, double-click in the marker timeline, and an area will be selected that includes all markers. If your start and end markers are the outermost markers in the session, double-clicking the Markers ruler selects everything in between, including those markers. Viola! You have the whole session selected accurately to the start and end SMPTE times for that reel. Also, once you have selected the whole session, Option-clicking on the Zoomer tool icon will zoom the session to show the entire selection.

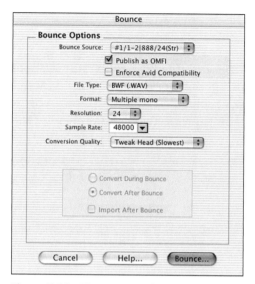

Figure 5.22   The Bounce dialog box. Here you can choose the type of file that will be created when you bounce the selected portions of your session to disk.

Recording Action Sounds (Foley)

Once the dialogue has been conformed from source tapes, AAF/OMF files, field recordings, studio voiceovers, and narration for animation and has been corrected with ADR and proper editing, it is time to record foley sounds. You'll recall that foley sounds are those made by the people you see on-screen and their direct interactions with the things around them, such as doors, guns, keys, and so on. Even the sound of clothing rubbing as the character moves is part of foley.

Using a Foley Stage

Most foley recording takes place in a studio that has a foley stage. Foley stages are usually larger rooms with a very low noise floor and low reverberation times to allow uncolored recording with a medium distance mic (3–6 feet). There can be pits in the floor that are filled with different materials, such as dirt, concrete, tile, wood, glass and just about anything else you can think of. The foley artist can walk, jump, and throw things into the pits in order to create all kinds of sounds. Almost anything can be used to make a foley sound. So much creativity and experimentation goes on in foley sessions in order to create the perfect effect. The choice of objects used to create certain sounds might not be as obvious as you think. A classic example is the recording of footsteps in cornstarch to imitate the sound of walking in snow. Try it yourself. It is amazing how real it sounds. But it is also much easier to get a bag of cornstarch into the studio than real snow!

When recording foley, you'll need to have a large monitor or (preferably) a projection system in order to allow the foley artist to see what's going on in the picture. Be careful of CRT video monitors; they create a high-frequency whine that can affect your recording. Headphones might not be needed, as the picture is primarily used for cueing. The foley artist can be distracted by dialogue. Watching a silent picture gives the artist the ability to focus on the sounds being created. However, a talkback system that allows anyone in the control room to speak to the foley artist will always be useful.

Basic foley can be broken down into three main items: moves, footsteps, and specifics. With a talented foley artist, these could take up as little as one track apiece. Specifics (sounds that are not moves or footsteps) will require more tracks, depending on how complex the scene is.

The Moves Track

The *moves track* is mostly made up of clothing sounds, such as the rustling of pants and shirts as the actors move around. It will be necessary to view the scene first to determine what type of materials are needed and which moves need the most attention. One foley artist might be able to do the moves for several characters at once if he or she is really good and the scene is not too huge. This is possible because the viewers typically notice only certain key actions that need a correlating sound in the moves track. If 12 people are all walking at once in a scene, you might notice only three or four of them that actually need moving sounds. The rest may blend in the background. Again, a talented artist may be able to make the sound of all four people walking. The moves track is a foundation layer of sound on which the rest of the foley is built. Consider this the *bed*, or ambience, of a scene.

During a moves track, the foley artist will most likely be sitting in a chair that does not squeak or make any undesirable noise. The mic can be anywhere from three to six feet away. Close miking of foley yields very unnatural sounds, as the proximity effect kicks in. You might have to find a compromise if your room is not acoustically optimal for this type of recording. Gobos and other sound-absorbing devices can be used to compensate for poor room acoustics. A typical moves setup is shown in Figure 5.23.

Footsteps

Next come the footsteps. After doing the moves track, the foley artist has a good idea about the general motion of the scene and can better re-create the footsteps. Footsteps are very difficult to re-create. The foley artist must do them while remaining stationary

Figure 5.23 Typical setup for recording a foley "moves" track.

so that the mic can pick up each step the same, and it's difficult to match the pace of someone running while you're standing still! When you can only see the torso or head of someone walking, figuring out where to put the footsteps can be tricky. Experienced foley artists watch the actors' shoulders to cue them how to walk. Try this yourself; it works quite well. Foley artists are sometimes referred to as "foley walkers," as the footsteps track is so critical. They can use many different pairs of shoes and even their hands sometimes. With animation, footsteps, as with other foley sounds, can be made up and not sound realistic at all. Many of the foot sounds in *Monsters, Inc.* were made using hands instead of feet. The monsters usually did not wear shoes, so the sound of skin hitting the ground or floor was more appropriate.

The technique for miking footsteps depends on the location of the scene. If it is an indoor scene, looser miking of around 6 to 10 feet helps create the feeling of being indoors. Hearing more room tone does this. Even adding a second mic farther away and mixing it in can help create a sense of space. Try not to go overboard and limit your choices later when mixing. For instance, if you mix too much of the distant mic in to the signal, you'll be stuck with an overly ambient recording that cannot be corrected during mixdown. With a dryer signal, it is possible to add artificial ambience later. When a scene takes place outside, tighter miking—around three feet—should work well.

Specifics

Specifics are any sounds that are not moves or footsteps. Anything the talent interacts with that makes a sound will need a specific recorded for it. This includes doors, guns, cars, furniture, fighting sounds, eating, and anything else you can think of. Recording specifics is easily the most complicated of the foley elements. Each one might require several layers of sound to create. Use as many tracks as you need to get it right. These sounds are the most creative and can define the "sound design" of a project. If you're running short on tracks, remember that you can always bounce the layers of a specific down to a new file.

Once you have recorded all the foley, it is time to create a rough foley track for yourself and other editors to use. Bounce the whole reel to disk as in the earlier example with dialogue tracks. The same SMPTE start and end times should be used so that importing these files into other sessions or even other workstations is painless and accurate.

Microphone Technique

Recording foley requires a very neutral style of recording. You're trying to capture a very natural sound so that it is believable to the viewer. Small diaphragm-condenser microphones are the first choice for recording foley. The directionality or pattern of the microphone depends on what type of sound you're dealing with. For instance, when recording small and quiet sounds close up, an omni directional microphone is preferred because of its lack of proximity effect. When recording things like loud footsteps, a more directional pattern, such as a cardioid microphone, will help focus the sound instead of capturing too much room ambience. Experimentation will determine the best choice.

Using FX Libraries

Using sound effects libraries to create foley can be a cost-effective solution for lower-budget projects. Libraries such as *The Hollywood Edge* and *Sound Ideas* offer a plethora of pre-recorded sounds that you can edit to picture to create a foley track. Doing so is no easy task, however. Editing precise footsteps for one scene could easily involve making hundreds of edits. What might take a foley artist one pass to disk might take you two hours to edit out of pre-recorded samples. You can find only so many samples of "male footsteps on concrete," so each footstep will not be as original as those created by a foley artist. Weigh these factors while budgeting in pre-production. Hiring a talented foley artist might save money and time in the long run.

If you do use effects libraries to create foley, you must import those files into Pro Tools first before editing them. To do this, you can use the Import Audio command from the File menu or drag audio files from the CD folder itself or from a Digibase browser into the region list. Pro Tools will automatically convert the file from 44.1kHz to 48kHz if needed in the background.

The Import Audio dialog box allows you to use Pro Tools to import, convert, copy, or reference any audio file on your system or on a networked drive. Many larger facilities have taken all their sound effect libraries and extracted the audio to data files and placed them on a server that is connected to the LAN (Local Area Network). Any workstation on the network can access the whole library remotely. Pro Tools can import audio from a network drive and copy the selected audio file into the session's Audio Files folder. After you select a file to import, choose Add if you want to reference the file or Copy if you want to copy the file into the current session's Audio Files folder. If the file you have chosen does not match the format of your current session, you can still add the file to the session, but it will not play back at the proper speed or bit depth.

You have the option to apply sample rate conversion during the import. After choosing the import method, click Done. If any files need conversion, Pro Tools will ask you where to put the converted files. The location of these converted files usually defaults to the Audio Files folder within the current session. Be sure to double-check that it does, as having the converted file in another location might make archiving difficult.

Examining Files with the Import Audio Dialog Box   The Import Audio dialog box offers a convenient way to examine and audition audio files. When a file has been selected, the file's attributes are displayed in the lower-left portion of the window. No matter what file type, sample rate, or bit depth the file is, you can still hear it by pressing the Audition Playback button. The file will play back through whatever Pro Tools hardware you are currently using.

On Location

In *The Godfather II*, the footsteps you hear when Fanucci is coming up the stairs, just before being killed by Vito Corleone, have an echoey sound while coming up through the stairwell. Walter Murch actually went to an old marble staircase and miked it up to record those footsteps. He had timed the pace from the film clip using a metronome.

With the metronome pacing him, he walked up the stairs, and that is what you hear in the movie.

This is an example of using locations to get very accurate and characteristic sounds for foley. Even without picture to look to for timing cues, it was still possible to record those footsteps and achieve a great result. Today, with systems such as Digidesign's Mbox 2 and laptops, portable computer recording has never been easier. If you wanted to record those footsteps in an old building, it would be much easier today than in the 1970s, when Walter used a metronome to get the job done.

First of all, the entire recording system—the Mbox, a laptop, and a couple of mics—can fit into a briefcase-size bag. Figure 5.24 shows the Mbox 2 family of interfaces, all of which have built-in mic-preamps and are capable of generating 48V phantom power for condenser mics, all while running off the battery in your laptop.

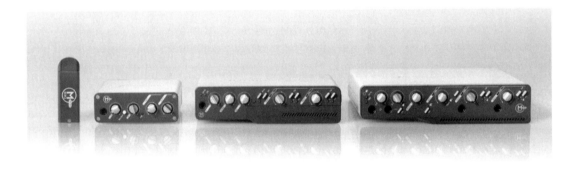

Figure 5.24 Digidesign's Mbox 2 Pro Tools recording systems. Using a USB connection, any Mbox 2 will run off of the computer's internal power supply.

And using the Mbox-laptop system, you would also be able to bring the movie with you in the form of a QuickTime file. This way, you would even be able to time the foley action with the action on-screen while in the jungle, hanging from a vine 100 feet up in the air. Now that's what I call a foley studio!

The movie *K19* used this idea to create the very realistic sounds from within a WWII submarine. Larry Schalit, one of the supervising sound editors on the movie, came up with the idea of doing all the foley inside an actual submarine. Using a laptop, MiniDV recorder, Pro Tools, an early USB interface (Sound Devices USBPre), and some Neuman mics, the crew set up in the submarine and created some stunning foley sounds for *K19*.

With or without a laptop, don't be afraid to get up out of the chair and go somewhere for that special sound you can't get in the studio. Getting into a real environment can stimulate the creative juices and help you make better soundtracks. On lower-budget projects, go on location and get the talent to run through the actions and moves without saying their lines, right after filming a scene. This way, you can record the actual foley sounds on location without the expense of using a foley studio. Early Francis Ford Coppola films used this method. Do it by yourself if no one else can help you. The director will thank you later.

Creating Sound Effects

The term *sound effects* can mean a wide variety of things. With regards to audio post-production, it refers to anything that could not be considered foley or dialogue. This might be extensions of foley sounds, such as gunshots. The sound of the trigger being pulled or the gun being cocked would be considered a foley sound, whereas the sound of the gun being fired would be a sound effect. These sounds are also referred to as *hard effects* and may come from a variety of sources, including CD libraries, field recordings, studio recordings, and even synthesizers and other electronic sources. Often a combination of some or all of these possibilities is used to create one sound effect.

Using Field Recordings

Field recordings can be the foundation for great sound effects. Going to the source for a desired sound effect is the most effective way of achieving realistic sounds. Junkyards can be great resources for sound effects—it's like having a gigantic foley pit with huge props.

Using a digital field recorder or Pro Tools on a laptop are two convenient ways of recording in the field; they allow you to import files directly into your main Pro Tools rig for editing. Although digital field recorders are designed from the ground up expressly for this purpose, the high-quality units can be quite expensive and might not be the right choice if only a small amount of field recording is needed.

Using an Mbox 2 as an interface, you can create a system that is also portable and can be operated by one person. Laptop cases are made that can be set up to hold your laptop in front of you while you're standing, allowing free movement while recording. The case shown in Figure 5.25 uses a special harness to hold the computer in front of you. The Mbox fits securely in the pouch, and microphones can be held in your hands.

Unless a field recording is tailored to meet specific sound-effects requirements, some editing and processing may be needed to alter the length or pitch of the recording. Many times, layering of different sounds together is used to create a single sound effect. Aspects of different sounds can be combined to create a complex and effective sound. For example, explosions are usually made up of several elements and can be created using many different sounds. The initial impact may come from an actual recording

Figure 5.25 A laptop case that allows you to support the computer while walking freely and using your hands to aim microphones.

of an explosion layered with other percussive sounds, such as close-miked thuds on a floor or even drums. Debris that is moved as a result of an explosion would also need to be layered in; the junkyard or foley stage can be a source for doing this. Fill a box up with all sorts of stuff, mixing different materials such as glass, metal, and wood. Find a slope steep enough to throw the material down, and record the sound it makes rolling down the hill. Edited into the impact sounds, this can create a dynamic and exciting sound for an explosion. The possible combinations are limitless.

Sometimes, however, realism is not the end goal, and you need to use other techniques to create fantastic sounds that are outside the realistic picture. Be creative and try sounds that are not so obvious. For example, crumpling tin foil, when pitched down an octave, can be a very interesting sound. That's just the beginning. Try anything that comes to mind. I am sure you will be surprised by the results.

Sound Effects Libraries

For the budget-minded, pre-recorded sound effects libraries offer an easy-to-use resource for creation of sound effects. These libraries try to provide complete, ready-to-use sounds for many common effects used in post-production. Certain libraries might be tailored for specific types of productions, such as commercials with "zip-bys," sparkle sounds, standard footsteps, cars, clocks, doors, and so on. More specialized collections can be found for historical uses, with sounds from vintage vehicles, airplanes, and home appliances. Other libraries include wartime, natural, mechanical, human, automotive, avionic, and animal sounds.

A full-featured library such as the *Hollywood Edge* has varieties of almost every kind of sound imaginable. The initial cost of such a library can be rather large, but it may be possible to buy portions of the library over time, when each part is needed. While the cost of a library such as this can be considerable, creating a library from scratch can take years and cost quite a deal more in time spent. However, the result of a custom-built sound-effects library will be more original soundtracks. Overuse of pre-made libraries can lead to mundane soundtracks lacking in dynamics and interest.

One method of extending the use of an existing library is to apply processing to create new sounds. It is very common to use pitch changing and time stretching processing to create new sounds from the original library ones. Pitch-shifted versions can be layered with other sounds to create new and original sound effects, thereby extending the life of your library. Don't be afraid to reinvent the *Hollywood Edge*.

Whenever you create an original sound effect for a project, keep a copy for your own sound effects library. Over the years of working on many different projects, you will amass a collection of unique sounds that you can call upon for your next project. The combination of original and library sounds should give you a large enough pallet to create unique soundscapes for your productions. Be sure to obtain any permission necessary to use original recordings made for a specific project. There might be copyright issues to deal with. Any legal rights to material generated by your work should be negotiated during pre-production. You don't want to get sued for using a sound effect that you created! Usually, sound effects by themselves do not fall under copyright laws, but there might be exceptions in certain cases.

Using Synthesizers and Samplers

Artificial creation of sound effects is a subject unto itself. The use of synthesizers and samplers to create unique sounds provides a whole universe of colors to paint with. The ability to generate tones, pitch samples, filter sounds, and reverse audio and audition these things on-the-fly gives you immediate feedback on how sounds will work in a particular setting.

Synthesizers

Anything that generates audio from electronic oscillators, small audio clips, acoustic modeling, or any combination of these can be considered a *synthesizer*. Pro Tools itself is a type of synthesizer. For our purposes, let's limit synthesizers to devices that are meant to create musical tones and that are controlled by a standard MIDI keyboard. These would include, but not be limited to, any type of electronic keyboard such as a Korg Wavestation or the Kurzweil K2000, shown in Figure 5.26.

Figure 5.26   The Kurzweil K2000 uses a combination of audio clips, oscillators, and filters to create musical sounds.

Today, many synths have migrated to the inside of the audio workstation. They have become computer programs themselves. It is possible to have a complete synthesizer with oscillators, filters, and envelopes that is a plug-in within Pro Tools. Access Virus, shown in Figure 5.27, is a good example of a plug-in or software synth, also known as virtual instruments.

Synthesizers can be used to enhance another sound effect. For instance, an explosion sound could be augmented by the use of a synthesizer playing a very low note that would, in essence, rumble like the sound of large chunks of debris falling to the ground. This subsonic enhancement could be layered with other explosion components to create a complete sound effect. By playing the sound on a keyboard, it is possible to audition different pitches of the tone in order to find one that complements the other sounds the best. The ability to do this quickly makes the synthesizer a valuable tool to the sound designer.

Samplers

A *sampler* is a device capable of playing back audio files instantly when receiving MIDI information. When a certain key is pressed on a keyboard controller, the sampler will play the correlating audio file. Additionally, samplers are capable of playing one audio file, or sample, in several different musical pitches. You can take one recording of a flute playing a middle C and play it back as a D or an E in real-time.

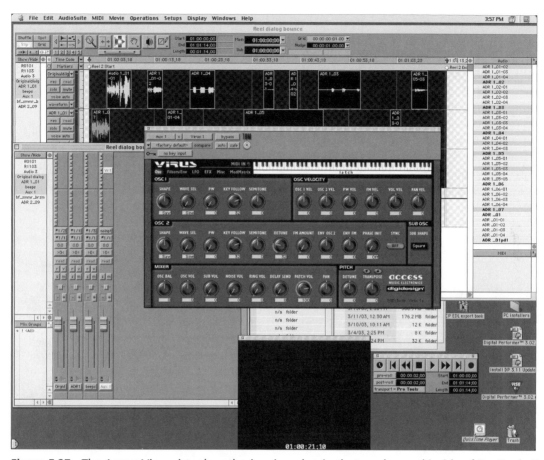

Figure 5.27 The Access Virus virtual synthesizer is a plug-in that can be used inside of Pro Tools. It is played with an external MIDI controller.

It would take much more time to accomplish the tasks common to a sampler inside of Pro Tools by itself. Every time you wanted a new pitch to be played you would have to process the file in order to raise or lower the note. Samplers can do this to multiple samples at once with different pitches for each sample. Samplers can be used for sound design as well. Taking an explosion sound and placing it within a sampler will allow you to quickly hear that sound in many different pitches, both lower and higher. This can help make a sound fit the picture better.

Programming a group of footstep recordings into a sampler can allow you to quickly play the footsteps while watching the video, as a foley artist would do. The ability to subtly alter the pitch of the footsteps can help keep variety in the soundtrack. Using traditional methods of editing each footstep into Pro Tools is much more time consuming and tedious. Record the footsteps into a MIDI track first. Then edit the MIDI track if there are any timing errors before recording the samples into an audio track. Doing so can help conserve disk space.

Commonly used sound effects for a TV show could be placed in a sampler for quick access during spotting sessions. Each sound effect could be assigned to a key. This could allow you to spot a show on-the-fly, coming back to fine-tune each effect.

Samplers, such as the Kurzweil K2000, and software samplers, such as the GigaStudio shown in Figure 5.28, also make use of synthesizer-type filters to further modify the sound of the original samples. Envelope filters can be used to affect the attack and decay of sampled sounds, and LFOs (low frequency oscillators) can modulate almost any parameter of the sampler as well.

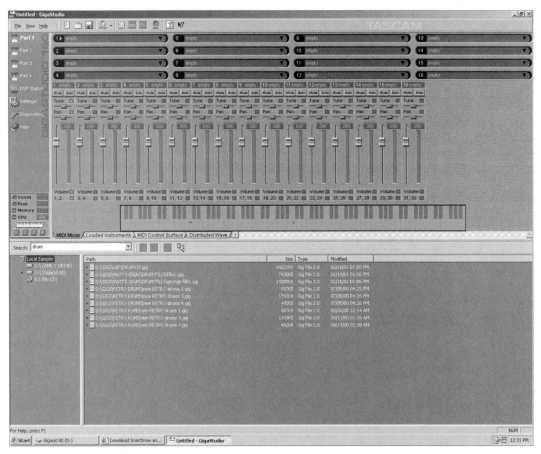

Figure 5.28 GigaStudio sampler is a program that runs on a Windows computer and is capable of playing back 160 voices of samples. These samples are played back directly from the hard disk and are not limited in size or length to the amount of memory in the computer. This allows the use of longer, more realistic samples.

Even though Pro Tools itself is basically a gigantic sampler, dedicated sampling tools offer another method for sound manipulation that can prove much more efficient for certain tasks.

Importing the Score and Incidental Music

Music plays an integral part in almost every visual production, from films and TV shows to corporate training videos. Music can come from CD libraries or from original music composers and recording artists. It might show up in the form of DAT tapes, audio CDs, CD-ROMs, or even as multi-channel audio files. I've even used MP3s, but the quality is very low with these compressed files. Try to get uncompressed files for use in any professional project; MP3s might be sufficient for demo or scratch purposes, but they should not be used in any final product, if possible.

Importing from CD, DAT, or Tape

Music commonly comes to you on an audio CD and can be imported directly into your Pro Tools session, including sample rate conversion, because video and film run at 48kHz.

DAT tapes are still a long-running standard in audio studios and are still occasionally used for music mastering. If the music was scored to picture and must be synchronized to your project, it must have SMPTE time code recorded on the DAT, or a 2-beep must be present in order to sync up the music to picture.

The same is true for analog tape. Some analog formats have a center SMPTE track to allow for synchronization. Often, a 2-beep is all that is necessary to sync the music up. With analog tape, two beeps may be required more often because of the inherent shift in tape machine transports.

Audio that is on any time-coded source, such as time code DAT or quarter-inch analog with center-track SMPTE, will need to be synchronized with Pro Tools. Connect the analog's SMPTE output to the input of your SMPTE-to-MIDI time code converter. Put Pro Tools online and record. Machine Control is not necessary for this operation. If sample-accurate sync is required for very long cues, a sync HD will be needed to maintain perfect sync.

Importing from CD-ROM

Audio files stored on a CD-ROM should be very easy to import directly into Pro Tools. Using the Import Audio function, you can access your CD drive just like any other drive on your system and then import the audio directly from the CD, assuming the CD-ROM is in a format that is readable by your computer.

If you're exchanging audio files across platforms—either PC to Mac or Mac to PC—using CD-ROM discs, the data format of the CD is important. The ISO 9660 format is readable by both systems. However, there are two naming conventions that can be used. The first is Joliet and is used primarily for backwards-compatibility with DOS systems. Joliet stores a list of names in two formats. The first format truncates every name to no more than seven characters. The second list contains Windows 95 long names, which are up to 32 characters in length. When descriptive names are truncated to seven characters, much of the information is lost. Programs that need to identify audio files by their full name, such as Pro Tools, will not be able to recognize these truncated names. OSX has built-in support for Joliet names. Most of these concerns are no longer issues with modern computers, but you still may run across one.

The second naming convention is called Romeo. Romeo is only recognized by Windows 95, 98, NT, XP, and later operating systems on the Windows platform. Macintosh computers can also read this Romeo format. Filenames in the Romeo format can be up to 128 characters in length. Using this method will ensure that programs can identify audio files by their original names.

Be sure to use the ISO 9660 format CD-ROM with the Romeo naming method employed. This will allow the filenames to have more than eight characters on the CD-ROM. Using the Joliet method results in filenames that are clipped if they exceed the eight-character limitation. This can make finding the file Star_Wars_cue_R1033. wav quite difficult. It might look like STAR_W~3.wav after being encoded onto a Joliet format ISO 9660 CD-ROM. Modern CD burning software such as Toast or Nero will deal with this automatically. It's only when you run into a very old data disc that these issues can arise.

Working with Film Composers   Film composers also work synchronized to picture. This allows them to create music that times out with the action on-screen, often accenting key moments with musical punctuation. In order for these accents to work correctly, perfect sync must be maintained from the composer's studio to your workstation. You must communicate with the composers to find out exactly how they synchronized to the picture. Did they run pulled-down or not? What SMPTE frame rate was used? What speed was their reference video running at, film or video? Did they use 44.1kHz, 48kHz, 88.2kHz, or 96kHz? Did they perform any sample rate conversion when outputting the files given to you? Again, these details should be worked out in pre-production, as unexpected discrepancies can wreak havoc when deadlines are closing in.

Importing Multi-Channel Music

Many composers will generate a surround sound mix of their music for you to import. It may come in the form of several mono tracks or as a self-contained, multi-channel audio file. If these files are not timestamped, the composer can include a cue list of time code addresses for the files.

Mono tracks can be imported directly into Pro Tools if they are of the same format and resolution as the current session. Once imported, these files must be placed together in the timeline and moved to the proper location for sync. Each file can be dragged from the Audio Regions List into the timeline while in Spot mode. When you let go, the Spot dialog box opens, and you can specify the same SMPTE start time for each file. Once the first file has been placed, Ctrl+drag the remaining files from the region list, and they will snap to the same position as the first. This ensures sample accuracy between each channel of a surround sound mix. You should then group all channels in the surround mix so they stay locked together, even if you edit them further.

If you import one multi-channel file, Pro Tools will have to convert it into multiple mono files first, but it will keep them associated as a surround group, as shown in Figure 5.29. You can create a surround channel with the same number of channels as the surround group you imported—in this example, 5.1 surround or six channels. It is then possible to drag the entire surround group into this track at once, as shown in Figure 5.30.

Using this multi-channel group ensures sample accuracy within the surround mix. This track can still be edited, and the relationship between channels will be maintained. Surround tracks behave just like stereo tracks but with more channels.

MP3 Files

MP3 files can be imported directly.

Understand that just because Pro Tools has converted an MP3 into another format does not mean that the inherent quality degradation in the MP3 codec is somehow reversed. Once an audio file has been converted into the MP3 format, the quality loss is permanent. MP3 files do contain some metadata but not timestamps, so they cannot be automatically placed at the correct position in the timeline. Other information regarding their location would be needed as written notes. Communication is the key to the most successful and creative productions.

Backing Up Your Data!

Now that you have recorded several terabytes worth of data for your current project, what happens when the power fails and your hard drive crashes? If you're like me, you don't even want to contemplate this possibility. To avoid the ultimate catastrophe, it is

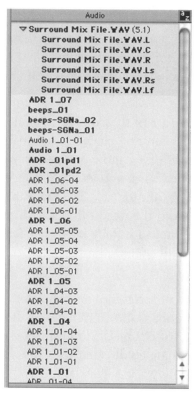

Figure 5.29   A multi-channel file once it has been imported into the Audio Regions List. The file has been converted into several mono files, but they remain associated as a surround group.

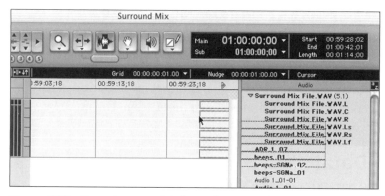

Figure 5.30   Dragging a multi-channel group of audio files into a surround track.

important to back up your data regularly. With the amount of data a project such as a film can generate, a simple CD burn is not going to cut it. It is necessary to come up with a secure backup plan that has even three or four levels of redundancy.

I talk to many people who say they back up their data only after a project is completed, in order to save time and space. This is foolhardy—the time to back up data is while you are working on it, because that's when a data loss will affect you the most. After the project is finished, you're safe, for the most part. You still must back up after finishing the project in case it comes back for revisions or you need to create a derivative work. This happens with commercials all the time. The client might want to re-create a commercial that is almost identical to the original minus a few changes in the price of a product or a telephone number. A complete backup will make this process much easier.

You Will Lose Data Eventually   It happens to everyone, given time. Hard drives fail, and power surges occur at the most inconvenient time. Power supplies are doomed to blow up without notice. No computer system is infallible. If you accept this truth and plan accordingly, you will be better off in the long run.

Backup Plan

When creating your backup plan, decide how much data loss is acceptable to you in the case of a system failure. Imagine your audio hard drive decides not to work today. What are you going to do? How much work can you afford to lose and still survive? Is one whole day too much? Is one hour acceptable? Once you decide where your threshold of data loss is, creating a plan to avoid it is simple. The decisions involve format choices and frequency of the backups.

An effective backup plan has several levels of redundancy, in order to ensure data recovery. They can be divided into three basic categories:

- Short-term or immediate backup
- Long-term storage and archiving
- Off-site fire protection backup

The short-term or immediate backup should be to a medium to which you can copy files quickly and that can be recorded over, as this is really a temporary backup. Hard drives make really good short-term backup devices. Re-writable DVDs and CD-RWs can also serve as short-term backups. Networked drive arrays that can have several terabytes available over a gigabit Ethernet network can be used by multiple Pro Tools workstations to provide a central facility-wide backup solution.

Long-term storage should have a long life expectancy. It should also have a large capacity, as this backup will never be erased and might contain several versions of a large project. This is the permanent storage for whatever projects it contains. Tape drives function well as long-term storage, as do DVD+/− discs. Remember that with only 4.5 gigabytes available on a standard DVD, it will take quite a few discs to back up a 60GB feature film. Toast and Nero support the spanning of data across multiple DVDs so that you can simply feed discs into your computer while creating a multiple disc archive of your project.

Off-site fire protection backups should be portable, to facilitate easy moving and storage. They should have a large capacity, as this backup is not updated as often as the first two. It should be able to contain all of your volatile data including samples, library sounds, and application settings. Anything that you cannot replace from a store should be on this backup. This is in case of a catastrophic loss due to the burning down and complete loss of the studio. Software can be replaced. Computers can be purchased at the store. Original data can't!

I hope you never have to use the fire protection backup, but it's good to know it's there. Imagine losing, in one fire, an entire sound library that took 20 years to amass, when the whole thing could fit on one small DLT tape cartridge. Enough said.

Automation of Data Backups

Manual backing up of data is not realistic, given the amount and complexity of day-to-day changes. Software designed to back up data is essential for smooth operation. Digidesign recommends using Mezzo software for backing up Pro Tools data. Retrospect, Chronosync, and Acronis are other popular solutions that will work for media files as well as other data on your computer (that is, contacts, calendars, email, and so on). Either software is capable of automating the backup process. They can analyze the data on your hard drive and determine which files have been created or modified since the last backup and copy *only* those files that have changed. This saves space and reduces redundancy in backup data. The software can use most storage devices, from VXA tapes to CDR and DVD discs. It is even possible to back up data to an Internet location, thereby keeping the backup off-site. This, however, requires a very speedy Internet connection.

You can schedule backups to take place in the late hours, when you are not working, or manually whenever you decide to. Each type of backup is completely customizable.

Once you have things configured, backing up should be as easy as sticking in a tape and pressing Start. Figure 5.31 shows a scheduling setup for Retrospect. You can determine how often the backup will occur and at what time of the day it will start.

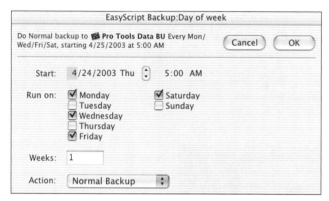

Figure 5.31   The scheduling setup window in Retrospect.

Possible Backup Scenario

A backup plan could work like this:

1. A secondary hard drive could be used to store data throughout the day. A script could be set up to copy any newly created or modified file to this hard drive automatically when the script is run. When you go to lunch or step out for some coffee, run the script. This will really help keep the downtime to a minimum in case of a drive or system failure.

2. A daily backup of the current project could be made to a DVD-RW. This could be written over every day and the media used again.

3. A tape-based storage system such as a VXA-1 drive could be used to incrementally back up the whole project every other day or so. This could be done at certain milestones in the process, such as when the dialogue has all been conformed and then again after ADR has been completed.

4. An off-site backup should be made once a week and taken to a remote location, to protect against fire and other catastrophic loss.

Note that any one of these backups can, and probably should, have two copies that rotate each time. That way you have an additional level of protection in case a disc or tape gets damaged.

Mass Storage Media

There are many mass storage devices available on the market today. Tape systems, such as the Ecrix VXA-1 drive shown in Figure 5.32, or DLT have traditionally been the only way to save vast amounts of data. Optical media such as DVD discs can compete with the size and cost of tape-based systems. Your choice should be based on how you like to work. Tape systems can hold more data in one unit than DVD. If you like to back up large quantities of data overnight without being at your computer, tape systems have the advantage. If your backups are smaller and you want to organize them in smaller chunks, DVDs might be the way to go. Ideally, a combination of media will yield the most dependability.

Figure 5.32 Ecrix's VXA-1 tape drive. One VXA tape cartridge can hold up to 33 gigabytes of uncompressed data.

Tape-based systems are usually proprietary—that is, you must have the drive on your system or on the network in order to restore information. Also, backup programs such as Mezzo and Retrospect save data to their own format, requiring you to use that program to retrieve the data.

DVDs can store proprietary info from Retrospect or Mezzo but can also store data in its normal format using programs such as Roxio's Toast or Easy CD Creator. DVDs created in this manner can be read by any compatible DVD drive, and the data can be copied directly to your hard drive. This type of backup is useful after the project has been completed to create a final copy for long-term storage. In the event that you need to go back to this project, simply copying the files directly off the DVD will restore the entire project. Any computer with a DVD drive capable of reading DVD-RAM or DVD-ROM discs can access this type of backup. No special software is required.

With the ever-increasing amount of data that we amass in audio and video workstations using hi-res sample rates and HD video files, backup solutions have not matched pace with increasing capacity in storage solutions. We are overdue for a revolution in backup technology. The device that is getting bigger and cheaper the fastest is the hard drive itself. DLT has managed to get up to 800 gigs on one tape and is convenient for creating copies of data very quickly to standard hard drives. Trusting these devices with long-term archival copies of your creative works seems quite tenuous at best. Be sure to devise an effective backup plan with any available technology and put it to use.

6 Editing to Picture

Editing in Pro Tools is a big part of the software's appeal. There are so many features that aid in the editing process that Pro Tools has become a standard in the post-production world. This chapter explores many of the techniques and features that help make Pro Tools the editor of choice for most audio post-production professionals.

Setting Up Pro Tools Sessions for Editing

Now that you have recorded all this great stuff into Pro Tools, it's time to edit everything to perfection. Post-production sessions can get quite large and visually cluttered when the track count gets high and the length is over a few minutes. Being able to focus on certain areas of audio with a simple and uncluttered screen will help you edit more efficiently.

Seeing the Information You Need

Pro Tools gives you the ability to hide elements that you don't need or want to see. You can customize the data that you see, whether it is rulers in the timeline or tracks that are not being used. You can resize tracks quickly so that you can see greater detail in certain areas. The Edit window is also capable of displaying mixing information—and if you only use one monitor, like me, getting as much information in one area as you can is very important.

Hiding or Showing Tracks

Even with all the options available from the Show/Hide window shown in Figure 6.1, sometimes you're looking for a quick and simple method of changing views without setting up groups or presets. And if you have much experience working in Pro Tools, you will find that key commands are paramount to working efficiently. The more mousing around you have to do, the less efficient you'll be.

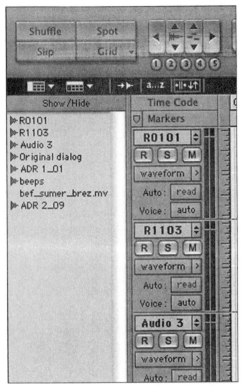

Figure 6.1 The Show/Hide window found on the left side of the Edit window.

A quick way to see only one track in the Edit window is to use the Option (Alt in Windows) key while selecting tracks in the Show/Hide window. When you Option-click on any track in the window, all the tracks will follow the same action. For instance, if all of the tracks are showing and you Option-click on one of them, all of the tracks will immediately be hidden. The reverse is true of Option-clicking on a hidden track—all of the tracks will appear.

Here's how to quickly make only one track visible in the Edit window:

1. Option-click on the track you want to see alone. All of the tracks will disappear, as shown in Figure 6.2. Track names in the Show/Hide window are not highlighted when they are hidden.

2. Immediately click (without holding down Option) on the track again, and it will reappear by itself, as shown in Figure 6.3. This track will be the only one highlighted.

Figure 6.2 Option-clicking on a visible track in the Show/Hide window hides all tracks at once. Hidden tracks are not highlighted.

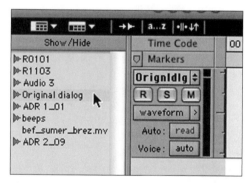

Figure 6.3 Clicking on that same track again causes it to appear by itself. Notice that Original Dialog is the only track name that is highlighted.

It's that simple. To return to seeing all of the tracks, reverse the process. Clicking on the track will hide it, and then Option-clicking on the track again will make all the tracks visible. Or you can just Option-click on an adjacent track that is not visible to achieve the same result. This trick only works when you want to view one track at a time.

You may also show or hide tracks by their type. If you want to view only audio tracks and hide any Aux, Master, or MIDI tracks, choose Show/Hide > Show Only > Audio Tracks, as shown in Figure 6.4. This also works for hiding tracks by type. If you only want to look at the Aux and Master tracks, choosing Show/Hide > Hide > Audio tracks will leave you only the Master and Aux tracks, provided you don't have any MIDI tracks.

Figure 6.4 Choosing Show/Hide > Show Only > Audio Tracks hides all other tracks except audio tracks.

You can sort the track listing in this window by name, type, group (I'll cover groups later in this chapter), or voice, as shown in Figure 6.5. This can help you locate a track quickly when you have a large number of tracks.

Figure 6.5 Show/Hide > Sort Tracks By. Here you can re-order the list of tracks in the Show/Hide window. This will also affect the order of tracks in the Edit and Mix windows.

In most cases you will likely need to see several selected tracks at any given point in time. The easiest way to do this is by using the Show Only Selected Tracks option seen in Figure 6.5. Select just the channels you need by Command-clicking on each one if they are non-contiguous and use the menu option to hide non-selected tracks. By only looking at the material you need to see, you can reduce your visual workload and work more efficiently.

Resizing Tracks

Once you have the tracks you want to work on in front of you, you might want to resize them for more accurate editing. You can do this by clicking in the vertical strip just to

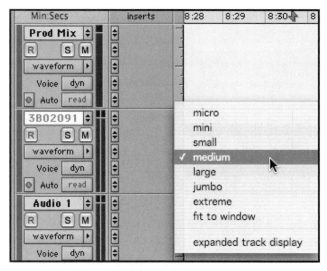

Figure 6.6   There are nine choices for resizing track heights, including the expanded track display for multi-channel audio. They are accessed in the marked area between the waveform display and level meters in the Edit window.

the left of the waveform display in any track, as shown in Figure 6.6. The choices are micro, mini, small, medium, large, jumbo, extreme, fit to window, and expanded track display.

- **Micro** is as small as you can make it.

- **Mini** is nice for reducing the on-screen clutter but keeping the track visible. Many tracks can be seen without scrolling, allowing you to get a view of the big picture.

- **Small** allows the same visibility as mini but with the ability to see some basic automation and audio regions clearly.

- **Medium** is what tracks default to when first created. This setting is very flexible, allowing most audio and automation editing tasks to be performed with precision. When tracks are very small, it's hard to actually see the audio or automation playlist you're editing. The medium size works well for most situations.

- **Large** is helpful with stereo files because it makes each side of the stereo waveform the same size as it would be on a mono track viewed at the medium height.

- **Jumbo** is very large and would only be used in very special situations where a high level of vertical detail is needed. I use this size when manually removing small digital clicks and pops with the Pencil tool.

- **Extreme** is useful when graphic editing of the waveform is needed or for precision editing of automation data.

- **Fit to Window** expands the waveform vertically to fill the entire available area in the Edit window as you have it sized—great for working on very detailed edits and editing digital pops or spikes.

- The **Expanded Track Display** applies to multi-channel files (for example, stereo, 5.1, and so on). When checked, each channel will occupy the same amount of space as the entire file alone did. For example, a stereo region using the Expanded Track Display will be twice as big—a 5.1 region will be six times as big.

It is possible to use the Option key modifier to resize all tracks at once. While holding the Option key, click in the resize area and choose a level. All visible tracks will be resized to that level. Individual tracks can be manually resized to any height by grabbing the dividing line between tracks and dragging up or down to size the track to your needs.

Global Modifiers   The Option key is a *global modifier*—it can be used to apply options to all tracks simultaneously. More global modifiers will be examined in this chapter. Try using Option+(any track operation) and see what the results are. Knowing and using global modifiers is one of the keys to high-speed operation of Pro Tools.

It is also possible to resize groups of tracks. Select several tracks at once, as shown in Figure 6.7. Press and hold Shift+Option and select a new viewing size; only the tracks you have selected will resize. This is an example of another global modifier. In most cases, when you use Shift+Option while performing an operation on several selected tracks, the same action will apply to all selected tracks.

Zooming, Scrolling, and Locating
An important part of using Pro Tools efficiently is being able to move around quickly and accurately within the timeline. Scrolling endlessly with a mouse can slow you down and make it much more difficult to get things done. The following subsections describe some ways to move around quickly through a Pro Tools session.

Zoom Commands. Being able to zoom to an appropriate level is important in Pro Tools. You should choose a method that helps you in the way that you work best. Instead of mousing up to the Zoom buttons as shown in Figure 6.8, try using the key commands Command+[for zooming out and Command+] for zooming in.

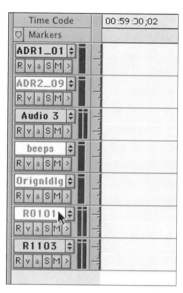

Figure 6.7 Selecting several tracks at once in the Edit window. By holding the Shift key and clicking on several track names, you can select them together. Selected tracks have their names highlighted in both the Edit and Mix windows.

Figure 6.8 The Zoom buttons in the Edit window. Using these buttons with a mouse can waste much valuable time.

You can leave your mouse wherever it will be used next and quickly press the key commands to zoom to the proper level. The time it takes to move the mouse up to the Zoom buttons and back down to where you're working might seem slight at first, but when you multiply it by the number of times you zoom in and out during a typical session, the time wasted becomes significant.

I use a multi-button programmable mouse from Kensington, the Turbo Mouse Pro, pictured in Figure 6.9. I have programmed two buttons for zooming in and out. Having those buttons right there in my hand helps me to see quickly what I need to see. This is just one example of how you can streamline your work methods.

Another tip for zooming involves a selected area on the timeline. Holding the Option key and pressing the Zoomer tool icon in the Edit window will automatically resize the Edit window to the selection you have made.

Figure 6.9   The Kensington Turbo Mouse Pro with a highly modified 8-ball installed. The weight of the 8-ball makes editing easier for me. This is one of many mice on which you can program buttons for frequently used commands. Mine has two buttons set up for zooming in and out.

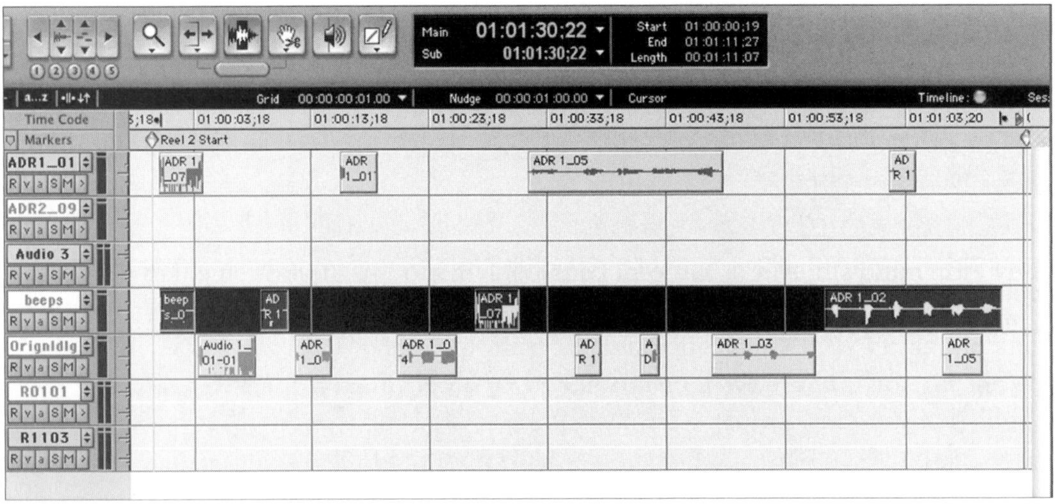

Figure 6.10   The Edit window after clicking on the Zoomer tool while holding Option. The Edit window will zoom to fit the selected area on the timeline.

In Figure 6.10, the selected area fills the Edit window after using Option-click on the Zoomer tool command. There is some margin on each side for convenience.

The Universe window, shown in Figure 6.11, is another way to view and navigate around a large session quickly. The highlighted blue area represents the area currently viewable in the Edit window. By clicking in non-highlighted areas in the Universe window, the Edit window will move to show that area.

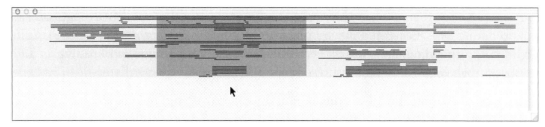

Figure 6.11 The Universe window. This window shows an overview of the whole session. By clicking in it, you can move the Edit window's view to a new location. The gray area is what is visible in the Edit window.

Locating within the Edit Window. Getting around the timeline accurately is possible in many different ways. One of the oldest Digidesign conventions, dating back to the days of Sound Designer II (Digidesign's original two-track digital editing application), is the use of the arrow keys to select and locate the start and end points on the timeline.

The down arrow key is used to set the start point. This can be done on-the-fly while playing. The up arrow key sets the end point. The left arrow key locates the Edit window with the start point centered. The right arrow key centers the end point in the timeline.

I don't use auto-scrolling because it makes it difficult to work on an isolated area and audition that area without the Edit window scrolling to some other location. I like to see only one area until I'm ready to move to another. I use the arrow keys all the time to function like auto-scrolling. Here's how to do that:

1. First, disable auto-scrolling by selecting Operations > Scroll Options > No Scrolling.

2. Start playback and wait until the cursor disappears off the right side of the Edit window.

3. Press the down arrow key. This sets the start point to wherever the cursor is at the moment you press the arrow button.

4. Press the left arrow key. The Edit window immediately centers on the new start point.

You can use the same method with the up and right arrows keys to center on the end point. It is also possible to press and hold the down or up arrow. As long as you're holding the button, the start or end point will be updated constantly to the cursor position. This can be handy for setting selections on-the-fly using your ears more than your eyes.

The use of the arrow keys is handy for setting punch-in and -out points if you're used to analog tape machine style operation. Pressing the down arrow key is like punching in, and pressing the up arrow key is like punching out, except that you are not recording, just preparing to. Once you have set the start and end points, putting Pro Tools into record with some pre- and post-roll time gives you the same results as punching in and out on an analog deck.

If you constantly press the down then left arrow keys over and over again, the window will keep moving along with the cursor as fast as you can press the keys. Try this and see how it works.

The Tab key is important for locating and selecting areas on the timeline. The Tab key will move the cursor to the next region boundary. If you are in the middle of a region, Tab will move you to the end of that region. If you press Tab again, you will move to the start of the next region on that track or the end of the session, whichever comes next.

If you use the Tab key while holding the Option key, the direction is reversed, and you will move to previous region boundaries and eventually to the start of the session. Using these two variants of the Tab key can get you to important editing areas of the session quickly. Arriving at region boundaries, where much editing takes place, can help speed things up a bit during your sessions.

Using the Shift modifier with Tab will select an area from your current position to the next region boundary. You can select areas to fade by starting at a point at which you want the fade to begin and pressing Shift+Tab to select from there to the end of the region, as shown in Figure 6.12.

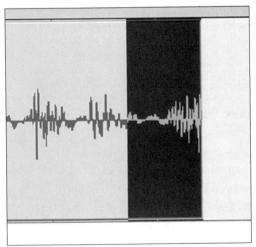

Figure 6.12 By pressing Shift+Tab, you can quickly select an area from a given point in the region to the end of the region.

If the cursor is across multiple tracks, then pressing the Tab key will move you to the next region boundary on any track in the selection. Figure 6.13 shows how a multiple track selection would move if you pressed the Tab key. Multiple tracks can be navigated through and selected in both directions using the Tab key technique.

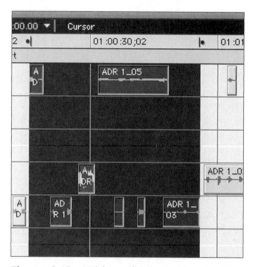

Figure 6.13 With multiple track selections, pressing the Tab key moves you to the next region boundary on any of the tracks selected. With grouped tracks, this can be very useful.

The Tab to Transient function is another way you can use the Tab key to move around in your session. To enable it, press the Tab to Transient icon shown in Figure 6.14. When this icon is outlined in blue, the function is active. Now when you press the Tab key, the cursor will move to the next transient waveform in the current region or the next region boundary, whichever is next. This can be quite useful when you're editing percussive material. All of the modifiers work the same way: Pressing the Shift key selects the areas in between, and Option reverses the direction. The best way to get an idea of how this works is to experiment. Import a drum loop, or any percussive sound file, and mess around.

Figure 6.14 The Tab to Transient enabling button. Use this to enhance the tabbing functions to include transient waveforms.

Auto-scrolling can be helpful in certain circumstances. For me, this is almost always during mixing—it's nice to have an updated view of where you are in the track while you're mixing. Having such a view can help you prepare for the next move or simply remind you where you are. The simplest form of auto-scrolling is Operations > Scroll Options > Page Scroll During Playback. This option will update the whole Edit window to a new location once the cursor has reached the right edge of the window. Be careful when editing with this mode enabled, as you could be about to edit a region when suddenly the screen scrolls to the next page, and you end up editing the wrong region. This is one reason I disable all scrolling while in Editing mode.

The nicest scrolling option to me is the Continuous Scroll with or without Playhead option (Operations > Scroll Options > Continuous Scroll with or without Playhead). This option keeps the cursor stationary in the middle of the Edit window, and the audio waveforms scroll by as they are played. This gives the most immediate sense of what is going on in the session. The only problem with this mode is that it is processor intensive and uses more resources than any other mode of scrolling. If you're viewing a Quick-Time movie at the same time, the strain on the CPU can potentially cause glitches in the GUI or video playback.

Keyboard Focus Mode   There are several Keyboard Focus modes in Pro Tools that allow the alpha keys (the letter keys) to function as single-stroke command buttons. The Commands Key Focus mode enables the alpha keys to perform editing commands with a single keystroke. There are also Keyboard Focus modes for the Groups list, the Audio Regions list, and the MIDI Regions list. As all of these functions are available without using Keyboard Focus, I will not cover all of them individually. You can get a complete list of these functions by selecting Pro Tools > Keyboard Shortcuts in OSX, or Help > Keyboard Shortcuts in Windows. This will open a PDF file that contains a complete list of all commands. I recommend printing this list and using it for reference, as it will help you learn the commands much faster. The Groups List Key Focus mode is discussed later in this chapter.

Edit Grouping

Pro Tools has very advanced grouping features that greatly help workflow in sessions. There are two types of groups: edit and mix. Edit groups link tracks in the Edit window, linking their editing functions together so that edits done on one track are also done on other members of the edit group. Mix groups link faders and other mixing functions for multiple tracks together in the Mix window. When you create a group, you are given the option to decide which type you're creating. You may also create a group that is both an edit and a mix group simultaneously.

Creating Groups

To create a group, select at least two tracks by Shift-clicking on their names in the Edit window, and then select Edit Groups > New Group (Command+G), as shown in Figure 6.15. The dialog box shown in Figure 6.16 will open, offering you a choice of making an edit, mix, or edit and mix group. Creating both an edit and mix group together is usually a good idea, as it is nice to have things grouped in a similar way later on, when mixing. If you make a dialogue group for editing, when it comes time to mix, there will be a mix group for the same dialogue tracks.

Figure 6.15 The Edit Groups submenu found in the lower-left area of the Edit window. Here you can create and organize your edit groups.

Editing Groups

Groups are used to help edit several tracks together in the same way. For instance, let's say you have six tracks of dialogue, and you need to move all of the edited regions to a new SMPTE location. Select all six of the tracks by Shift-clicking on each name in the Edit window. Then choose New Group from the Edit Groups submenu and assign a name, such as DIALOG, to this group. Now, click somewhere on one of the dialogue tracks. Notice that the cursor is now across all of the grouped tracks, as shown in Figure 6.17. Any selection you make in any of the tracks will also be made in all of the grouped tracks. Moving all the edits is as simple as selecting an area that includes all the regions you want to move. Figure 6.18 shows several regions selected in a group.

You can use the Shift+Tab method with edit groups to select areas starting exactly at the region boundaries. Here's how I selected the particular area shown in Figure 6.18:

1. First I grouped the four tracks together. I called the group DIALOG.

2. Next, I placed the cursor before the first region and on one of the tracks in the DIALOG group.

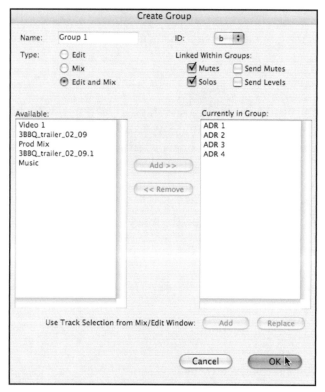

Figure 6.16 The Create Group dialog box. Here you can decide whether to create an edit or mix group. It is common practice to create an edit and mix group together.

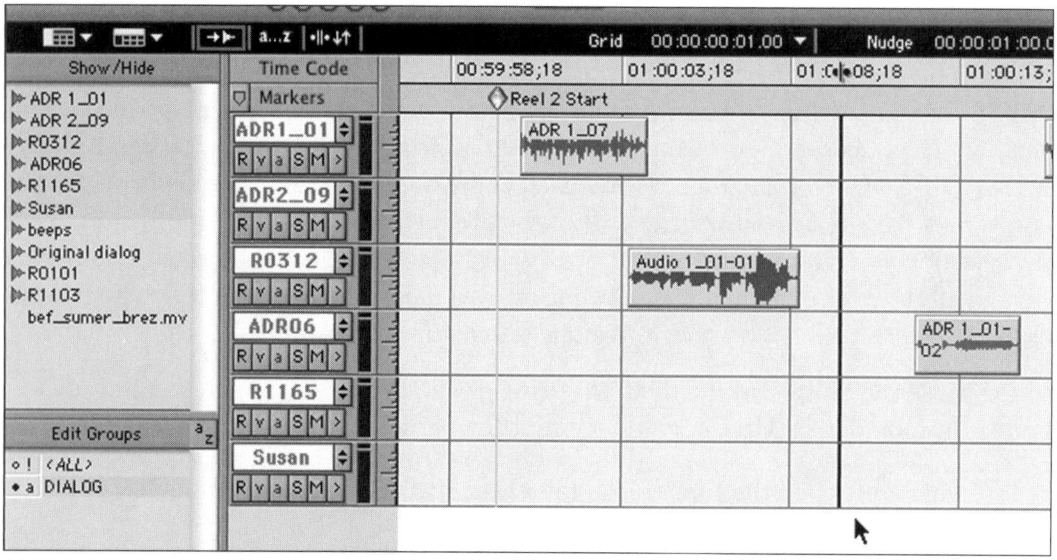

Figure 6.17 The cursor has been placed inside an edit group. Now, the cursor sits across all six members of the group.

3.   Then I made sure the Tab to Transient mode was off.

4.   I pressed the Tab key. The cursor moved to the start of the first region.

5.   Finally, I pressed Shift+Tab until all of the desired regions were selected.

Once you have grouped all of the regions you'd like to move, you can simply grab and move any one of them, and the whole selection will move. You can also use Spot mode and click on the first region and then input the correct SMPTE number; all the regions selected will move relative to this new SMPTE position. This is just one example of how techniques can be combined to yield quick and accurate results.

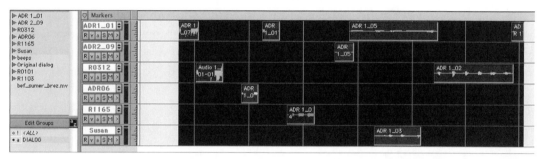

Figure 6.18   Several regions have been selected in an edit group. Notice that all selections occur on all the tracks.

Anything that can be done to a single track can be done to a group of tracks. Cutting, pasting, copying, erasing, repeating—you name it. Grouping also becomes very important during mixing. I'll discuss that process in Chapter 9, "Delivery of Master Recordings."

Enabling and Disabling Groups

When you're working with grouped tracks, it is often necessary to edit one of the tracks individually. There are several ways to disable the grouping in order to work with one track at a time.

First, you can disable the group entirely by clicking on its name in the Edit Groups area of the Edit window, as shown in Figure 6.19. The groups that are highlighted are active; clicking on a name will disable that group, leaving the name not highlighted. When the group name is not highlighted, you can edit any track that is a member of that group without affecting the other tracks.

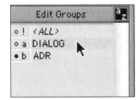

Figure 6.19 Clicking on the name of an edit group here toggles the enabling of that group. Highlighted group names represent active groups, and non-highlighted group names represent inactive groups.

You can also use the Key Focus mode to enable and disable edit groups. Activate the Group Key Focus mode by clicking on the Group Key Focus button just above the Edit Groups window shown in Figure 6.20. When you first created a group, a letter was assigned to it in the Create Group dialog box (refer to Figure 6.16). In Key Focus mode, this letter refers to the alpha key, or letter key, you can now use to enable or disable the group. In Figure 6.20, the DIALOG and ADR groups are labeled a and b, respectively. If Key Focus is enabled, pressing the A key will disable group A (Dialog). Pressing the B key would enable the ADR group (as in Figure 6.20, it is disabled already).

Figure 6.20 The Group Key Focus enabling button shown here in the upper-right corner of the Edit Groups section of the Edit window. When highlighted, Group Key Focus is enabled, allowing you to turn edit groups on and off by using the letter keys.

Regrouping Tracks and Renaming Groups

Pro Tools has now added the ability to easily modify existing groups. The addition of the Modify Groups option from the Edit Groups menu, shown in Figure 6.21, will allow you to add or remove tracks from the group, rename the group, and alter the linking properties of the mix group.

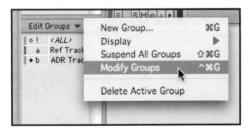

Figure 6.21 The Modify Groups option is available from the Edit Groups menu.

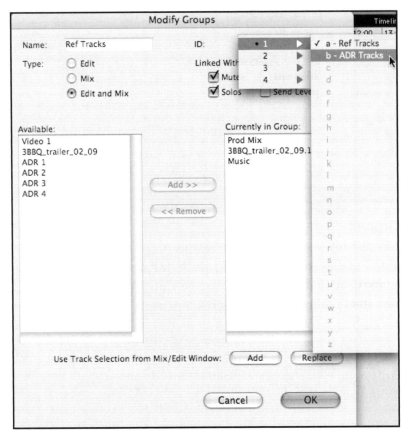

Figure 6.22 The Modify Groups window, showing the group ID submenu.

The Modify Groups dialog box is similar to the Create Groups dialog box. You can add or remove tracks from the group, change the type of group, and alter the linking of mutes and solos between group members, as seen in Figure 6.22. You may choose which group to modify by selecting it from the ID pull-down menu.

Creating edit and mix groups at the same time facilitates soloing and muting of whole sections of your project. If you just want to hear all the dialogue tracks, press the Solo button on any dialogue track with the dialogue group enabled. Similarly, you can mute whole aspects of a production quickly and without any fuss. Disabling the group is as easy as pressing the appropriate alpha key, if Group Key Focus is enabled.

Managing groups in a large session (more than 32 tracks) will enable you to concentrate on more important aspects of the sound. Preparing your sessions with grouping can speed up workflow and allow for more creativity. That's always my goal! The tools should help you get to the creative aspects of sound design and leave the technical chores behind.

Color Coding by Group   You can now color-code both tracks and regions by their associated group. Go to Setups > Preferences and look at the display pane. There are two default coloring-coding settings. If both are set to Groups, the tracks and regions on those tracks will be color-coded by the group they belong to. If a group is not active, regions will have black audio on a gray background. Color-coding related tracks can help you visually organize your work. This can really make a difference in a large session with over 100 tracks that lasts over an hour or so for feature films. Any time your eyes can work less, you ears can work more…

Using Counters and Rulers

Counters and rulers are used to represent time in different formats. Rulers appear at the top of the Edit window and can be used as a visual guide for position and duration information. The counters appear in a number of window throughout Pro Tools, but most notably in the Transport and Edit windows, where they can be used to position the cursor, the start time, and the end time.

Rulers and counters both share the same choice of formats, from bars and beats to time code and even samples. Counters and rulers provide different ways of viewing time in a Pro Tools session. It is essential that you be able to see the timeline from different time references. Depending on what operation you are performing, different counter and ruler formats can aid your efforts. For example, if you're placing music cues in the timeline, the time code ruler and counter will be much more effective than the samples format. Viewing time in samples requires very large numbers that won't make much sense in terms of video time, which is measured in frames. However, the samples format is much more useful during mixdown if you have to compensate for latency within the mixer. I'll go into the details of DSP latency in Chapter 8, "Mixing to Picture in Pro Tools."

Counters

Pro Tools offers two counters that can each have a different format, allowing you to view time in two ways at once. The Main counter is the larger of the two. These counters are visible in the following three locations:

- In the Transport window, shown in Figure 6.23. You may have to choose Display > Transport Window Shows > Counters to display the counters in the Transport window.

- At the top of the Edit window, shown in Figure 6.24.

- In the Big Counter window, only the Main counter is visible, as shown in Figure 6.25.

Figure 6.23 Both the Main and Sub counters in the Transport window. The Main counter is the larger of the two and is set to Time Code. The Sub counter is set to Samples.

Figure 6.24 The Main and Sub counters in the Edit window.

Figure 6.25 The Big Counter window shows only the Main counter. Choose Windows > Show Big Counter (Command+3) to see the Big Counter.

In the Transport and Edit windows, each counter has a pull-down menu to the right of it that allows the format to be changed to one of five options, as seen in Figure 6.26. Each counter can display a different format. The Big Counter window will always display the format of the Main counter only.

In the Edit window, there are additional readouts for counter numbers. These are used to view the Start (in-point), End (out-point), and Length (duration) of the current selection, as seen in Figure 6.27. Select an area in the Edit window and watch the in and out points change as you move. The duration also changes as you increase or decrease the size of your selection.

Figure 6.26   The five choices for counter formats are Bars:Beats, Minutes:Seconds, Time Code, Feet. Frames, and Samples.

Duration Counter as a Stopwatch   Use the duration (Length) number to analyze the length of voiceover takes. It is very easy to get an accurate length by setting the Main counter to Minutes:Seconds, switching to Slip mode, and selecting the voiceover you want to measure with the Selector tool. Be very precise about the start and end points, in order to get an accurate measurement. The duration number will be the length in minutes and seconds. It is possible to do this on-the-fly while recording. Simply use the up and down arrow keys to mark the start and end of the voiceover take while recording. You can even hold the up arrow to continually update the running time of the recording. The Length indicator will increase just like a real stopwatch.

You can manually set the in and out points by typing in values for them, as shown in Figure 6.27. This is useful when you have precise instructions about the length and location of an edit you need to perform. Just click the in-point area of the Edit window, and you can enter a number in the format currently enabled in the Main counter. The same is true for the out point.

Figure 6.27   The Start, End, and Length indicators in the Edit window. These values can be manually entered by clicking on the number itself.

If you enter a value for the Length indicator, the End indicator will be modified so that it is equal to the in-point plus the value you enter for the Length. For instance, if you want to copy an area starting at 01:30:22;17 and lasting for 10 seconds and two frames, enter 00:00:10;02 into the Length area. The End indicator will be updated to 01:30:32;19, as shown in Figure 6.28.

Figure 6.28   After entering a value for Length, the end point is updated to reflect the new length.

The in, out, and duration will all update when you use the arrow keys for selecting as well. The duration will update on-the-fly continually as long as you press the up arrow key. This can give you a live counter for a relative position that is counting from any point in the timeline starting at zero. In this way, the arrow keys can function something like a stopwatch. While playing, press the down arrow as you would a stopwatch start button. You can press the up arrow at any time to get a revised time, as you would use a lap timer, or press and hold the up arrow to have the duration display a continuous running time.

Rulers

Rulers also help you get around and edit in Pro Tools. In TDM systems, the time code ruler is obviously going to be helpful when working with video. If you're working with music and video, the bars:beats ruler will be invaluable.

Use the Ruler pull-down menu, shown in Figure 6.29, to select which rulers should be visible. There are 10 choices for ruler formats. In addition to the formats available as counters—Bars, Minutes, Time Code, Time Code 2, Samples, and Feet:Frames—there are four other Ruler formats that can be viewed: Tempo, Meter, Markers, and Key Signatures. Tempo, Meter, and Key Signatures rulers are used primarily for music. The Markers ruler can be used in just about any application. I typically view Time Code and Markers rulers in a post-production session.

The Markers Ruler. Markers are helpful to anyone working with picture. They can help outline areas and give editors direction when spotting audio to picture. Pinpointing frame-accurate locations with markers helps you perform complex editing with precision and speed, without the need to memorize SMPTE numbers and keep lengthy logs and notes. Keeping your ears tuned to the sound without bogging down your mind with details allows for a more creative work context. I'll explain how to use markers in detail later in this chapter.

Figure 6.29 The Ruler pull-down menu in the upper-left area of the Edit window. Here you can select what types of rulers will be visible above the waveform display.

The Time Code Ruler. The Time Code ruler displays the SMPTE format of the current session. Knowing the SMPTE format is essential when working with time-coded material and picture. The ability to see the exact location of the cursor in SMPTE numbers also helps when spotting audio to picture. You can use a cue sheet with SMPTE times in conjunction with the Time Code ruler to accurately create markers where sound effects need to be placed. This will give you visual references in Pro Tools for spotting audio.

The Time Code 2 ruler can be set to a different frame rate from the current session frame rate. This ruler is used for referencing another video frame rate that is being used in the production. For example, the session time code might be set to 29.97fps, but the HD video frame rate of the final production could be running at 23.976fps. The secondary Time Code ruler can be set to 23.976fps so that you have a visual reference of where the actual video frames line up in relation to the audio. However, the secondary Time Code ruler is only for reference and cannot be used in the Spot dialog box or as the main counter format. You can set the frame rate of the secondary Time Code ruler in the Session Setup window (press Command+2).

The Feet:Frames Ruler. The Feet:Frames ruler performs the same functions as the Time Code ruler but should be used only when all timing references are being created in the Feet:Frames format for film editing.

The Minutes:Seconds Ruler. The Minutes:Seconds ruler is helpful for dealing with real clock-time editing. This ruler goes down to the millisecond level and thus is essential when you need a higher resolution for very precise editing. The Minutes:Seconds ruler is also useful in measuring lengths in a clock-time format instead of SMPTE frames. Many music-recording engineers are more familiar with durations measured in milliseconds and might find this ruler of more use.

The Samples Ruler. The Samples ruler has the finest resolution of any of the rulers. Neither Pro Tools nor any other PCM digital audio system is capable of editing with smaller increments than one sample. These values will give you the highest degree of accuracy available to the system. Using this ruler is cumbersome for editing in any real-time sense, though, because the numerical values are so high (48,000 values for one second alone at 48kHz).

The Bars:Beats Ruler. The Bars:Beats ruler is obviously used for music. Unless you're recording the music yourself, this ruler might not have any relevance to your session. If, however, the composer gives you a MIDI file that you can import into Pro Tools, this Bars:Beats ruler can add valuable information, such as where beats in the music fall in relation to frames in the video.

For instance, if, during a car chase scene, the music plays a large role in the pace of the action, this ruler could be used to help place sound effect in sync with the beat of the music. An old example of this comes from the original *Batman* TV series. The sounds heard in the intro to the show, such as "Bam!," "Smack!," "Boom!," and so on, have been placed in sync with the musical punctuation and film editing. These sounds certainly weren't placed with Pro Tools, but you can see how the Bars:Beats ruler might help with such a task.

The Tempo Ruler. The Tempo ruler is also mainly for music. It can be helpful for an editor to see where the tempo changes relative to the picture and other audio elements. If the music can be heard, these changes should be obvious, but having a visual clue can help out when you're trying to work quickly. Film composers can make much use of this ruler, as tempo changes are commonly used for dramatic effect. The ability to visually reference these changes against picture is very helpful.

The Meter Ruler. The Meter ruler is almost exclusively for music composing. Film composers make use of this ruler in placing meter changes to specific picture changes.

Using Grid Values

The grid is a system that restricts cursor movements, selections, and region boundary placement to values larger than one sample. As one sample is the smallest increment available to any Pro Tools operation, the grid is used to divide the timeline into larger segments, allowing users to move in pre-defined steps rather than continuously through each sample. These larger increments can be based on a number of different timescales, which are as follows:

- Clock time in minutes and seconds.

- Musical time in bars, beats, and tics. (There are usually 400 ticks per beat. Pro Tools has 960 ticks per beat.)

- SMPTE time code in frames and subframes.

- Film measurements in feet and frames.

- Samples.

- Markers and regions, which includes both region boundaries.

Each timescale has several preset choices for values that would typically be used. For instance, the Bars:Beats grid has preset values for whole notes, half notes, quarter notes, and so on. The Time Code grid has set values for quarter frames, frames, seconds, minutes, and hours.

Setting the Grid Value

Grid values are somewhat dependent on the setting of the Main counter. Setting the format of the Main counter changes which values are available in the Grid setting, as shown in Figure 6.30. This option can be disabled by unchecking it at the bottom of the Grid submenu.

Figure 6.30   Here are the grid value choices for time code. The option to have the grid value follow the Main counter can be turned off at the bottom of this menu.

Each timescale has preset choices for grid values. For instance, the Bars:Beats grid values start at one bar and divide equally down to a 64th note. There are also options to include dotted and triplet notes. This timescale has the most possible grid values. In audio post-production, the Time Code scale is used most often. The choices available for grid values are as follows:

- 1 second
- 10 frames
- 1 frame
- 1/4 frame (25 subframes)
- 1 subframe (1/100th of a frame)

Enabling Grid Mode   In order to use the grid values, Grid mode must be enabled. Press the Grid button in the upper-left area of the Edit window, as seen in Figure 6.31, or press F4. Now, all cursor movement is limited to the specified grid value.

Figure 6.31   The Grid mode button in the Edit window. Alternatively, you can press F4 to enable Grid mode.

I spend most of my time using a grid value of one frame. One frame is the smallest increment by which the picture can be edited. Using the same grid value can help you line up sounds to the actual video or film frames in your project. For instance, imagine you have just imported some score music from the film composer, and you have been given an SMPTE start time and a 2-beep in the audio file. Let's say the start time of the music is 01:00:21;23 (the semicolon indicates you are using 29.97 drop-frame SMPTE). Here's how you can place the audio file in the correct location:

1. Enter Slip mode (F1).

2. Assuming you have already imported or recorded the audio into Pro Tools, either drag the audio file from the Audio Regions list into a new stereo audio track or go to the audio you have recorded.

3. Select the Trim tool (F6).

4. Make sure the Trim tool is in Standard or Scrub mode, not TCE (Time Compression/Expansion). Figure 6.32 shows how to manually select the proper Trim tool.

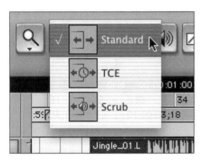

Figure 6.32   Manually select the Trim tool in Standard or Scrub mode.

5. Trim the music file close to the 2-beep.

6. Zoom in to at least the millisecond level and fine-tune the trim to *exactly* the start of the 2-beep, as shown in Figure 6.33.

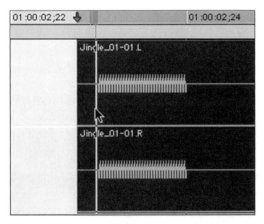

Figure 6.33   Fine-tuning the trim to the exact start of the 2-beep tone.

7. Enter Grid mode (F4). Using the Time Code format, choose a value of one frame.

8. Zoom out so that you can see at least one second or so of time.

9. Using the Grabber (F8), drag the region so that the start of the 2-beep lines up with the frame number that is two seconds ahead of the start time. Grid mode will force the region to "snap" to each frame. If there is no 2-beep to use, simply line up the start of the music waveform to the given SMPTE start time in the same manner.

10. Look up at the Main counter to see what your current start time is.

11. When you reach 01:00:19;23, stop and let go of the region.

12. The 2-beep is now lined up two seconds before the actual starting frame of the music. Press Play, and the music should be in sync.

13. Once you have checked that the music is playing in sync, trim off the unwanted 2-beep.

Relative Grid mode is a secondary function of Grid mode accessed by the Grid mode pull-down menu or by pressing F4 repeatedly to toggle between Relative and normal Grid modes. In Relative Grid mode, movement of regions is constrained to grid increments but not actual grid points on the timeline. In other words, you may move a region *relative* to grid points but not necessarily *aligned* to any grid points. This option is discussed later in the chapter in greater detail.

Grid and Relative Grid modes can also snap to other points *inside* the region boundaries. These points are called *sync points;* they are also discussed later in this chapter.

Using Memory Locations

Memory locations are formatting options and timeline locations for the Edit window. The position, visible tracks, zoom level, and selection boundaries are just a few of the items that can be stored in a memory location. They make it easy to put lots of information inside your session where you need it the most and allow you to move quickly to key points within your session. They can also be used to resize your tracks and go to a new zoom level, hide tracks and enable groups, or select an area and adjust pre- and post-roll times. There are many uses for memory locations, and I'll only be able to touch on a few within the confines of this chapter. With continued use and experience, you will find new uses for memory locations every day.

Creating Memory Locations

To create a memory location, simply press the Enter key while playing, recording, or stopped. As long as there are no other dialog boxes open at the time, pressing Enter will call up the New Memory Location dialog box, shown in Figure 6.34.

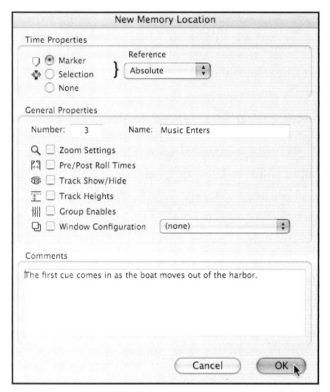

Figure 6.34 The New Memory Location dialog box. You can create a memory location by pressing the Enter key at nearly any time. In addition to the name of the memory location, you can also enter comments about it for more information.

As you can see in Figure 6.34, memory locations can affect many aspects of the Edit window's appearance. Three memory locations options exist: Marker, Selection, and None. All three options can include the current zoom level, pre- and post-roll times, visible tracks, current height of visible tracks, group enabling, and even window configuration. The None option is used for saving only appearance information, such as the zoom level and visible tracks, and not timeline information such as location and selection values.

Selection Memory Locations

Creating selection-type memory locations saves the current start and end times as part of the location. Recalling a selection's memory location will move the cursor to the start time and extend the selection to the saved end time. If you had checked any other options, such as zoom level or visible tracks, these would be recalled as well.

None Memory Locations

Using the None option saves only the data formatting of the Edit window. Whatever aspects you choose can be stored in this memory location. Creating a memory location that hides all other tracks except dialogue, resizes the dialogue tracks to medium, and disables the dialogue group, for example, could instantly set up the Edit window for dialogue editing.

Memory locations like this could be created for each type of editing you do—dialogue, foley, sound effects, or music—so that switching between them does not require a lot of resizing, hiding, and group enabling.

Marker Memory Locations

When creating Marker memory locations, the position of the marker is determined by the exact position of the cursor at the moment you press the Enter key. Even if you take several seconds to type a name for the marker, it will be placed at the point in the time-line where you first pressed the Enter button. When stopped, any markers created will be placed at the current cursor location.

A yellow tab will appear at the current cursor location in the Markers ruler with the name of the marker to the right of the tab. You can use the yellow tab in many ways to affect the marker position.

- Clicking on the tab once will locate the cursor to the exact marker position.

- Clicking and then dragging the yellow tab will move the marker to a new location. This function will also follow the editing mode, whether Grid, Spot, or Slip is used. Shuffle does not affect the marker moving.

- Option-clicking on the tab will delete the marker immediately.

- Double-clicking on the tab allows you to modify the name and characteristics of the memory location.

Using the Cue List to Create Markers

Cue lists are created by viewing video with a time code burn-in window and noting at certain time code values when sound effects are needed. A sample cue list is shown in Figure 6.35. These cue lists can then be transferred to Pro Tools markers for editors to use and follow. The time code value for each cue can be entered into the Main counter window, thereby locating the cursor to that position. Pressing Enter will bring up the Create Memory Location dialog box. The name of the cue or description of the sound can be entered as the marker name. This process could be repeated for each cue,

"SuperSuds Soap" - Country Style :30 TV

CUE LIST

TC	Cue Name	Description
01:00:00;23	Barnyard walla	Misc. barnyard animal noises creating realistic rural background
01:00:04;03	Screen Door	Light screen door squeak open then clapping shut
01:00:05;21	Basket squeak	Light creaking of the woven basket as she is carrying it across the lawn
01:00:11;20	Soapy Bubbles	Over the top "sudsy bubbles" sound as she plunks the clothes in the tub emphasizing the wholesomeness of SuperSuds
01:00:21;23	Music	SuperSuds Country Fresh jingle with :02 vocal tag

Figure 6.35 A sample cue list. The first cue in this list is used in the following example.

resulting in a session that has all the necessary information for editors to use when creating sound effects for the project. The markers are a road map for creating the soundtrack. This is just one example of how using markers can help smooth workflow.

Here are the steps for creating markers from cue lists:

1. Enter the time code value for the first cue into the Main counter. (See Figure 6.36.)

2. Press Enter to create a marker. The New Memory Location dialog box will open.

3. Type in the marker name and information that will assist editors. (See Figure 6.37.)

4. Click OK. The marker will be created. (See Figure 6.38.)

Figure 6.36 Entering the time code value for the first cue. You must press Enter or Return in order for Pro Tools to locate to this position.

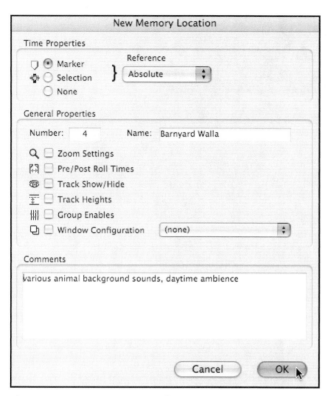

Figure 6.37 Entering cue information into the marker name.

Once all the cues have been entered into markers, the editors of the session have a clear road map for the placement of sound effects, as shown in Figure 6.39. You may also view all memory locations in one window by choosing Windows > Show Memory Locations (Command+5).

Recalling Markers and Memory Locations

Once markers or memory locations have been created, recalling them or getting to them easily is important. The Memory Locations window (Command+5) is a convenient way to view, organize, and recall markers and viewing setups. Memory locations can be organized by name, location, or type. Each one is assigned a number when it is created. This number can be seen at the left of the Memory Locations window, as shown in Figure 6.39.

The Memory Locations Window

To recall a memory location, simply click on the number to the left of the location's name. This will locate to the marker and/or reformat the data that is viewed in the edit window to reflect the settings of the location. Any aspects of the edit window that are

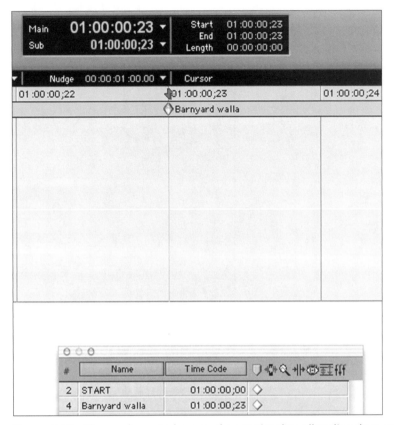

Figure 6.38 The newly created cue marker. Notice the yellow line that extends below the marker's tab. This line can be seen on any visible track, helping you to see where the marker lines up on all tracks.

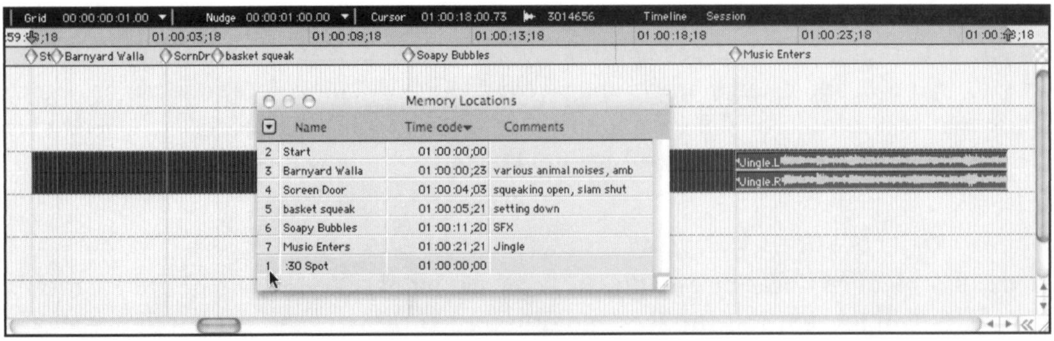

Figure 6.39 The entire example cue list has been entered into markers in Pro Tools. The Memory Locations window (Command+5) displays all memory locations of any type in the current session.

not part of the location will not be modified. If the location is just a marker point, Pro Tools will move to a point where the marker is centered in the Edit window. If the location does not contain a marker but does specify track sizes, group enables, and pre/post-roll amounts, the Edit window's location will not change, but the data will be formatted to the memory location's parameters.

Selection Markers   Notice in the example shown in Figure 6.39 that Marker 1 is named ":30 Spot." This is a selection marker. The Edit window in Figure 6.39 shows this selection. The selection starts at exactly 01:00:00;00 and ends at 01:00:30;00, making the length exactly 30 seconds. I created this selection so that when the commercial gets bounced to disk as a final mix, it will make it easier to create a perfect selection of just the 30-second spot and no more or less. This is just one use of a different type of marker in Pro Tools.

It is also possible to recall a memory location by using the keypad. The Memory Locations window does not have to be open in order for this function to work.

1. Type a period (.) on the numeric keypad, not on the regular alpha keyboard.

2. Type the number of the memory location you want to recall.

3. Type a period (.) again on the keypad. The memory location will be recalled.

This method provides quick access to any memory location. In order to use the keypad method without the Memory Locations window open, you must have the number of the location memorized. I typically set up formatting locations that I commonly use in the first few numbered locations. They are more easily remembered. Markers in the timeline can be accessed via the Markers ruler.

The Markers Ruler

The Markers ruler contains only memory locations that have marker values in them. Selection and None locations are unavailable in this ruler.

The Markers ruler behaves in very much the same way as audio tracks do when it comes to editing. Selections can be made within the Markers ruler just like with other tracks. Markers can be cut and pasted to other areas of the Markers ruler as well.

If you click on a marker tab while in Play, the audio is interrupted, and playback starts at the marker point. If you are in Stop, clicking on a marker tab will locate the cursor to that spot without playing. If you click somewhere within the Markers ruler but not on a tab, the cursor will appear there but only inside the Markers ruler. You can then use the Tab key to move to the next marker or Option+Tab to move to the previous one. The Shift modifier works as well in the Markers ruler, allowing you to select larger areas of the timeline using markers as in and out points. Tabbing through markers can move you through a session accurately and quickly to points of interest.

You can also use markers to cut and copy large sections of audio and paste them in other locations. This can be useful when you're asked to conform to a change in the editing of the video. If the editor has suddenly decided to add three more seconds of video starting at a specific time code, you will need to move all the audio from that point on by three seconds to accommodate the new video. This is called *conforming to picture changes* and is covered in more detail later in this chapter.

Perform a Save As Operation   When you are about to drastically modify a session, it is wise to save the file with a new name so that if something goes terribly wrong, you can return to the previous session. Use the File > Save As function and rename your session, perhaps using a numerical modifier at the end to signify a new version—Dialog Session 2, for example. This should also be done periodically upon reaching certain milestones in a project. When the foley editing is complete, rename the session so that you can always return to a completed foley session if you need to. Also, it can be helpful to be able to import data from an older session without opening the session, reclaiming only the data you need.

Pro Tools also offers the Auto Backup feature to automatically save incremental versions of the session to your own specifications. These backups can be reverted to in case you lose data or want to return to a previous state of the session.

Here is how you could use markers and the Markers ruler to insert three seconds of silence across all tracks at a given point in the timeline:

1. Perform a Save As operation and give your session a different name.

2. Create a marker at the point at which the new three seconds of video has been added.

3. You could name the memory location "insert 3 secs" or something else descriptive.

4. Enable the default group ALL. Make sure that every single track in your session is visible. Otherwise, this editing operation will be performed only on visible tracks, leaving others unchanged and out of sync with the picture change.

5. Click in the Markers ruler ahead or to the left of the "insert 3 secs" marker. You will see a small cursor flashing in the Markers ruler.

6. Now Shift-click in any track. The cursor should blink across all tracks plus the Markers ruler.

7. Press Tab. The cursor should be right on top of the Edit marker, blinking across all tracks and the Markers ruler, as shown in Figure 6.40. You will not be able to see the cursor flashing in the Markers ruler anymore, as the yellow tab blocks this from view.

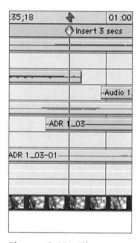

Figure 6.40 The cursor is now located at the marker and across all tracks, including the Markers ruler.

8. Press Option+Shift+Return. This extends the selection from the cursor position to the end of the session. When you move this audio three seconds later, you want everything from that point until the end of the session to move as well. You should see all tracks and the Markers ruler highlighted from the "insert 3 secs" marker until the end of the session, as shown in Figure 6.41.

9. Choose Edit > Cut or press Command+X. All audio and markers to the right of the marker should be gone. Don't worry—they are now in the Clipboard's memory, and all you have to do is paste them at the new location three seconds later.

10. Enter the new SMPTE location into the Main counter three seconds after the edit point and press Enter (or Return). This will move the cursor to the right place for pasting the audio back into the session.

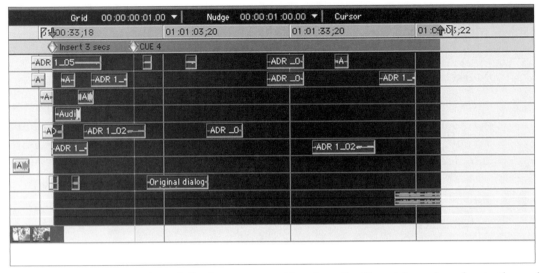

Figure 6.41 By using Option+Shift+Return, everything from the "insert 3 secs" marker to the end of the session has been selected, including the Markers ruler.

11. Choose Edit > Paste or press Command+V. All the audio and markers should now be in a new location exactly three seconds later than the original position, as shown in Figure 6.42.

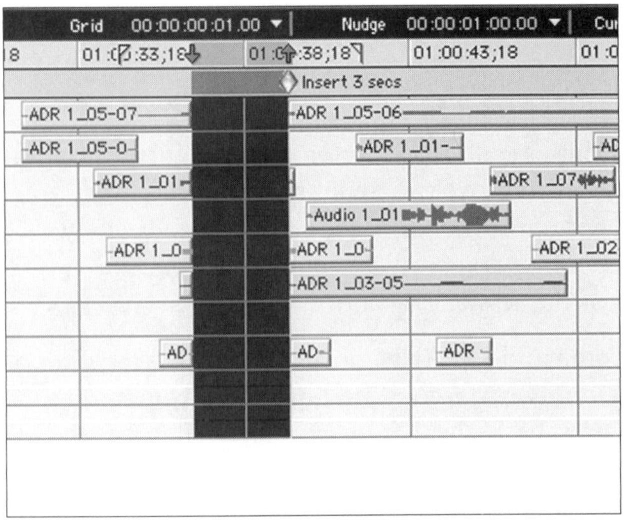

Figure 6.42 All the audio and markers that were removed in Step 9 are now exactly three seconds later than before, in order to accommodate the picture addition. The three-second gap has been selected to make it easier to see.

Note that unless you require markers to move with your edit, several other ways to move a large selection rather quickly do exist. First, you could use the ALL group to select an area on all tracks. Enter Spot mode and click on any region in the selection. Type +300 into the Spot dialog box and then press Enter; the selection will be moved three seconds later (to the right). To clarify: If you typed +314 into the Spot dialog box, the audio would be placed three seconds and 14 frames later. There is no need for the semicolon. You could also enter a whole new time code value in the Spot dialog box to achieve the same result. You could even move the selection in Relative Grid mode, set to one second. You could take the same selection and use a nudge value of 1 second three times in a row.

There are many ways to slice a fish—or to edit in Pro Tools. Depending on your style and needs, you will find methods that work the best with experience.

Marker Placement   Make sure your markers are exactly on a frame boundary. If the marker lies somewhere between frame boundaries, using them for editing, as in the previous example, will result in a big mess. You might easily place audio out of sync with the updated video.

When you're creating markers on-the-fly while playing, they'll be placed wherever you press the Enter key. Even if you're in Grid mode, markers created on-the-fly will not be restricted to grid values. Very rarely will markers created on-the-fly land exactly on a frame boundary, even if the grid is set to one frame. When viewing the time code in the Main counter, you will not be able to see subframes and will not be able to tell whether you're exactly on a frame boundary by looking at the counter.

The quick fix for this is to enter Grid mode with a value of one frame and manually grab each marker tab and move it until it "snaps" to the nearest frame boundary.

Aligning Regions to Markers

Once you have markers in place, they can be used to align audio regions. By placing the grid into Regions/Markers mode, regions will "snap" their starting boundary to markers or other region boundaries.

Placement of an audio region at a marker or at another region's boundary might not be precise enough to achieve a smooth-sounding track. When finer adjustments are needed, the Nudge function comes into play.

Using Nudge Commands

Nudge commands are used to "bump" or push audio regions around the timeline by preset amounts. This is handy for fine-tuning audio placement to video by nudging regions frame by frame until they line up with the correct video frame in a QuickTime movie. When set to very small amounts such as one millisecond, nudging can finesse audio editing for more subtle effects. At the sample level, nudging can be used to offset tracks and compensate for very small TDM mixer delays induced by plug-in processing. This complex topic will be covered in Chapter 8.

Nudging is done by selecting one or more regions in the Edit window and using the plus and minus keys (+, −) on the keypad to move the region(s) forwards (+, to the right, later in time) or backwards (−, to the left, earlier in time). When you nudge a region, the QuickTime movie will update its location to reflect the new start position of the earliest region boundary in the selection. This happens very quickly so that you can repeatedly press the plus or minus key to move through several nudge amounts and see exactly where you currently are in the movie. Pressing and holding the plus or minus key will activate key repeat, and the region will nudge rapidly through each value along with the QuickTime movie.

Nudging Is Relative   Nudging an audio region does not align that region's boundary with the nearest grid value. It merely adds (+) or subtracts (−) the nudge value to the start time of that region. Nudging can be used just like the Relative Grid mode. The normal Grid mode will *snap* regions to the nearest grid value, whereas Relative Grid mode will move regions by grid increments relative to grid values. If you want your audio file to start exactly at a certain video frame, you must use normal Grid mode to snap the region to an absolute frame point on the timeline.

Setting Nudge Values

Nudge values are set in much the same way as grid values, as shown in Figure 6.43. They can follow the Main counter's format if that option has been checked. All the preset values are the same as the grid values for each time format.

You may manually enter your own custom nudge value by clicking in the nudge value number itself, as shown in Figure 6.44.

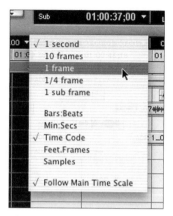

Figure 6.43   You can select nudge values from the Nudge pull-down menu.

Figure 6.44   You can manually enter nudge values by clicking on the number itself.

Aligning Regions to Video Frames

A common nudge value to use when working with video is one frame. This increment matches the smallest increment by which the visual image can be adjusted. Using the one-frame nudge value makes it easy to nudge through each and every frame of a short sequence to find the key frame to which the current sound you are editing applies. When a baseball bat is swung and hits the ball, there might be 15 frames in the last part of the swing leading up to the hit. If you are placing the "crack" sound of the bat hitting the ball, you must find the exact frame at which the bat connects with the ball.

A common practice is to place your sound effect somewhere close to where you think it should be. Then using the nudge keys (+ and −), nudge the sound by one frame until you see the precise frame where the effect should begin. I'll break it down.

1.   Enter Grid mode with a value of one frame.

2.   From the Audio Regions list, drag the sound effect into the timeline to a place that is close to where you think it should be. The important thing to remember is not to take too much time when initially dragging the sound effect into the timeline. Nudging the region later will provide more accuracy. Just get it close. (See Figure 6.45.)

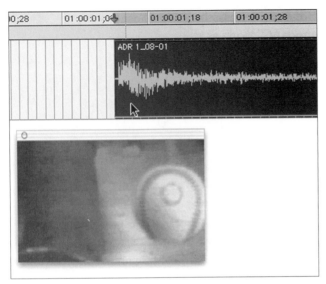

Figure 6.45 The "crack" sound is placed near to the frame in which the bat actually touches the ball. Notice that the ball is not touching the bat yet.

3.   Make sure your nudge value is set to one frame.

4.   While watching the QuickTime window, nudge the sound back (−) or forward (+) until you see the frame where the sound should start. (See Figure 6.46.)

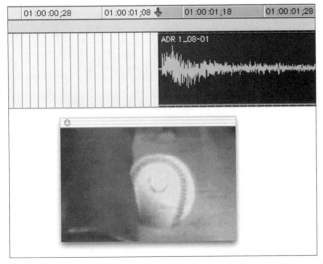

Figure 6.46 Notice that the QuickTime window shows the ball actually touching the bat. After being nudged, the "crack" sound now starts on this exact frame.

5.   Play the result to see how it syncs up. It should be quite close. Even though the waveform is visually lined up exactly with the frame that shows the ball touching the bat, it might not be in the exact position yet. I'll explain what I mean in more detail in the next section.

Subframe Nudging

Two factors must be taken into consideration when nudging audio regions by one frame. Just because one particular frame of film happens to have the ball in contact with the bat does not mean that the bat first connected with the ball exactly when that film frame was exposed. The ball could have contacted just prior to the opening of the shutter within the film camera. That frame caught the ball still touching the bat, but some small amount of time after they actually hit. Granted, this is a very small amount of time, but human hearing is far more sensitive to timing cues than human eyesight, and so the difference in timing is perceptible. Secondly, just because an audio region begins at its left boundary does not mean that the valid audio event occurs right at the start of the region itself. Often there is a small amount of silence before audible sound begins, or the sound is structured so that the critical timing portion occurs later in the region.

Human eyesight has time accuracy down to about one-thirtieth of a second or so. That's about 33 milliseconds. At this speed, the brain is not making clear distinctions between successive images in the video. The brain is capable of constructing motion out of repeating images up to 130 milliseconds apart. This is the basic principle upon which film making has been developed.

To the ear, 130 milliseconds is slap-back echo. The human ear is capable of discerning much smaller time increments—down to about 10 milliseconds (much smaller for audio professionals with trained hearing). If you take into account stereo-imaging delays, the factor decreases to below sub-millisecond values. For our purposes, the 10-millisecond threshold is the most relevant.

While the eye is constructing smooth motion and continuity out of still images passing by every 1/30 of a second, the ear is busy correlating sounds relating to those images. However, the ear is using much smaller increments in creating a smooth perception of time than the eye. The bottom line is that one-frame accuracy in editing for picture is just not good enough in many instances, especially in action scenes.

Using subframes, milliseconds, or samples will allow subtler placement of sounds. Click on the nudge value itself and manually enter a small number, such as five milliseconds, to fine-tune a region's placement once you have found the correct frame. You will be surprised how much difference a few milliseconds can make.

How to Use Sync Points

Sounds are not like Legos, where one always fits into another at regular intervals. Sounds are intertwined. Trying to place sounds using a standard anchor point, such as the start of a region, can be limiting. Sometimes you need to make an anchor point where you feel the important aspect of the sound lies. This is where sync points come in to play in Pro Tools.

A good example of a sound that needs a sync point would be a "swoosh" type sound, such as that made by a sword swinging through the air. "Swoosh" sounds usually have a peak point, where the sound is the most intense, toward the end—the sound begins quieter than it ends. When placing such a sound, the action might be timed to this peak point in the "swoosh" and not to the very start of it. In such a case, nudging the starting boundary of the region to the key frame to which the sound applies might be an exercise in futility, as the frame of video you see at the start of the region is not aligned to the critical section of audio. You need to create a sync point within the region that defines the critical moment of the sound so that nudging this sync point will align the sound properly.

Creating a Sync Point

Creating sync points is easy. Here's how it's done:

1. Decide what point within the region is the critical point of interest. This should be the defining moment of the sound, the point that would sync up to a key frame of video.

2. Place the cursor at that point within the region.

3. Choose Edit > Create Sync Point (Command+comma). A small tab appears at the bottom of the region at the sync point, as shown in Figure 6.47.

Figure 6.47 A small tab at the bottom of a region indicates that a sync point has been created there.

Using Sync Points and the Grid

Now that a sync point has been created, it can be used to align the sound with a key frame of video. In most editing commands, the sync point will act as the region's start boundary. You can nudge the sync point. It can be snapped to grid values. It can be copied and pasted.

If you move a region with a sync point while in Grid mode, the sync point will snap to grid points instead of the region start. A classic example of how to use this is with vocals in a piece of music. Many vocalists will take a breath before the downbeat of a new section. By using a sync point on the downbeat in the region that contains the vocal, you can copy that vocal part to any downbeat in the song and the breath will still be heard before that down-beat. Sync points allow regions to have start times in odd places but still be referenced to a grid location. The end result is similar to how the Relative Grid function works.

Once a sync point has been created, it will be used until it is deleted. In order to delete a sync point, you must first select the region that contains it and then choose Edit > Remove Sync Point (Command+comma). The sync point will be deleted.

Relative Grid   Relative Grid allows you to move regions relative to grid points. In other words, it is as though each region has been assigned a sync point exactly on a grid point. When you move that region, the starting boundary is not auto-matically aligned with a grid point—the temporary sync point is. If the region start was 17 milliseconds before the nearest grid point, when you move it to another grid point, the start of the region will still be 17 milliseconds ahead of the new grid point. Figures 6.48 and 6.49 show how one region moved in Relative Grid mode maintains its relationship to the grid. To use Relative Grid mode, select the Relative option from the Grid button pull-down menu, as seen in Figure 6.50.

Figure 6.48   Region A starts at 1.347 seconds. The grid value is one second, and Relative Grid mode is on.

Figure 6.49 After moving Region A one second to the right in Relative Grid mode, the new start time is 2.347 seconds. Relative Grid maintained the relationship of the region to each grid point.

Figure 6.50 The Relative Grid mode can be selected from the Grid pull-down menu.

Playlists

Playlists are one of the most useful and most misunderstood features of Pro Tools. They allow you to have much more information in one session. You can try many more radical types of editing and processing without risk of losing the original source material.

A Pro Tools *playlist* is an ordered list of all the regions, edits, and crossfades that occur on a single track. It is the list of things to play in a certain order and at certain times. Information such as type of automation, available plug-ins, or any other mixer data is not stored in a playlist. Only the audio regions and any crossfades associated with them are contained within the playlist. Each track can have essentially an unlimited number of playlists (128 possible in LE). This makes it possible to use multiple playlists for all sorts of things described in these subsections.

The playlist functions are accessible from the Edit window in the left area, where the name of the track is listed, as shown in Figure 6.51. You can duplicate a playlist by creating an exact copy of the current one. Duplicate playlists can be used to perform radical editing without losing the original source material. If you want to return to the source material, you merely have to return to the original playlist.

Figure 6.51 The Playlist pull-down menu lists the playlists linked to this track. You may also create new or duplicate playlists and delete any unused playlists.

You can also create a new, blank playlist. Blank playlists can be used for recording additional takes onto one track. Each take can be recorded into a new playlist. Each track can have a virtually unlimited number of playlists, even though you will only be able to listen to one of them on any single track. Blank playlists can be used to extend the tracking capabilities of Pro Tools LE beyond the 32 (48 with DV toolkit) track limit (I'll describe a detailed, step-by-step method for doing this later in this chapter). Playlists that are created in one track will be visible in the pull-down menu for that track. Playlists created but not used from other tracks will also be available from the secondary pull-down menu, Other Playlists, shown in Figure 6.52. One playlist cannot be played on two tracks at the same time. Only unused playlists are available from the Playlist submenu.

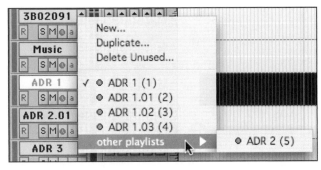

Figure 6.52 This secondary pull-down menu lists all unused playlists that are linked to other tracks.

If you select one of these other playlists, the playlist you select will now be played on the current track, regardless of what track it was created on. Once any playlist is made active (*active* meaning that you will actually hear it) on any track, it will no longer be available to other tracks in the Playlist menu. This might be confusing at first, but it provides a high degree of flexibility in managing playlists while keeping the clutter on each Playlist menu to a minimum.

Here are some suggestions for playlist use:

- Record multiple takes on one track. Create a new playlist for each take.

- Use the Duplicate function to create backup copies of edited playlists before performing radical processing or editing.

- Move a playlist from one track to another accurately. Create a new "dummy" playlist on the current track, and then go to the destination track and use the secondary pull-down menu and find the first playlist. The dummy playlist frees up the original, making it accessible to other tracks.

- Exceed your system's track count or voice capability. Each playlist can function as a virtual track. You will not be able to hear extra playlists that are not active in a track, but you can still keep the data within one session.

- Use inactive playlists to store source material that does not need to be heard in the final mix, such as sound effect source files and production audio material.

Being able to export a session with more than 32 tracks to a Pro Tools LE system is helpful for people who have a TDM system in one location and a Pro Tools LE system in another and want to exchange sessions between them. The larger TDM session must be prepped for this to work.

Following is a step-by-step method for transferring TDM sessions with high track counts to smaller LE systems limited to 32 tracks (or 48 tracks with the DV toolkit), without losing any data:

1. Organize the TDM session so that the first 32 tracks are the ones you would like to open first in the LE system. You will not be able to immediately play any tracks after the first 32 in the LE system. Don't worry—they won't be lost.

2. On each subsequent track after 32, create a "dummy" playlist by choosing New from the Playlist menu, as seen in Figure 6.52. You can Shift-select all of these tracks and use the Command+Option+Shift modifiers to create the new dummy playlists for all selected tracks at once. These dummy playlists should be blank, as they will be deleted. Again, don't worry....

3. Select all of the tracks that contain the dummy playlists starting from Track 33 on up.

4.   Choose File > Delete Selected Tracks. I swear, don't worry!

5.   Here's the trick: A dialog box opens that gives you the option to delete playlists that are not assigned to any track, as shown in Figure 6.53. Just click No! All of the playlists will remain available to the first 32 tracks of the session even when it is opened in Pro Tools LE.

6.   Open the session in LE. All of the extra playlists from the larger TDM session will be available as other playlists in the Playlist menu. Voila!

Figure 6.53   This dialog box appears whenever you are deleting tracks that have multiple playlists assigned to them. In order to keep playlists as part of the session when transferring to Pro Tools LE, click No to retain these extra playlists in LE.

Grouping and Playlist Functions   Performing playlist functions on grouped tracks will affect all members of that group. If you choose New Playlist from one member of a group, all other members will have new playlists created for them at the same time. You will not be given the chance to manually name each one. They will be given automatically generated names with appended numbers, such as .01, .02, and so on. If you have several playlists for all members of a group with the same suffix for each playlist, switching from one to another on one track will switch all of the grouped tracks to that same numbered playlist. This technique can be used to switch between the original dialogue playlists and the new, sweetened playlists on several tracks at once.

Conforming to Picture Changes

You are bound to want (and need) to make changes during your project. These changes can become necessary at the most inconvenient times. If the director makes any changes to the video edit, the audio session must follow those changes. When these changes are required in the midst of audio post-production, conforming the audio to match the new video can be complicated. Each change can either add video to the timeline or take some away. If you have already edited dialogue tracks and added effects and maybe music before these changes occur, you will have to conform all of your new tracks to these picture changes. This is also known as "balancing."

When a picture change is made, the editor will usually create a *change note*. This could be as simple as a handwritten note or as complex as a multipage edit-decision list that outlines each change in terms of time code. The change note will specify at what time code values the change takes place and exactly what was added or deleted. You can use this information to edit your session and match the new video edit. However, change notes are notorious for being inaccurate in some respect and may not always help in making accurate edits. Referencing the newly edited video is the only way to be truly accurate.

Virtual Katy

As evidence for this difficulty, sound effects editor John McKay, whose work can be heard on the first two *Lord of the Rings* movies, had this to say about how to deal with picture changes:

> "This question has occupied my working days for the past two years. I have been a sound effects editor on the first two *Lord of the Rings* pictures, and this problem was evident from day one. The picture was never locked, and for instance, we went through 50 conforms for Movie One alone, with reel rebalancing also. We found Avid change notes to be variable in quality, depending on who actually did them, and they seem to take an age to make."

For the first movie, *Fellowship of the Ring*, conforming to picture changes was done manually. By the time the second picture, *The Two Towers*, was started, John had developed a method of utilizing QuicKeys to expedite the conforming process. This process has been refined and turned into a standalone software solution called Virtual Katy (now called VK Premium Collection). The software is capable of analyzing two EDLs and creating an accurate change list that describes the differences between them. Virtual Katy can then be used to auto-conform the Pro Tools session to the new picture changes. It does this by remote controlling Pro Tools. The newly conformed audio will be placed at another SMPTE hour in the timeline so that the original material is not altered in any way. If you are involved in conforming to last-minute picture changes on a regular basis, this type of software is a necessity.

QuicKeys   QuicKeys is a Macintosh program designed to make complex keystrokes and procedures accessible via a single keystroke. It can be useful for the automating of repetitive tasks such as conforming to picture changes. You can think of QuicKeys as a macro editor.

Manual Rebalancing

Manually conforming to picture changes requires a new guide track as a reference. When you are given a picture change, you'll need to digitize a new video and import it into Pro Tools. Hopefully, a guide track will be included in the new copy of the video. Once you have imported the new video, import the audio from the guide track as well.

Using the change note, find the first change by time code location. Listen to your edited audio and the new guide track together. They should match one another until the first change occurs. The time code number where the new reference audio diverges from your edit should match the time code value listed in the change note. Make sure you are set in Grid mode with a value of one frame. Try to pinpoint the exact frame where the change occurs and create a marker there. You can listen to the audio and hear where it fails to match up or notice when the lip sync is lost. The next part gets a little tricky.

These steps should be followed when the picture change has added a portion of video. The same principles apply when a change removes a section of video, but the method would be different.

1. Save your session with a new name just in case you need to return to the unaltered original.

2. Create an edit group that contains every track *except* the new guide track you imported from the movie. Try clicking to the left of the ALL group in the group window, in order to select every visible track in the session. Then Shift-click on the guide track to deselect it and press Command+G to create the new edit group.

Performing Large Edits   When performing edits on a large numbers of tracks, keep all the tracks visible, as editing will occur only on visible tracks. Grouping is also affected. Edits performed on grouped tracks will be applied only to the visible members of that group.

---

3. Select this new group in order to edit all but the guide track at once.

4. In Grid mode, place the cursor right on the change marker you have created.

5. Choose Edit > Separate Region (Command+E). This will cut all audio tracks at that point, creating new regions if necessary, as shown in Figure 6.54.

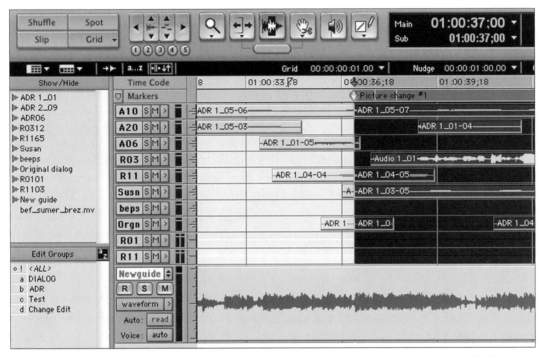

Figure 6.54 The Change Edit group contains all the tracks except the new guide track. The Separate Region command has been used to cut all audio tracks exactly at the change marker.

6. Press Option+Shift+Return (not Enter). This command selects everything from the current cursor position to the end of the session.

7. Now use the Grabber tool and move the selection down the timeline to where the change note says the new edit should end, as shown in Figure 6.55. If you do not have a change note or think that it is inaccurate, move the audio far enough so it is beyond where you *think* the change should end. If the Markers ruler is included in the selection, you will receive an error message indicating that the operation is not supported in the Conductor rulers. It is not clear that Pro Tools considers the Markers ruler a Conductor ruler, but it is true for this instance. Choose to continue the operation without affecting the Conductor (including Markers) rulers, as seen in Figure 6.56.

8. Assuming that you are very familiar with the material you're working on (and I bet you are by now!), watch the video and listen to the guide track through the change period and notice where it returns to the original video edit. Try to be frame-accurate if possible, but don't sweat it. You'll be able to check this afterwards and make adjustments. Create a marker here for reference.

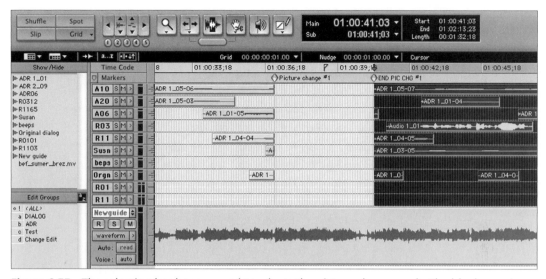

Figure 6.55   The selection has been moved to where the picture change ends. The blank area is now available for new audio that goes with the inserted video.

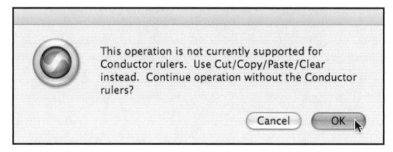

This operation is not currently supported for Conductor rulers. Use Cut/Copy/Paste/Clear instead. Continue operation without the Conductor rulers?

Cancel   OK

Figure 6.56   You might get this error message if the Markers ruler is part of your selection. Continue with the operation without affecting the Conductor (and Markers) rulers.

9. If you have not lost your selection of audio from the previous step, move all of the audio to the end mark you just created. If you lost the selection, get it back by clicking on the first frame of the remainder of audio and using the Option+Shift+Return command.

Link Edit and Timeline Selection   A very useful but seldom-used feature in Pro Tools is the ability to link or unlink the edit and timeline selections, using Operations > Link Edit and Timeline Selection (Shift+/). You might have discovered this option by accident, because the key command is easy to press inadvertently. I've had many calls from engineers wondering why they can't locate to a new position the way they normally do when this option has been changed. In the default setting, the edit selection and timeline selection are linked. That is, whatever selection you make in any track is duplicated in the timeline selection at the top of the Edit window, in the ruler section. Figure 6.57 shows the start point, end point, pre-roll, and post-roll markers that define the timeline selection. When they are unlinked, you can select areas in tracks, but the play cursor will not automatically locate to the start of that selection. It will remain wherever it was last set up in the ruler. To change the timeline selection, you must click inside the ruler and drag from the start point to your end point. Or, you can manually enter values in the counter windows. This way, you can move around the timeline without losing the selection you have in the tracks area.

10. Now play from before the change start and listen. When the original audio returns, is it in sync with the guide track? This should be obvious. If not, try soloing the guide and dialogue tracks to eliminate any effects and music from the mix. You can pan the guide tracks hard left and your edited dialogue tracks hard right to get a better idea of how the two are syncing together.

11. If everything is in sync, congratulations—the change note was accurate, and you are lucky. Save your session and go take a break while the rest of us figure out why this thing won't play in sync!

12. If things are not sounding right and the sync is off, try nudging the entire selection by one-frame increments until you have lined it back up. Always use grid and nudge values of one frame to ensure that you are staying on frame boundaries while editing.

13. Hopefully, by nudging around a few frames, you will be able to find the correct spot where the edited audio will line up in sync with the new guide track. Once you have found this spot, save the session.

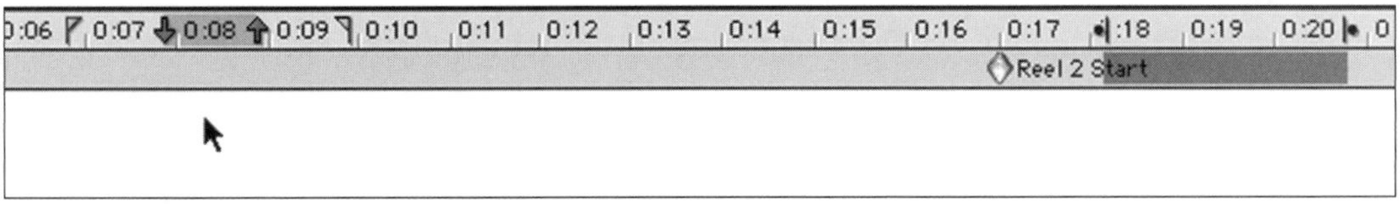

Figure 6.57 The pre-roll, start, end, and post-roll marks are visible at the top of the ruler section. When the timeline and edit selections are *not* linked, you may select areas in the timeline by clicking in the topmost ruler and dragging. Any edit selection that you might have will remain unchanged.

Okay, now you have created space where video has been added. The next step will require an accurate EDL of the source tracks for dialogue and any other sounds the picture editor used. This might require creating a new session for conforming just the picture-change portions of an EDL and then importing them into your master session. Doing this can save much time and confusion without loading up a large session with conforming tracks.

Different Dialogue Takes Be aware that a picture change may also affect the dialogue takes that overlap the change area. Different takes might have been used. You will need to check the new EDL thoroughly to make sure you have the correct audio files.

Once the edit is complete and you have all new dialogue tracks conformed to the picture change, you will need to edit any other tracks, such as foley and music. The hole created by the picture addition must be filled with the necessary sounds in order to make the transition across the edit a smooth one. You might have to eyeball these things, as the foley studio might not be available at the time, or the film composer could be booked on another gig. If the change is minor, fudging it around might just work fine. Major picture changes require major additional work for the sound designer.

The Fellowship of The Ring went through 50 revisions of the film before it was finalized. Each sound editor had to conform to each one of these versions before continuing editing. John McKay developed a whole set of QuicKeys that helped automate the conforming process. This solution evolved into the Virtual Katy software that can analyze two EDLs and conform the Pro Tools sessions to the changes found between them. This saves an incredibly large amount of time on a project of that scale.

With the inaccuracy of change lists, conforming to picture changes is a difficult and arduous task. If pre-production is planned out well, these changes can be kept to a minimum. Constant communication, again, is the key to a smooth post-production process.

7 Processing Audio Using Audiosuite Plug-Ins

During editing, it might be necessary to process audio files and make changes for editorial reasons. These changes to the audio files could include time compression or expansion, reversing, pitch changing for certain effects, and envelope alignment for matching dialogue takes. These changes should be permanent and cannot run in real-time like TDM or RTAS plug-ins used during mixing.

Pro Tools allows offline processing of audio outside of the mixing abilities of TDM and RTAS plug-in environments. The Audiosuite versions of plug-ins are used to perform this offline processing; they can be accessed from the Audiosuite menu. In most cases, every plug-in in either TDM or RTAS will have an Audiosuite equivalent. Certain plug-ins, such as reverse, time compression/expansion, and tone generator, are only available as Audiosuite plug-ins due to the nature of how they operate.

The processing of Audiosuite plug-ins is not audible. Processed files are written directly to disk. Portions of the processed file may be previewed in order to make parameter adjustments. Once the parameters have been set, the file will be processed and saved under a new name that reflects the plug-in used during processing. For instance, if a file called Region A_01 is processed with the Reverse plug-in, the resulting file will be named Region A-RVRS_00. Similar abbreviations are made for other plug-ins. This way, you will be able to identify the type of processing that has been applied to a certain region or file.

Operation of Audiosuite Plug-Ins

To operate an Audiosuite plug-in, you must first select one or more regions to process. Then you can open an Audiosuite plug-in window, as shown in Figure 7.1. Clicking the Preview button will cycle a portion of the region you selected first, so that you may adjust parameters of the plug-in while listening to the results. You will only be able to hear that one portion of audio. The amount of this portion you hear is determined by the Audiosuite buffer setting, which you can access by selecting Setups > Preferences > Processing to access the Pro Tools Preferences for Audiosuite Processing. There, you will find five options for the Audiosuite buffer size, ranging from mini to jumbo. Larger buffer settings will allow you to preview long portions of your selected audio in order to adjust parameters. Once you have made any adjustments to the plug-in's parameters, you have several options for processing the file.

You may want to replace the original audio with the newly processed file. In this case, make sure that the Use in Playlist button is active, as in Figure 7.1. This is the default setting, because the processing you do will most likely replace the original sound in the timeline.

The second option concerns how you would like the selection of several regions to be handled. Pro Tools can process each file separately, creating a new processed file for each region selected. Or the entire selection can be processed as one continuous file, with the processed audio showing up in the exact same place as it was originally. Both the Region by Region menu and the Create Individual Files menu will toggle from one option to the other.

Finally, you can select either Region List or Playlist from the top-center menu. When this option is set to Region List, you can choose a region that is not currently used in any track or playlist and process that file, placing the new file into the Audio Regions List only. No audio on any track will be affected. When in Playlist mode, the processed files will replace the original ones on the track.

Figure 7.1   The Reverse Audiosuite plug-in window.

Reversing Files

Reversing sounds is a common technique for creating new and interesting sound effects. Common sounds such as dog barks, water splashes, and even speech can be reversed to create some interesting effects. Reverse reverb is a classic example of this type of effect.

Following is a step-by-step guide for creating reverse reverb for a group of sound elements. In this example, the reverse reverb is not continuous and happens only once, preceding the group of sounds you have chosen.

1. Choose the sound or group of sounds for which you want to create reverse reverb.

2. Pick a point in the timeline at which you want the reverse reverb to end. This point will probably be just before the original sounds begin. The reverse

reverb will lead up to this point. Create a marker there. This point will be used as a reference point for placing the reverse reverb when it is done. Figure 7.2 shows the selection of three regions on three separate tracks. The marker has been created just before the first of these three regions. Once the reverse reverb has been created, it will be placed just before this marker so that it culminates right at that point.

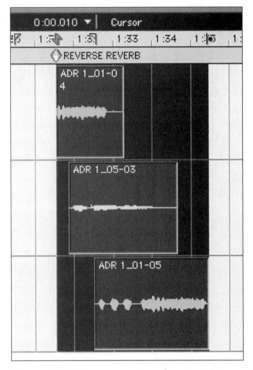

Figure 7.2 In preparation for creating reverse reverb, three regions have been selected, and a marker has been placed at the beginning of the first.

3.   In the Mix window, create sends on each track that contains audio you want to include in the reverse reverb effect and assign them to the same buss. I use buss 1 and 2 for this example, as shown in Figure 7.3.

4.   Create a stereo Aux track in the mixer and assign buss 1 and 2 to its inputs, as shown in Figure 7.4.

5.   Instantiate your favorite reverb plug-in in one of the inserts of the Aux track.

6.   Make sure the sends on the three tracks are turned up. Listen to how the reverb sounds and adjust any parameters to taste. With reverse reverb, it is much

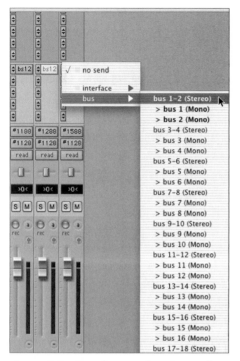

Figure 7.3   Creating sends going to busses 1 and 2.

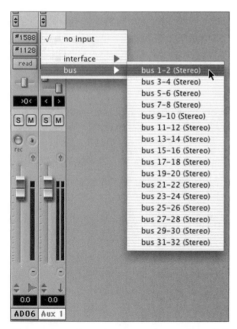

Figure 7.4   Creating an Aux track with busses 1 and 2 as its inputs.

harder to hear the low-level fade of reverb when it is reversed. Setting a longer reverb time than you think is necessary will allow you to have some editing control after the reverb is reversed.

7.   It might be necessary to automate the sends or edit the audio around this point so that any unwanted sounds are not reverberated. You want to be able to record the reverb tail without having any additional sounds coming into the reverb plug-in causing unwanted reverb. Figure 7.5 shows the automation playlist for the sends after automating them to send only the first bit of audio to the reverb Aux. Typically with reverse reverb, only the very first transient sound should be used to create the reverb tail. If you're using dialogue, the first word should be the only thing sent to the reverb in most situations.

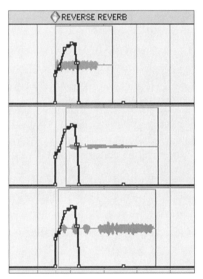

Figure 7.5   Send automation playlists showing the volume automation sending only a small portion of the audio to busses 1 and 2 from each source track.

8.   Assign the output of the reverb Aux track to another set of busses, such as buss 3 and 4, as seen in Figure 7.6.

9.   Create a new stereo audio track and assign busses 3 and 4 to its inputs, as shown in Figure 7.7.

10.   Record-enable the track.

11.   Start recording the reverb from a point just before the first region, as seen in Figure 7.8. Make sure you record the entire reverb tail. Record until a few

seconds after the meters have stopped registering a level. If you automated the sends well, you should hear one clear reverb tail as it is recorded.

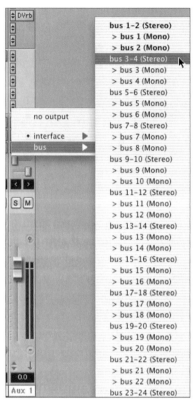

Figure 7.6 Assigning the Aux track to another set of busses for recording the reverb into another track.

12.   Choose Audiosuite > Reverse to open the Reverse plug-in.

13.   Enable the Use in Playlist button.

14.   Select the region of reverb you just recorded and press the Process button. The waveform should be similar to Figure 7.9.

15.   Move the reversed reverb region so that the ending boundary lines up with the marker you created in Step 2.

16.   The finished edit should look something like Figure 7.10. Play the section and see how it turned out. You may have to nudge the reverb around to get the timing right. After hearing the reversed reverb in context, you might want to adjust some parameters of the reverb and record it again.

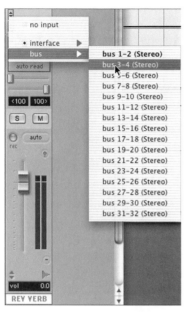

Figure 7.7   Creating a stereo audio track for recording the reverb.

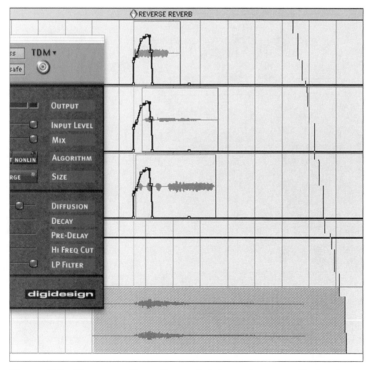

Figure 7.8   The recording of reverb into a stereo audio track.

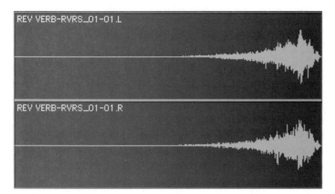

Figure 7.9   The reversed reverb's waveform.

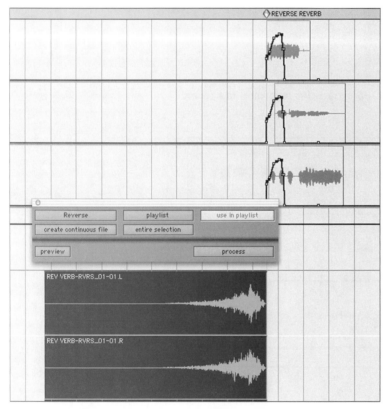

Figure 7.10   The finished reversed reverb edit with the reverb leading up to the marker.

Time Compression/Expansion

Time compression and expansion is the process of lengthening or shortening a piece of audio without altering its pitch or timbre in any significant way. Time compression and expansion are very useful tools for sound design. You will often find sounds that are perfect for a certain situation except that they are not the correct length. Expanding or compressing them to fit the necessary space can save the day. Many times musical cues need some time adjustment to fit into a 30- or 60-second TV spot. Time compression or expansion can be the answer to these and other problems.

Audiosuite Time Compression/Expansion

The Digidesign time compression/expansion Audiosuite plug-in, shown in Figure 7.11, has many parameters and functions that will help you alter the length of just about any sound without affecting its pitch or timbre. You must define how much compression or expansion needs to occur for your particular use. In most cases, your goal will be to correct the length of a sound to fit the visual timing.

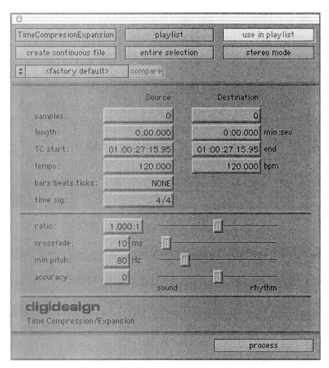

Figure 7.11 The time compression/expansion Audiosuite plug-in.

Although the only parameters that affect the processing are the ratio, crossfade, minimum pitch, and accuracy, Pro Tools allows you to use other methods to define what the ratio will be. The ratio parameter is a function of the desired length of the audio file divided by its original length (x:1). Thus, a ratio of 0.993:1 will create a shorter file than the original. Conversely, a ration of 1.237:1 will yield a longer file once processed.

The upper parameters are all used to generate a proper ratio for processing. With the measurements of the original region appearing in the left column in the plug-in window as source parameters and the destination parameters appearing in the right column, it is possible to enter numbers in the Destination column and alter the ratio. Take the ratio slider and move it around and see how the destination numbers change. This is not really intuitive, but you'll understand it as you gain experience working with this plug-in.

Directly inputting numbers in the Destination values will change the ratio as well. Using this method, very precise time compression and expansion are possible with accuracy down to one sample. Here's how to generate a time compression ratio to match a video accurate to one millisecond:

1. Measure the visual timing to get an accurate idea of how much compression or expansion will occur.

2. Use the Selector tool and set the Main counter to either time code, minutes and seconds, or samples.

3. Using Grid mode, select the area that you would like the resultant audio file to completely fill.

4. Look at the Length (duration) number at the top of the Edit window, as shown in Figure 7.12. Write this number down somewhere handy.

Figure 7.12 Selecting the desired length for an audio file about to be processed. Write down the duration length for handy reference. In this example, it is 10.567 seconds.

5. Select the region to be processed, making sure it is edited to your liking.

6. Choose Audiosuite > Time Compression Expansion. The plug-in window will open.

7. Check to see that the numbers on the source side of the parameters reflect the region you have selected.

8. Manually input your destination length you jotted down into the appropriate value, as shown in Figure 7.13. (With time code, only the end time should be changed to reflect the new audio length. The Destination value is not a length value but an end time.)

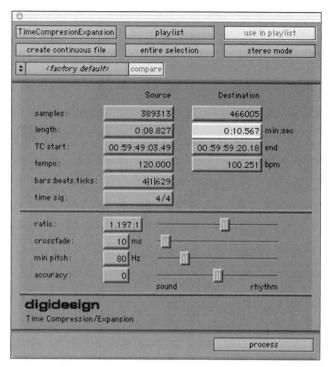

Figure 7.13 Manually entering the desired length into the min:sec Destination value of the time compression expansion plug-in.

9.   Press the Preview button to listen to the processed audio and tweak the settings below to achieve the desired sound quality. For dialogue, the accuracy slider usually sounds best set to Sound, not Rhythm.

10. Decide if you want the processed file to replace the original in the playlist or just placed in the Audio Regions List. Set the options accordingly.

11. Click the Process button. Viola! Your audio file should now be the desired length.

Compression and Expansion Limits Time compression and expansion will degrade the sound quality as the ratio increases or decreases further from 1:1. The degradation will vary according to the type of program material. A good rule of thumb is that if you are expanding, ratios above 1.2:1 will start to sound strange, and compression will get a little funny below 0.8:1. But there are circumstances in which such degradation is the desired effect. Try processing with ridiculous ratios and see what happens. You could come up with a really cool effect.

Trimmer Tool Compression/Expansion

The Trimmer tool can be used to compress or expand audio files just like the Audiosuite plug-in but using visual methods. You can select the Time Compression Expansion (TCE) Trimmer tool from the Trimmer tool's pull-down menu or by pressing F6 repeatedly until the cursor changes to the TCE Trimmer tool's icon. Once selected, the TCE Trimmer tool looks like the Trimmer tool but with a small clock icon in the center, as shown in Figure 7.14.

Instead of you having to manually enter values, the TCE Trimmer will simply change the length of the audio file by the amount you trim or open up the region. This can be a really convenient way of quickly resizing audio files to match picture. When resizing a region, you will see a processing progress bar after letting go of the region, indicating that the time compression or expansion is occurring.

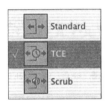

Figure 7.14   The Time Compression Expansion Trimmer tool.

When you choose Setups > Preferences > Processing and select a preset for the Time Compression Expansion plug-in from the Pro Tools Preferences window, the parameters of that preset will be used each time you perform a time compression or expansion with the Trimmer tool, as shown in Figure 7.15. You may even choose additional time compression plug-ins, such as Time Shift, Serato Pitch 'n Time Pro, or Wave Mechanics Speed, to do the processing.

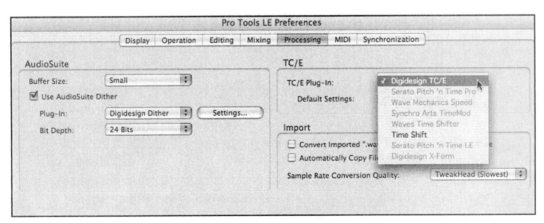

Figure 7.15   The Pro Tools Preferences window. Here you can determine what plug-in will process the Trimmer tool's time compression or expansion mode and what preset will be used.

Pitch-Changing

Pitch-changing, or pitch-shifting, is closely related to time compression and expansion. Similar algorithms are employed in a different way to achieve pitch changes without altering the length of an audio region.

Digidesign's Pitch Shift plug-in allows you to change the pitch of an audio region up or down by as much as two octaves (plus or minus 24 semitones) with or without altering its length. As you can see in Figure 7.16, there is a checkbox for time correction in the Pitch Shift plug-in window that also enables the quality parameters at the bottom of the plug-in window, just like the Time Compression Expansion plug-in.

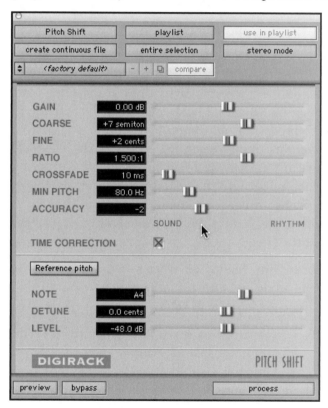

Figure 7.16 Digidesign's Pitch Shift plug-in.

Pitch-shifting is very useful as a sound design tool. All sorts of weird sounds can be made by shifting ordinary sounds outside their normal range. You can pitch-change dialogue to deepen someone's voice or create imaginary voices for animated characters.

There is a very famous use of pitch-shifting in the original *Star Wars* movie. The Ti Fighter sound was created by hitting a tension wire on a telephone pole and shifting the sound very low. This created the unique screaming engine effect.

If you happen to own Pro Tools HD, you can take advantage of higher sample rates. When pitching down sounds recorded at higher sample rates, ultrasonic harmonics that were inaudible in the original recording will come down into the audible spectrum, creating some very interesting effects. This process was used extensively by sound designer Dane Davis on *The Matrix Reloaded*. Strange mechanical sounds were created by pitch-shifting high-resolution recordings of loud metal clangs to reveal their ultrasonic spectrum.

Try experimenting with any sound you can think of, shifting it up or down. Even subtle pitch changes can help sounds fit into the overall mix of elements in ways that EQ or other processing cannot.

Digidesign's Time Shift Plug-In

Digidesign has added a new time compression and pitch-shifting plug-in called Time Shift, shown in Figure 7.17. This plug-in has the capabilities of both the Pitch Shift and Time Compression/Expansion plug-ins, together with the added capability to alter the formant of a sound during the process. The *formant* of a sound is the specific harmonic content that helps differentiate its timbre regardless of the pitch. The ideal example of this is the difference between the male and female voices. A man and a woman singing the same note will have noticeably different timbres to their voices. When applying time compression or pitch-shifting, the formant quality can be altered, rendering the voice unnatural sounding. With plug-ins such as Time Shift, this formant quality can be retained or even altered for effect.

The formant setting is available only when Time Shift is set to the Monophonic mode in the Audio section of the plug-in. You can adjust the formant in semitones if you want to alter the harmonic signature of the sound or leave it at 0.00 to preserve the current formant. Preserving the formant will make pitch-shifted voices sound more natural than simple pitch-shifting.

In polyphonic and rhythmic modes, Time Shift provides additional control over how transients are handled by the time compression and pitch-shifting algorithms. Because this type of processing involves separating cycles or segments of audio to create the effect, transients can become corrupted if the cycle lands right on the transient. Using transient detection can help avoid these aberrations in the processed sound.

Aligning Dialogue

When you're working with dialogue, it might be necessary to adjust the timing of certain lines to compensate for camera moves, tricky edits, or even ADR recording.

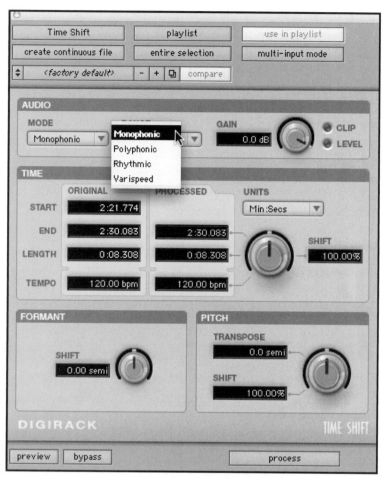

Figure 7.17 Digidesign's Time Shift Audiosuite plug-in with formant processing. Formant processing is only available in Monophonic mode.

When camera angles change in a scene, sometimes directors will use a person's spoken line from another camera angle, and therefore a line from another take. This alternate take might overlap images of the character performing the same lines from the original take. When this happens, editing between the two takes right when the camera angle changes might work, but often the continuity is lost, and the first take must overlap the image of the second take. If luck is with you, the lip sync will match. If not, you might have to alter the take to match the image. Likewise, sometimes an actor is not able to re-create a performance in the ADR studio that matches well to the picture. In a case like this, you might need to alter the dialogue audio to match the original.

Plug-in tools such as Synchro Art's VocALign plug-in are created for matching the timing of one recording to another. This plug-in can analyze an existing vocal take and conform a similar one to match the timing of the original. This can help a problematic ADR session by taking a good performance and aligning it with the original take.

As you can see in Figure 7.18, the VocALign plug-in has two windows in it. The top window is used to analyze the original or reference audio, and the lower window is used for the audio that will be processed to match. To align one dialogue take to another, follow these steps:

1. Choose Audiosuite > VocALign to open the plug-in. This is an Audiosuite-only plug-in and will not be found in the mixer's inserts.

2. Select a region that contains the dialogue take you want to reference. This region will be used as a guide to how the new take will be aligned.

3. Press the top Guide button, indicating that the file to be analyzed is a Guide track.

4. Press the Guide button. A waveform display of the selected region should appear in the Guide window, as seen in Figure 7.18.

5. Select the region that contains the new dialogue that you want to align.

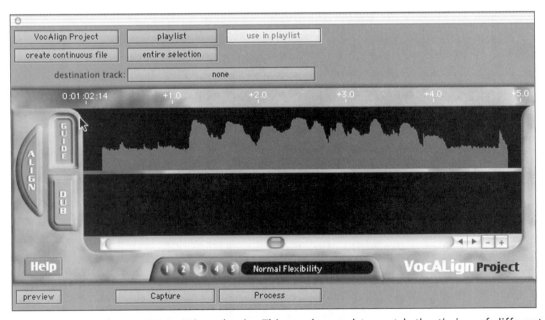

Figure 7.18 Synchro Art's VocALign plug-in. This can be used to match the timing of different vocal takes of the same line. A source file has been analyzed and displayed in the Guide window.

6. Click the Dub button to indicate that this is the audio to be processed.

7. Click the Align button. An outline of the processed file will appear above the Guide track, indicating where each peak and valley will line up in the new file, as seen in Figure 7.19.

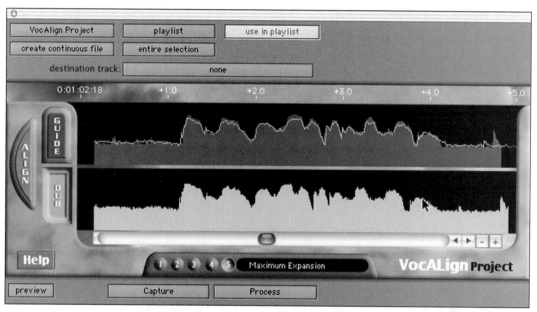

Figure 7.19 Once the Align button has been pressed, this outline appears above the Guide track, showing where the new file will line up.

8. In order to hear the result, press the Preview button.

9. Click on the buttons in the flexibility setting along the bottom of the window to see which one yields the most accurate match to the guide. You will have to press the Align button again after choosing another flexibility setting.

10. Decide whether or not you want the new file to replace the unprocessed file. There are several choices. You can leave the processed file in the Audio Regions List without placing it in a track, you can place the new file on another track specified in the Destination pull-down menu, or you can replace the file on the same track. Create a duplicate playlist and append the name with "-align" to indicate that you have aligned all the regions that are necessary and that the track is complete. This way, you can quickly return to the unmodified version of the track if you need to.

11. Click the Process button. Done.

As with any plug-in, overuse is not a good idea. It is always best to get a better performance than to "fix it in the mix." VocALign is a tool, not a crutch.

Noise Reduction and Restoration

As you're editing dialogue, you might find that the recordings have unwanted noise on them. In lieu of re-recording them in an ADR session, it might be possible to clean up the tracks using plug-ins that analyze noise content and filter it out, leaving the dialogue relatively untouched.

Digidesign's DINR and the Waves Restoration Bundle are two popular systems for removing noise. Sonic Solutions NoNOISE is one of the oldest developers of this type of technology, and it too is available to TDM systems. Sonic Solutions and Waves plug-ins have more sophisticated tools for removing hum and clicks, but all three have a similar broadband noise reduction plug-in that will analyze the noise content of a signal and create an inverse noise-canceling algorithm to remove the noise while leaving useful program material intact.

You must have a section of audio without any dialogue that contains the same type and level of noise as the areas you want to clean up. A second or so of background noise will usually do nicely. You should be able to find a section of this background noise prior to or just after a take. You might have to return to the source tapes to find such a section. Most professional production sound mixers will record long sections of background ambience for use later on in dialogue editing. Although these recordings are primarily used to create seamless background ambience for sections with many dialogue edits, they can also be used for noise analysis and removal. Here's how the process works using Waves' X-Noise plug-in. The process is similar with Digidesign's DINR and Sonic Solutions' NoNOISE.

In this example, you have some production dialogue audio that was recorded on a set using several fans to create wind for the scene. These fans made a decent amount of noise, which was recorded through the boom mic. The director would like to keep the original dialogue recording for this scene because the performance was very special. You must remove as much of the fan noise as possible in order to make this recording usable. Here's how:

1. Instantiate the Waves X-Noise plug-in on the dialogue track in question.

2. Find and select a section of audio that is just the background noise without any dialogue. A second or two will do.

Noise Samples   The noise you select is critical. Analysis of the noise sample will be used to subdue noise in audio that has dialogue in it. If the noise floor changes between shots in a scene or even between different takes in one shot, reanalysis will be needed in order to accurately remove the noise. Changes in the noise floor could be from movement of the fans, in this example. Air conditioners will often create noise that changes when the unit cycles on and off. Make sure the noise you analyze is the same noise you want to remove.

3.   Open the plug-in window and press the Learn button at the bottom. The button should flash yellow and say "Learning," as shown in Figure 7.20. The plug-in needs to analyze this noise sample in order to create a profile that will be used to remove the noise. This is what the Learning mode is for.

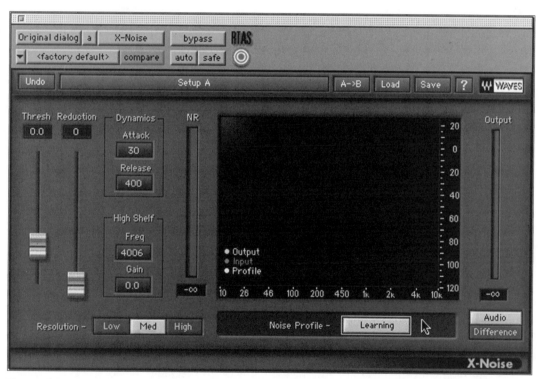

Figure 7.20   Waves' X-Noise plug-in set up in Learning mode in order to analyze the noise sample.

4.   Make sure that both pre- and post-roll are disabled. This ensures that when you play the selection, only the selected audio will be analyzed by X-Noise. Any audio outside your selection might contain desired program material and should not be part of the noise profile.

5. Play the portion of audio. You will notice a spectral display of the audio inside the X-Noise window while playing.

6. After playing through the whole selection, press the flashing Learning button again to end the analysis and stop playback. In the spectral display you will see a noise profile that represents the noise components in that portion of audio.

7. Play the section from which you want to remove noise. Putting it in Loop Playback mode (Command+Shift+L) might help while adjusting the X-Noise parameters. If you have other tracks playing along, you might notice that the one with X-Noise on it is severely out of sync with the rest. This plug-in has a large amount of latency. It takes more time to process the audio, and therefore it is delayed in playback. For now, just solo this track so as not to be distracted by its lack of sync.

8. Adjust the threshold (Thresh) slider up. As the threshold increases, more noise will be removed. The function is similar to a noise gate or downward expander. The threshold is the level at which the signal will be allowed to pass through and be heard. If the signal is below the threshold, it will be gain-reduced. The amount of noise reduction is determined by the Amount slider. Adjust these two parameters until you achieve the desired noise reduction. As noise reduction increases, you will see two moving lines and one stationary white line in the spectral display. The white line is the noise profile curve adjusted to the threshold setting. When you raise the threshold, the noise profile curve moves up. The red moving line indicates the signal input to the plug-in. The green moving line is the result of the plug-in's processing. In sections where there is only noise, the red line should appear below the green, indicating reduction of the noise floor, as seen in Figure 7.21.

How X-Noise and Other Noise Removers Work   X-Noise uses a large number of downward expanders on individual frequency bands to achieve this quality of noise reduction. The noise profile sets relative thresholds for each frequency band. The Resolution setting determines how many individual bands there are. The higher the number of bands, the more precise and accurate the noise reduction will be. The trade-off is that the higher resolution creates larger amounts of latency. The method in this example will avoid the latency issue by processing the files offline with the Audiosuite X-Noise plug-in. With that in mind, using high resolution will yield better results in most cases.

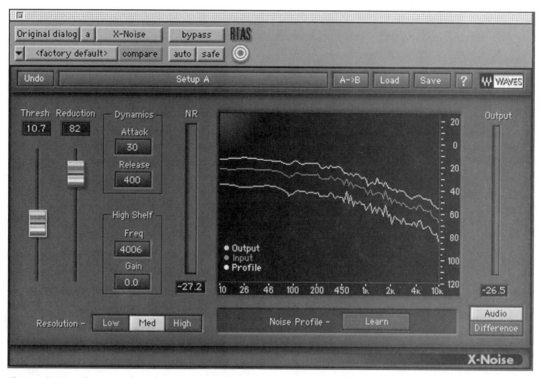

Figure 7.21   The X-Noise plug-in in action. The green line shows the result of processing; the red line shows the noise floor being reduced from its original level.

9.   The High Shelf frequency and Gain parameters allow you to adjust the threshold of higher frequencies in the noise profile. The higher frequencies in dialogue can sometimes be close to the same energy level as other noise components in the signal. Reducing the threshold at these frequencies by entering negative values for the Gain parameter can help maintain clarity when performing a large amount of noise reduction. Raising the high-frequency threshold can help reduce noise components in the more audible ranges when the program material itself is mainly in lower frequencies. The result of this equalization can be seen as changes in the shape of the white line. Figure 7.22 shows the same noise profile as in Figure 7.20, with the addition of −30dB of gain with a corner frequency of 4006Hz. Notice the right side of the white line is lower. The threshold of frequencies above 4006Hz has been reduced by a maximum of 30dB, thus allowing more high frequency detail to come through.

10.   The Dynamics section of this plug-in controls the speed at which the noise reduction operates. The Attack parameter determines how long in

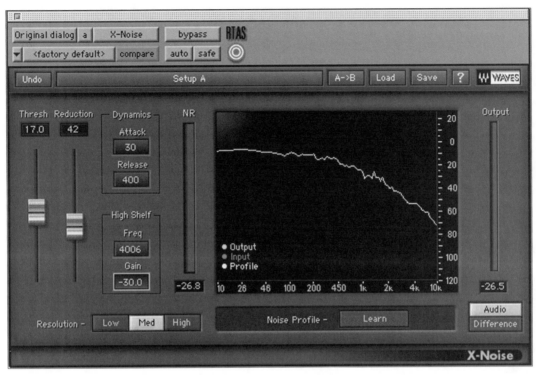

Figure 7.22 The noise profile has been adjusted by the High Shelf parameters. Notice the right side of the noise profile is lower than in Figure 7.20.

milliseconds it takes for noise reduction to occur once the signal goes below the threshold. Conversely, once the threshold is exceeded, the Release parameter determines how long it takes for noise reduction to cease. Quicker attack and release times will improve clarity in most situations. However, the quicker these times are set, the more noticeable the processing becomes. At very fast settings, the processing starts to sound rather robotic and mechanical.

Listening to the "Difference" You can use the Audio and Difference buttons located at the bottom-right side of the plug-in window to hear exactly what noise is being removed. When you click the Difference button, you will hear only the noise components that are being removed. Anything you are hearing will not be in the processed signal. This is a good way to ensure that you aren't removing useful program material. If you are listening to the difference and hear any clear dialogue, your settings are too severe. Try backing off the reduction and lowering the threshold.

---

11.   Once you have adjusted all the parameters and come up with a setting that achieves the best noise reduction versus sound quality, you must save the setting as a preset. This preset will be used to perform offline processing using the Audiosuite version of X-Noise. This offline process eliminates the latency issues that arise when using X-Noise in real-time as a TDM or RTAS plug-in without delay compensation. To save the preset, choose Save to New File from the Save submenu in the upper-right corner of the plug-in window, as shown in Figure 7.23. It is also possible to save settings from the standard preset menu in the upper-left side of the window, but with Waves X-Noise, the only way to save the parameters *and* the noise profile is to use this other submenu. Try to use a descriptive name for the preset that you can identify as applying to this particular section of audio. You might be saving many more noise presets before an entire film is completed. Being able to refer back to these settings can be very important if you decide to alter the settings at a later time or additional dialogue material is added in a revision.

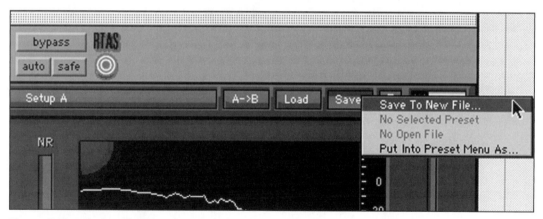

Figure 7.23   Choose the Save to New File option under the Save submenu.

Using X-Noise in RTAS or TDM   If you want to use the RTAS or TDM version of X-Noise, you will have to compensate for the extreme latency that this plug-in will create. Please refer to the plug-in latency compensation section in Chapter 8, "Mixing to Picture in Pro Tools."

---

12.   With the preset saved, you are now ready to process the files offline. Choose Audiosuite > X-Noise to open the Audiosuite version of X-Noise.

13. Click the Load button and choose Open Preset File. Locate the preset you saved in Step 11.

14. Click the Load button again, and you should see the name of your preset file listed in the middle section of the submenu, as shown in Figure 7.24. Select the Both option to load both the noise profile and the parameter settings from the preset file. Your plug-in should look the same as it did in the RTAS or TDM version.

Figure 7.24 Once a preset has been loaded into the Audiosuite version of X-Noise, you have three choices available. You can choose to load the noise profile by itself, the preset by itself, or both at once.

15. Before you process these files, you should create a duplicate playlist in which the processing will occur. This gives you a quick way to return to the unprocessed files in case you want to make a change. Understand that once you process the files with any Audiosuite plug-in, only those portions of audio that are visible inside the regions will be processed. The parent files these regions belong to will not be entirely processed. It will not be possible to "open up" the regions with the Trimmer tool once they are processed. Using an alternate playlist allows you to go back to the originals, which will retain any handles they might have had, allowing you to tweak edits if need be and then reprocess with X-Noise.

There are other plug-ins that help remove different types of noise. The Waves Restoration Bundle has X-Hum, shown in Figure 7.25, which is designed to remove unwanted hum generated by electrical grounding problems, portable generator noise, and even air conditioning and fan noise. Most steady-state noises like these can be dealt with using X-Hum. Using a series of tight notch filters placed in the harmonic series, X-Hum attacks not only the fundamental tone of hum but also all the subsequent harmonics it generates.

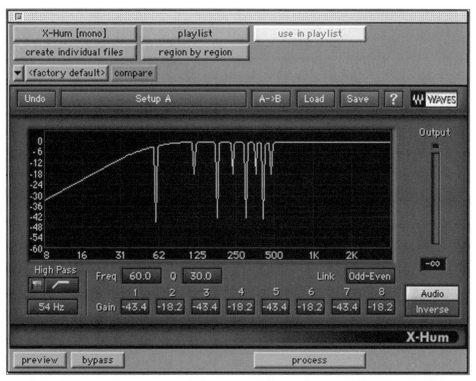

Figure 7.25 The Waves X-Hum plug-in is designed to remove 60-cycle and other types of hum, including their harmonic components.

X-Hum's controls are very intuitive and can be used in the same way as in the X-Noise example above. Typically, removing hum would be done prior to broadband noise reduction. When performing offline processing, simply use the X-Hum Audiosuite plug-in first, and then apply X-Noise to the files already processed by X-Hum.

Noise reduction tools like the ones presented in this chapter are powerful and complex. Experiment with some noisy material to get a feel for how each one works before processing critical files. It is often a trade-off between the amount of reduction realized and the number of artifacts introduced into the de-noised signal. In some instances, you will find that one plug-in works better than another on a particular piece of audio. In other instances you may find that processing the signal twice with slightly lower amounts of noise reduction in each pass will result in a greater total noise reduction with fewer artifacts than you could get with a single pass. The controls are very intuitive and can easily be mastered with experience. The ability to remove much of the unwanted noise can drastically improve the resulting soundtrack, leaving more space and dynamics while improving clarity.

Surgical EQ

Sometimes the dialogue tracks will have small anomalies in them, such as mic "thumps," where someone accidentally touched the microphone or the boom operator was unsteady and bumped the microphone against something else. If this occurs during a word or phrase, it could potentially make that dialogue recording unusable. It is possible, using Audiosuite plug-ins, to process just a very small portion of the audio file in the affected area to treat these anomalies.

Using the example of the mic thump, you can select the affected area of the sound file and then open an Audiosuite EQ plug-in that has a high-pass filter in it such as the Waves Q1. Using the Preview function, adjust the parameters of the Q1 to filter out the low-frequency thump in the sound. You will not be able to entirely eliminate the thump sound, but you may greatly reduce the effect it has on the overall mix using this high pass filter. Process only this small portion of the audio file, creating a new region in its place without the pronounced thump. You might have to create crossfades on either side of this newly created region in order to smooth the transition between the original recording and the newly processed one.

This same type of process can be achieved through the use of automation. That technique will be explained in Chapter 8. Although both methods can potentially achieve the same results, by using the Audiosuite plug-in you can affect very small portions of audio easily. Using the automation method might not yield the same results with very small audio segments due to priorities in the automation structure of Pro Tools and how certain plug-ins react to automation data. In addition, the Audiosuite method frees up DSP power for other tasks, as the file is processed offline.

Once you've completed any offline processing and all editing tasks are complete, it is time to start mixing.

8 Mixing to Picture in Pro Tools

ixing is one the most challenging and creative stages in any recording project. Combining all the recorded material into one finished presentation requires all the skill, experience, and expertise an engineer can provide. With so much material being presented in surround sound these days, the mixing task becomes even more complex. Arranging all the sounds among six speakers instead of two provides many more opportunities for creative expression and at the same time creates the potential for more pitfalls and trouble spots.

Pro Tools provides an environment that is capable of exploiting all the possibilities in a simple stereo mix or in a full 5.1 surround mix. From a simple narration with music to a complete film mix, Pro Tools has the capabilities to provide you with the ultimate control and flexibility in all of these mixing situations. In this chapter, I discuss preparations for mixing, the pre-mixing stages of creating "predubs," the use of automation throughout to create a dynamic and compelling mix, the use of reference levels in order to maintain industry standards, and preparation of your mix for use in multiple formats.

Stereo and Surround Formats

In the audio post-production world, you must be prepared to mix down your project to just about any format, from mono through 7.1 surround. One project will often be mixed down to several formats at the same time. Specialized tools are needed to perform these down-mixing routines. In today's ever-changing consumer world, you never know how your original 5.1 mix is going to be heard. It might end up coming out of a mono television speaker, an audiophile home theater system, or anything in between. Being able to preview all these possibilities is an important part of your mixdown procedure.

Encoding and Decoding with Dolby Technologies

Dolby Laboratories is the leader in multi-channel sound-encoding techniques. They have pioneered methods for bringing multi-channel surround sound into theaters and into the home. You should be familiar with the encoding processes that certain Dolby formats require.

Dolby Stereo and Pro Logic

The original Dolby surround format is known in theaters as Dolby Stereo and in the home as Dolby Pro Logic. This format encodes a center and surround channel within a stereo signal. The stereo signal can then be recorded onto 35mm optical film, VHS tape, DVD, or even broadcast over stereo television without losing any of this encoded material. The stereo signal is then decoded into left, center, right, and surround (LCRS) channels when played back through a proper Dolby Stereo cinema processor or Dolby Pro Logic AV system. In addition to manufacturing over 70,000 Dolby Stereo capable cinema processors, Dolby has licensed this technology to nearly every manufacturer of consumer playback equipment, making it the most widely used encoding technology for surround sound.

The encoding process requires four discrete inputs that are processed into a resulting stereo output file. The center channel information is simply added equally to both the left and right channels of the stereo output at the appropriate level. The surround channel is band-limited and encoded as a +90 degree phase signal in the stereo mix. This is called *phase-matrixed encoding*. The decoder can then take any completely out-of-phase signal within that band and send it to the surround channel. Similarly, any signals that are equally present in both the left and right speakers will be redirected to the center channel. This is an oversimplification of the process, but it will suffice for the purposes of this book.

This encoding-decoding process can provide surprising results in certain situations. Stereo synthesizers are notorious for creating false surround images through the decoder because of the radical phase manipulation used to create these sounds. In order to be sure of what your mix will sound like once it's been through the encoding and decoding process, you must mix while listening through an encoder and decoder. Dolby provides hardware units that will encode and then decode the signal for you, allowing you to hear the results of the process. For TDM users, there are the Dolby Surround Tools plug-ins, which will encode and decode Dolby Surround signals right inside Pro Tools.

As is often the case these days, the Dolby Pro Logic mix will be derived from a discrete 5.1 master. The process is called *downmixing*, whereby the extra channels in a 5.1 system are blended together in certain ways to create an LCRS or Dolby Pro Logic Master. Downmixing is discussed later in this chapter.

5.1 Surround and Dolby Digital

Dolby 5.1 surround formats have a left, center, right, left surround, and right surround channel plus an LFE channel, making a total of six. These channels can be encoded using the Dolby Digital format for theatrical presentation and a DVD home-theater presentation.

This encoding scheme differs from that of Dolby Surround (Pro Logic) in that each channel is discrete, and there is no matrixing of the surround channels into a stereo-encoded signal. It is a digital process rather than analog. This digital encoding can occur in the studio with the proper equipment. There are certain parameters affecting levels that can be encoded into the metadata that the mix engineer should have control over.

If encoding the Dolby Digital signal is not possible, the audio studio can provide a six-channel discrete mix, with time code, to the film transfer house or DVD-authoring studio for encoding. Being present at the encoding stage is advisable for quality control purposes. It might also be necessary to prepare a Dolby Stereo or Pro Logic downmix of the discrete channels for compatibility with older systems. This downmix will also be compatible with simple stereo and even mono broadcast chains. It is always a good idea to preview your mix in all of these formats.

Multi-Channel Processing and Format Confusion   Take care to differentiate between the different Dolby recording formats and the various bass management systems. If these get confused, improperly formatted mixes will be the result. Dolby Stereo and Pro Logic must be encoded during mixdown. Dolby Digital signals will not be encoded during mixdown, but will be encoded from an all discrete, six-channel master when the optical film print is created or in the DVD authoring suite. Bass management systems are only used for playback calibration and monitoring, not for processing the actual audio recording.

Downmixing for Other Formats

As described previously, downmixing is the process of taking multi-channel surround sound mixes and recombining the channels for compatibility with systems having fewer channels. 5.1 Surround mixes will often need to be downmixed to Dolby Surround or Pro Logic formats, regular stereo, and even mono in some broadcast applications.

Dolby Digital decoders have the ability to perform downmixing during the decoding process. Using the same preprogrammed algorithm as found in a Dolby Surround encoder, center, and surround, channels will be recombined with the left and right signals to create a stereo signal encoded in Dolby Surround. The Dolby Stereo signal is also compatible with stereo and mono playback systems. So creating one downmix provides compatibility with every type of playback system at once.

This automatic downmixing involves some dynamic processing to avoid overloading the stereo channels caused by combining the other various channels. The results of the automatic process might not be desirable in every situation. The Dolby Digital encoder offers a wide degree of flexibility to the encoding engineer in how such dynamic range processing is applied to the signal by the decoder. Often, these powerful tools are preset and ignored. Creating downmix files in the studio is an alternative that allows predictable results with more control. Plug-ins, such as the Waves Surround toolkit, have been developed to facilitate this process easily. But unless the delivery system offers both the 5.1 and the two-channel soundtracks, the users may not have access to the "hand made" downmix and will hear the Dolby downmix instead. In that case, it is worthwhile taking time to best exploit the internal downmix options within the Dolby encoder as much as possible.

Preparation for Mixing

Before you begin mixing, there are several steps you must take in order to be prepared for the final mix. Depending on what type of mix you are creating, whether a stereo or surround mix, there are several considerations to be made regarding speakers, their placement, and the input and output configuration of your Pro Tools system.

The I/O Setup

The I/O Setup in Pro Tools (shown in Figure 8.1) is a very helpful section that is often overlooked. Choose Setups > I/O Setup to access this feature. Here you can create custom names for different inputs, outputs, and even busses that you would use for certain purposes. For instance, the first six outputs of your system can be labeled as 5.1 Surround Mix. The next pair could be called Pro Logic Stereo, and so on. Now, each time you select an output for a specific track, aux send, or master fader, you will see 5.1 Surround Mix and Pro Logic Stereo as available options. It is possible to label all your inputs and hardware inserts with the devices that are connected to them, such as Line 1, Synth 3, Plate Reverb L, and so on.

Outputs

When mixing in surround, labeling of outputs and busses is more important because of the complexity of the surround mixer. In order to be able to use the surround capabilities of the Pro Tools mixer, you must first create a surround sound output or buss that a track can be assigned to. Figure 8.2 shows the pull-down menu where you can determine what types of output paths are available.

Create a 5.1 output path and call it 5.1 Surround Mix. Assign different hardware outputs of your system to the different channels of the surround path, as shown in Figure 8.3. This will determine what physical outputs of your system will be connected to each speaker in your playback system. You will have to deactivate any other output path that overlaps the outputs used in this new surround path.

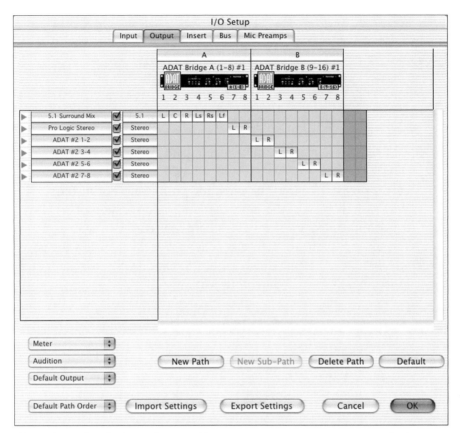

Figure 8.1 The I/O Setup feature. Here you can create custom names for inputs, outputs, hardware inserts, busses, and mic preamps connected to your system.

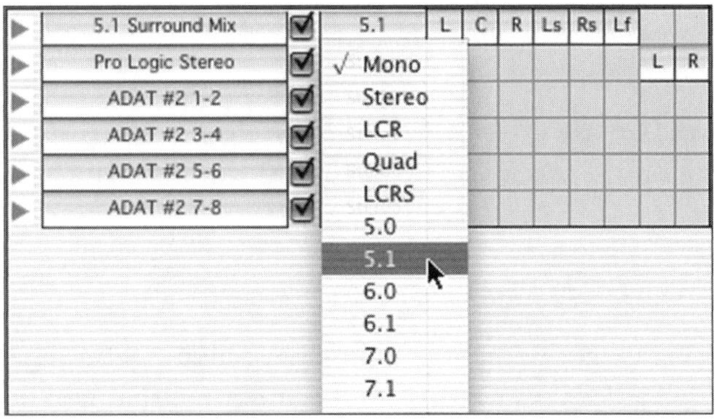

Figure 8.2 The Output to Path Type pull-down menu. This menu determines what type of output path you are creating, whether stereo or 5.1 surround.

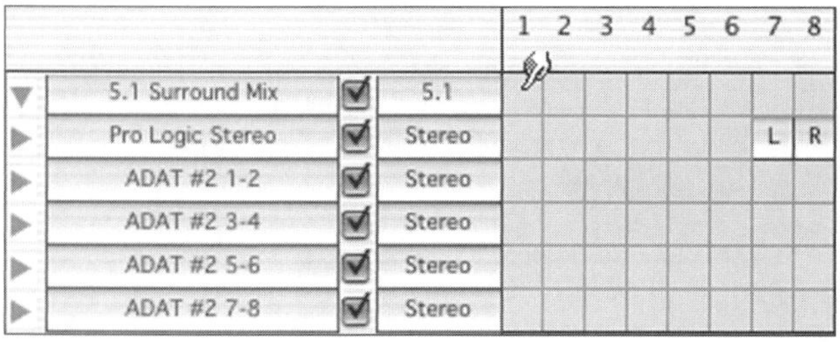

			1	2	3	4	5	6	7	8
▼	5.1 Surround Mix	☑	5.1								
▶	Pro Logic Stereo	☑	Stereo							L	R
▶	ADAT #2 1-2	☑	Stereo								
▶	ADAT #2 3-4	☑	Stereo								
▶	ADAT #2 5-6	☑	Stereo								
▶	ADAT #2 7-8	☑	Stereo								

Figure 8.3 Assigning physical outputs to members of an output path.

It is also possible to create a sub-path within the surround path itself. For instance, you might want to create a sub-path that is just the stereo left and right speakers. This allows you to assign tracks to just the stereo speakers. This can help conserve DSP and also simplify your mixer. A mono sub-path for the center channel speaker makes it easy to assign dialogue tracks to just the center channel. Figure 8.4 shows the two sub-paths that have been created underneath the 5.1 Surround Mix.

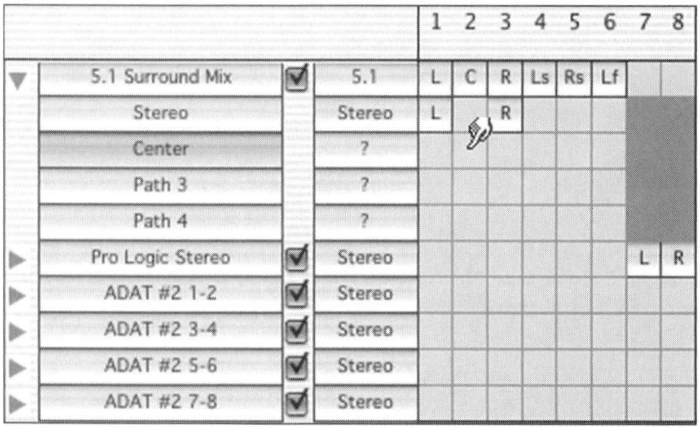

			1	2	3	4	5	6	7	8
▼	5.1 Surround Mix	☑	5.1	L	C	R	Ls	Rs	Lf		
	Stereo		Stereo	L		R					
	Center		?								
	Path 3		?								
	Path 4		?								
▶	Pro Logic Stereo	☑	Stereo							L	R
▶	ADAT #2 1-2	☑	Stereo								
▶	ADAT #2 3-4	☑	Stereo								
▶	ADAT #2 5-6	☑	Stereo								
▶	ADAT #2 7-8	☑	Stereo								

Figure 8.4 Creation of stereo and mono sub-paths allows signals to be routed directly to the center channel or the left and right speakers discretely.

When assigning outputs for a track, you will be given the option to select 5.1 Surround Mix, Stereo, or Center CH. Depending on the track you are working with, one of these choices will be most appropriate.

Busses

Busses can also be grouped together to create multi-channel pathways. These can be helpful when combining large numbers of related tracks to form a mix sub-group that will be used to create a mix "stem." Figure 8.5 shows the formation of a 5.1 surround buss for effects. All the effects tracks can be routed to this buss and maintain their positions in the sound field. This helps in mixing later, when you want to balance levels between dialogue, foley, effects, and music. If each group of sounds is routed together on its own buss, balancing their respective levels is as simple as grabbing one fader. Later in this chapter, I talk more about grouping channels and creating mix stems this way.

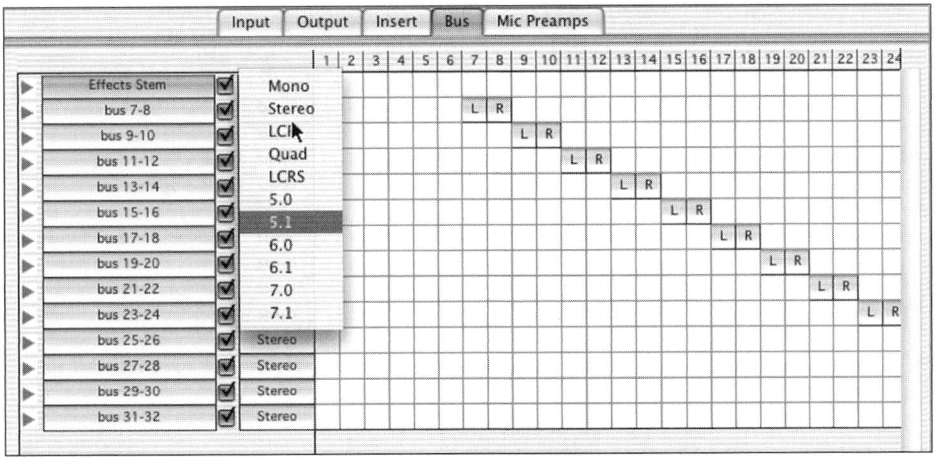

Figure 8.5 Creating surround busses for sub-grouping related sounds together in a surround configuration.

Mix Stems   *Mix stems* are finished master recordings made from a post-production mix session. A stem is created for each facet in the production: dialogue, foley, effects, and music. These stems can then be combined at unity gain to create the different print masters for each format the project will end up on: Dolby Digital, Dolby Pro Logic, and even foreign language versions that do not include dialogue tracks.

Inserts

It is possible with Pro Tools to patch in your favorite external hardware processors on channels in the same way that you use plug-ins. Each channel of external processing requires an I/O pair from your Pro Tools hardware. Keep in mind that when mixing in surround, at least the first six outputs of your hardware will be used for monitoring only. These outputs, and their corresponding inputs, will not be available for external inserts.

Let's say you want to patch an external reverb that has a unique sound you would like to use in your Pro Tools mix. Assuming that this reverb unit is stereo in and stereo out, you will need two I/O pairs to patch the unit in. Because I use an ADAT bridge in my system, I will use that as an example. The ADAT bridge is connected to two 8-channel AD/DAs for a total of 16 I/O pairs. The first six outputs are connected to my monitoring setup. Here's how to patch the reverb unit in I/O pairs 7 and 8 and create a hardware insert for it.

1. Physically connect outputs 7 and 8 to the left and right inputs of the reverb unit.

2. Connect the left and right outputs of the reverb units to inputs 7 and 8.

3. Choose Setups > I/O Setup.

4. Click the Inserts tab.

5. If there are no inserts already created, click New Path.

6. As this is a stereo reverb unit, select Stereo from the pull-down menu, as shown in Figure 8.6.

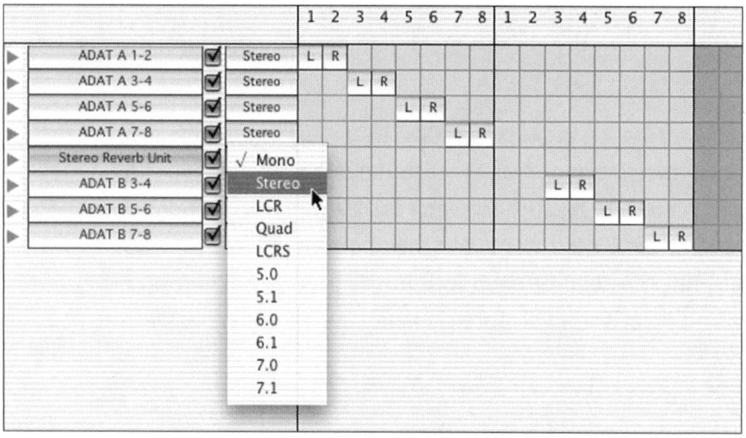

Figure 8.6 Creating a stereo insert path from I/O Setup.

7. Double-click in the Name field and enter the name for your stereo reverb unit.

8. Select the appropriate I/O pairs that are connected to the reverb. In this case, ADAT A, channels 7 and 8.

9. Go to any stereo channel or aux in your mixer and click on an Insert button. You will now be able to go to the Insert submenu, where you'll see the reverb unit listed as an insert, as shown in Figure 8.7.

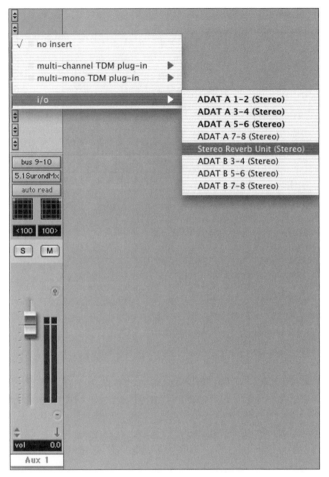

Figure 8.7   The reverb unit is now available as an insert on any channel. It will function like a plug-in. However, it can be used only once in any mixer configuration.

Insert Latency   Understand that when you program a hardware insert and use it on any track, aux channel, or master fader, a certain amount of latency will be introduced into that channel. On TDM systems, this amount is 96 samples. That might seem small, but it can wreak havoc on the phase relationships of different signals in a mix. Latency is covered later in this chapter.

Now that you have set up your input and output configurations, it is time to connect the speakers to your monitoring system and calibrate them for ideal listening.

Speaker Systems and Layouts

Depending on what type of format you're mixing, the speakers' size and relative positions to your ears are very important. If you are mixing music that listeners will enjoy in cars or on small portable radios, smaller speakers will help you achieve the best results. If you're mixing for home stereo listening, larger, full-fidelity speakers will be appropriate. If you're mixing for a home-theater system with four or perhaps six different speakers including a subwoofer, having a similar setup in your mix room will help you achieve the best results. Finally, if you're mixing for a theatrical presentation, being able to listen to the actual type of system that is found in theaters will help you get a realistic idea of what your mix will sound like in its final form. In any situation, proper alignment and test level calibration will help you achieve the best results.

Mixing in Stereo

The main consideration when mixing in stereo is the proper angle between the two speakers in your listening position. The standard is a 60-degree angle from the left speaker to the right speaker, as shown in Figure 8.8. Although placing the speakers at a wider angle can be effective, loss of the phantom center image might be the result of placing the speakers too far apart. Angles of up to 90 degrees can be used effectively if the acoustic treatment in the control room is sufficient to maintain a strong center image.

You can set up this type of monitoring configuration using a tape measure. If the distance between the listener and each speaker is the same as the distance between the

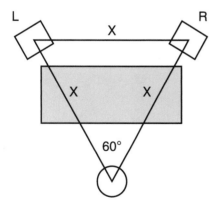

Stereo Speaker Configuration

Figure 8.8 A diagram of the standard stereo speaker configuration using a 60-degree angle. X is the distance between the listener and each speaker.

speakers themselves, you will have created a 60-degree angle between the speakers. This forms an equilateral triangle between the listener and the two speakers and will allow you to effectively hear signals in the stereo field. The stereo image you create should remain intact when played back on many other types of systems.

Mixing in 5.1 Surround

5.1 Surround is the most common form of surround mixing being done today. It's used in theatrical presentation, DVD releases, and HDTV broadcasts, making it the most-used configuration for surround sound. The basic equilateral triangle that is used for stereo mixing forms the basis for the 5.1 surround setup. Four additional speakers—center, subwoofer, left surround, and right surround—are then added to the stereo pair.

The Center Channel. It is often said that the center channel is primarily used for dialogue, and while it is true that its proximity to the center of the screen makes it the most appropriate location to put dialogue, this channel is also a primary carrier of key sound effects. Also, people in the audience who might not be sitting towards the center of the room will still perceive dialogue coming from the center channel as being very closely tied to the center image on-screen. The center channel should be placed so that it is aligned with the center of the screen, as shown in Figure 8.9.

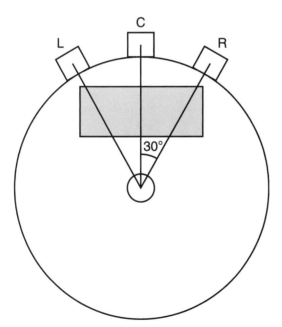

Figure 8.9 The center channel speaker should be aligned with the exact center of the viewing screen. If possible, all three speakers should be on the same horizontal plane—that is, level with each other.

Sometimes, for practical reasons, the three front speakers cannot be on the same horizontal plane. In order to accommodate a convenient screen location, the center speaker will often be lowered so as not to be in front of the screen. When this is necessary, you must endeavor to keep the tweeters of all three speakers as aligned as possible. Figures 8.10 and 8.11 show two common alternatives for center-channel placement when accommodating a large viewing screen.

Stereo creates a phantom center image by having equal volumes of a signal in both the left and right speakers (panned in the middle). In a large viewing room, audience members located off to one side of the room will perceive a shift in that phantom center image that will disassociate the dialogue from the images on-screen. The center channel speaker eliminates this problem. Only in very limited circumstances will you hear dialogue elements in either the left or the right speaker. These cases are primarily instances when a character enters from the extreme left or right of the film frame while talking or for special effects.

The center channel speaker should be placed equidistant from the listener, the same as the two left and right speakers. This places the front three speakers on an arc in front of the listener, as shown in Figure 8.10.

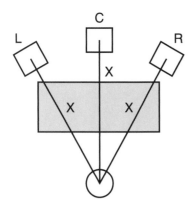

Center Speaker Configuration

Figure 8.10 Placement of the center channel speaker. Notice that the distance from each speaker to the listener is the same, placing all speakers on an arc in front of the mix position. This keeps all signals phase coherent or arriving at the same time.

Take care to keep each speaker equidistant from the mix position. This keeps signals phase coherent from all speakers, allowing accurate level and pan information to reach the listener. If the center channel were to be placed forward of this position to accommodate a monitor or viewing screen, signals coming from it would arrive at your ears earlier than signals emanating from either the left or right speaker. If this happens, sounds that pan across L-C-R might not follow a smooth movement. Phase coherence between all speakers in a surround sound setup is critical for accurate monitoring. If the center speaker must be a different distance than left and right, compensating time delays may be used to achieve coincident arrivals.

The viewing screen often becomes an obstacle for placement of a center channel speaker. There are several options that will allow for accurate monitoring while still giving space for a sizable viewing screen. The center channel speaker may be tilted on its side 90 degrees in order to be lower and more out of the way, as seen in Figure 8.11. The center channel speaker may be inverted and placed over the viewing screen in some situations. When this is done, be sure to make every attempt to align the high-frequency drivers in each speaker in the same horizontal plane, as shown in Figure 8.12. This allows for a more seamless soundscape. Figure 8.13 shows the optimal position for the center channel speaker in the same horizontal plane as both left and right speakers.

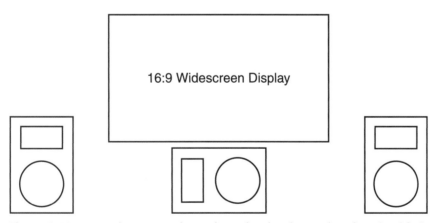

16:9 Widescreen Display

Figure 8.11   Here, the center channel speaker has been placed on its side in order to lower it to accommodate the viewing screen. If possible, the left and right speakers should be lowered somewhat to maintain alignment with the high-frequency driver of the center channel speaker.

Surround Speakers. Surround speakers are intended to provide an immersive experience by creating a 360-degree sound field in which the listener is placed. In order to provide such an encompassing sound field, these speakers must be placed behind the listener. ITU-R specifications outline the position as 110 degrees off axis from the center channel

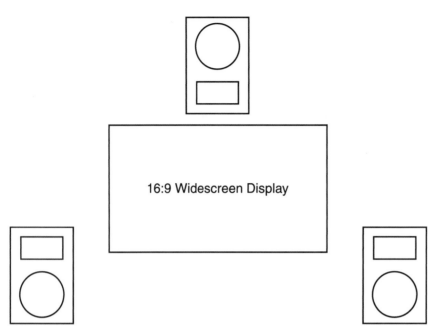

Figure 8.12 In this setup, the center channel speaker has been inverted and placed above the viewing screen. Notice that the left and right speakers have been raised in an attempt to align high-frequency drivers in the same horizontal plane.

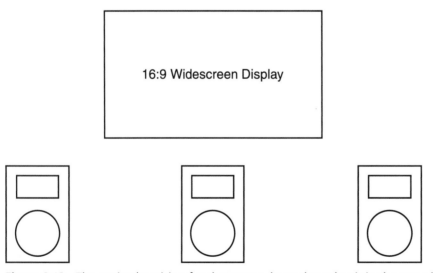

Figure 8.13 The optimal position for the center channel speaker is in the same horizontal plane as both the left and right speakers.

speaker position and equidistant from the listener. Figure 8.14 shows the complete 5.1 surround configuration.

Dolby Stereo versus Dolby Digital or 5.1   The Dolby Laboratories reference material (found at www.dolby.com) suggests that surround speakers not be aimed directly at the listening position but rather at a point that is approximately two feet above that position and mounted higher than the front speakers if mixing material that is to be encoded in the Dolby Surround protocol. Dolby Surround differs from Dolby Digital and 5.1 in that there is only one surround channel. When mixing a Dolby Digital or 5.1 Surround with two surround channels, all of Dolby's recommendations follow the ITU-R specification.

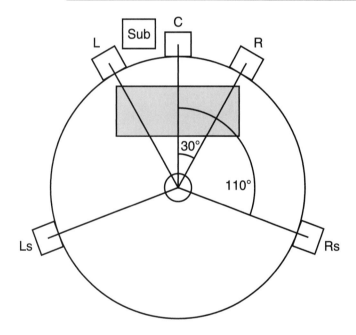

5.1 Surround Speaker Configuration
ITU-R

Figure 8.14   The ITU-R specifications for 5.1 mixing environments. The geometry of placement of a 5.1 surround configuration has been specified in this setup.

What Is ITU-R?   The International Telecommunications Union (ITU) is an organization that coordinates government and private sector management of telecom and network services. The "-R" refers to the Radio Communications Sector.

Subwoofer and Low Frequency Effects (LFE) Channel. The subwoofer is perhaps the most difficult speaker to place properly in a mixing room. As low-frequency information is not very directional in nature, the position of the subwoofer does not necessarily have to be in the center of the front speaker array. Placement of speakers should be based on the acoustics of the room to provide accurate frequency response from the subwoofer.

Figure 8.14 shows the typical placement of the subwoofer just off-center and behind the front speaker array. A practical technique for placing the subwoofer is to initially put the subwoofer at the mix position. Then while playing program material that has a significant amount of low frequency information, walk around the room until you find the most pleasant and accurate low-frequency sound. Place the subwoofer there. This process is more accurately done with pink noise and an RTA analyzer. Now, when you're sitting at the mix position, you should hear the same type of response. Subwoofers will excite the low-frequency room modes, and unless acoustic treatment has been applied professionally, there will always be some anomalies in the low-end response of any small mixing room. Placing the subwoofer a great distance away from the other speakers can cause some phase problems with signals that are sent to both the LFE channel and another speaker in the array. Even small changes of a foot or so in subwoofer placement can dramatically affect the response of the system. Try lots of different positions until you find one that is most satisfying.

Bass Management and Sub Position   Before you determine the position of your subwoofer, refer to the section entitled "Bass Management," later in this chapter. Bass management can affect the relative level between the subwoofer and the other speakers. Your system must be properly set up before you can accurately determine the bass response of your subwoofer's position.

Loudness Calibration

When mixing for film or television, the level at which your monitor is set can drastically affect the outcome of your mix. Theaters have calibrated playback systems that are designed to reproduce a wide frequency range. The levels you generate during your mix session should be faithfully reproduced in theaters due to this calibration. If your mixing system is not calibrated to the same reference points, there is no way of telling how it will be reproduced in the theater. Similarly, television requires a slightly different reference point due the nature of home viewing. Listening levels in the home are lower than those in the theater. As such, your mixing system should be calibrated to this lower volume in order to create a mix that will translate well into the home listening environment.

Calibration of the playback system involves pink noise that can be generated by the Signal Generator plug-in in Pro Tools. You also need an SPL meter, such as the one pictured in Figure 8.15. A pink noise signal will be generated at the reference operating level of your system, in this case −20dBFS. This is the standard digital reference level in the industry. Calibrate this signal at a certain volume in the mix room so that it will correlate to the same volume when the material is reproduced later. The SPL meter is used to measure the acoustic output of each speaker channel in order to adjust a gain stage in the monitor chain to the correct volume in the room.

True Pink Noise at −20dBFS RMS?   Some people have questioned the accuracy of the pink noise generated by Digidesign's Signal Generator plug-in. The key to proper calibration of your studio starts with proper test tones. A highly respected collection of test tones developed by Tomlinson Holman (creator of THX), including a tutorial for its use, is available for a modest investment. Most basic calibrations can be accomplished using only the Radio Shack SPL meter. There is also a professional edition with many other tests and complete documentation. If you are serious about calibration (and you should be), owning one of these is a must.

Figure 8.15   The Radio Shack SPL meter. This common and relatively inexpensive meter can be used to accurately calibrate your surround speaker system. This one is set up for C weighting, with a slow response. Any decent recording studio should own one of these meters.

−20dBFS RMS and 0VU Reference Levels   In the old analog days, VU (Volume Units) meters were used to calibrate levels. The nominal recording and playback level was set at 0VU. The VU meter is a slower-reacting meter that does not respond to transient signals. As a result of this response, VU meters more accurately reflect the average level of a signal, or RMS (Root Mean Square), value.

When creating test signals, the average or RMS value of the signal is the most significant. That is why 0VU is used to define the reference or average level of a system. Signals can exceed this 0VU amount to a certain degree without creating distortion. This is the headroom of a given system.

With digital systems, all levels are absolute. Levels are measured in decibels at digital full scale, or dBFS. The maximum level any digital signal can reach is 0dBFS. The nominal, or 0VU level, in digital systems had to be set lower than 0dBFS, so there would be headroom available for transient signals to use. This point is set at −20dBFS for film and post-production work, leaving 20 decibels of headroom above the nominal operating level before distortion.

When calibrating signal levels, be sure to set any meter you are using to a VU or RMS type of response. Peak meters will register higher levels than a VU meter for the same signal.

Metering is a subject unto itself. A basic audio handbook can give much more detailed information on this subject.

Film-Style Mixing

Film-style mixing requires a slightly different calibration than when mixing for television or home theater applications. All calibration tests will use the pink noise signal at −20dBFS RMS. Here are the steps:

1. Create the test signal using the Signal Generator setup, as shown in Figure 8.16. Create a tone that is five to ten seconds long that you can loop for continuous playback. Or, you can use test tones from a reference CD such as Tomlinson Holman's TMH Digital Audio Test and Measurement Disc Series, available from www.HollywoodEdge.com.

2. Route that track to the first channel you want to calibrate. In this example, we will start with the center channel. Simply assign the track directly to the center channel's output. Figure 8.17 shows the direct routing of the test track to the center channel.

3. Set Loop Playback mode to play the test signal repeatedly. Press Play.

4. Place the SPL meter right at the mix position at head level. If you're holding the meter in your hand, keep it at arm's length distance to avoid coloration from sound reflected off of your body.

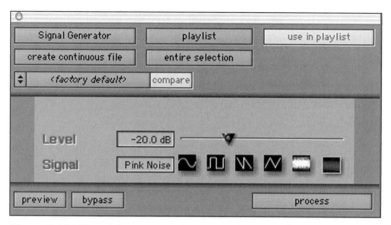

Figure 8.16 Signal Generator set up to create a pink noise signal at −20dBFS. Make this signal five to ten seconds long in order to loop it for continuous playback.

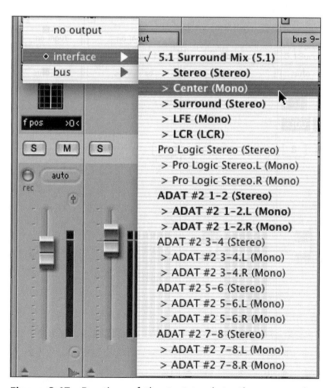

Figure 8.17 Routing of the test track to the center channel speaker only. Each speaker is tested independently.

Also, hold the meter at a slightly upward angle of roughly 45 degrees. Use this meter position to calibrate all the speakers. If possible, use a microphone stand to hold the SPL meter.

5. Using the SPL meter setup for C weighting and slow response (refer to Figure 8.15), adjust your monitor level until you get a reading of 85dBC (the C stands for C weighting of the meter).

6. Repeat this for both left and right speakers. All front three speakers are calibrated to the same level.

7. When calibrating the surround speakers, set the individual monitor volume to get a reading of 82dBC. With film mixing, this sets the surround speakers at a slightly lower volume. If you're holding the meter in your hand, turn your back 90 degrees towards the speaker you're calibrating so as to avoid obscuring the sound from it with your body. Aim the meter at the wall closest to the surround speaker you are calibrating.

8. LFE level adjustment is more complex. To properly calibrate the volume of the LFE channel, you must have a real-time analyzer. However, a simple SPL meter can work in a pinch. For film mixing, the LFE channel will play back 10dB louder than any of the front three speakers for the same input level. The reason for this is to give the LFE channel more headroom for low-frequency sounds such as explosions. Signals sent to the subwoofer should be band-limited from 25 to 120Hz. When using a simple SPL meter, it should read about 89dBC when feeding pink noise at an RMS level of −20dBFS. Due to the C weighting of the SPL meter and the limited bandwidth of the subwoofer, this level will not quite reach the 10dB increase specified. It is an approximation and can be more accurately determined with a real-time analyzer (RTA).

Adjusting Volume When calibrating reference levels for any speaker, the adjustments should be made so as not to affect the level of a Pro Tools output path directed to that speaker channel. Otherwise, if you make playback monitor calibration adjustments within Pro Tools, you will be calibrating the levels of your mix buss to your speakers and not your speakers to a reference acoustic SPL level, thereby throwing away the benefits of calibration: accurate reproduction of your mix on other calibrated playback systems. The level adjustment should be made outside of the mixing environment. Using the volume knobs on your power amps is a very effective way of adjusting the volume and also maintaining the highest degree of signal to noise ratio in the playback system.

TV and Home Theater Applications

When mixing material for television, each speaker, including the surrounds, is calibrated to a reference level of 79dBC. This is due to the lower average listening level used by consumers. Referencing at this lower level will provide a better dialogue mix for in-home viewing. The subwoofer should be calibrated 10dB higher, just the same as in theatrical mixing.

Surrounds in a Small Room   It should be noted that when you are mixing in a very small room where the surround speakers are less than six feet away, they should be turned down 2dB to compensate for their proximity to the mix position. This method has proven to be very effective when mixing on location in a remote truck where space is definitely limited.

Bass Management

Okay, this gets complicated. The reason you need a bass management system is because many consumer systems use five small satellite speakers combined with a subwoofer to supplement the low frequency response of the system *and* act as the LFE channel. The low frequency information that is directed to any of the five satellite speakers, but that cannot be reproduced by them, is redirected by the bass management system to the subwoofer. Because lower-frequency sounds are less directional, the spatial image does not suffer drastically.

The amount and crossover frequency at which this redirection of low-end occurs is fairly standard among consumer playback systems. Typically, the crossover frequency is 80Hz, meaning that frequencies below 80Hz in any channel will be diverted to the subwoofer.

Theatrical Sound Systems   Sound systems in movie theaters do not have or use bass management. The front three speakers are full range and can handle deep bass. The surround speakers are full range as well, but they typically are not as powerful. The subwoofer in theaters reproduces signals only from the LFE channel. No signals from any other channels will come through the subwoofer. Consumer systems use bass management for economic and aesthetic reasons, not sonic integrity. 5.1 Surround is best heard with five full-range speakers and a dedicated LFE subwoofer.

Bass management can also be used to enhance the performance of smaller speakers used in the studio. Many times, studios will purchase surround and sometimes center speakers that are smaller than the main left and right ones and thus are ill equipped to handle lower frequencies. This is usually due to budgetary considerations, as the cost of a full-range 5.1 surround speaker system can be formidable. Bass management can compensate for the low-frequency response of the smaller speakers by redirecting the low end to the subwoofer channel (not to be confused with the LFE channel). If you must use some smaller speakers in your system, make them the surrounds and try to keep the left, center, and right speakers matched in response and size.

In addition to this low-frequency content from the five satellite speakers, the subwoofer must also reproduce the signals for the LFE channel. For film mixing, the LFE channel must be regarded as a separate entity from the low-frequency content of the bass management redirection. Even though the subwoofer will reproduce these two signals, they must be treated independently as two discrete sources.

The way you treat the two signals as two separate sources is through the use of a bass management system while you are mixing. Waves offers the 360 degree Surround Toolkit, which, among many other tools, has a bass management plug-in that can be used on the master fader to assist in calibrating your system with bass management. There are other software and hardware solutions for bass management, but I will use the Waves plug-in as a common example.

As bass management is basically acting as a home-theater emulation system, it should be used as the last item in your signal path. Consider it a part of your speaker system. And, as you would never record the mix you create by miking the speakers, you must disable any bass management before you record your mix (or bounce to disk). Recording with bass management on will yield unpredictable results based solely on your mixing environment and not the real world.

Disable Bass Management when Printing Final Mixes! All bass management does is calibrate your speakers so that they react like a home theater system; it does not encode or decode any Dolby or other surround information. It should *not exist in the audio mix going to tape or disk, only in the room's monitor path.*

Calibration

Using the Waves M360 plug-in shown in Figure 8.18, I will outline how to calibrate the bass management system. It is similar to the calibration steps outlined earlier in this chapter, with certain exceptions. The plug-in has the ability to divide each channel into frequency bands and divert the low-frequency band to the subwoofer. The amount of signal that goes to the Sub channel can be varied independently for each channel. The crossover frequency and slope of the filter used to divide the signals are also adjustable. The LFE, or .1 channel of 5.1 surround mix, is dealt with separately from this bass management redirected signal. The result is that the subwoofer will act as the low-frequency driver for each speaker in the system, in addition to providing discrete LFE signals.

Here's how to calibrate the bass management system:

1. Set the crossover frequency to 80Hz. This is also the default setting. The default setting for the slope of this crossover filter is set to 24dB/octave for the subwoofer channel and 12dB/octave for all satellite channels, as shown in Figure 8.18. This setting should be fine for most situations. If your satellite speakers are particularly small, you might have to use a higher crossover frequency so that all of the low end that is missing from the satellites is present in the subwoofer. Experiment to find the best setting for your speakers.

2. Engage the high- and low-pass filters on every channel by clicking the All button, as shown in Figure 8.18.

3. Place a multi-mono instance of the Signal Generator plug-in on the surround master channel ahead of the Bass Management plug-in. Set it for pink noise at the reference level of −20dBFS. This will provide a continuous pink noise signal to all speaker channels.

4. Using the solo buttons on each satellite channel, proceed with the calibration setup as outlined earlier in this chapter. There are some additions and changes to the procedure that relate specifically to the subwoofer channel.

5. When you've calibrated the volume for all five of the satellite speakers to 85dBC, mute every one except the center channel, as shown in Figure 8.19.

Calibrate One Speaker at a Time   Remember that when you're calibrating, you should hear only one speaker at a time. If you hear more than one speaker, your meter reading will be inaccurate. The Waves plug-in provides convenient mute and solo switches to help in this process.

---

6. Solo the Sub channel, as shown in Figure 8.20. Make sure you don't accidentally solo the LFE channel instead.

Figure 8.18 The All button will engage all the high- and low-pass filters, thereby directing all low frequency energy to the subwoofer. For custom setups, individual channels can be filtered without affecting the others. This can be helpful when you have one pair of speakers that are full range and several others that require bass enhancement.

Remember, the Sub channel and the LFE channel are two distinct signals, even though they're both reproduced by the subwoofer speaker.

7. With only one satellite speaker unmuted, adjust the Send to Sub control, shown in Figure 8.20, to get a meter reading 6dB lower than its corresponding satellite channel (79dBC if using 85dBC as a reference). The 6dB difference is due to the fact that the Sub channel contains fewer frequency bands and is therefore not as loud.

8. Repeat this Sub channel calibration process for each satellite speaker.

9. Next, mute the Sub channel and all satellite channels.

Figure 8.19 Mute buttons are engaged on every satellite channel except the center.

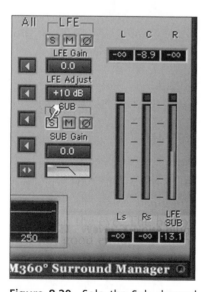

Figure 8.20 Solo the Sub channel, not the LFE channel above the Sub. With all but one satellite speaker muted, the Sub channel will contain only the low-end content from the unmuted satellite speaker. The Sub channel should be calibrated 6dB less than the satellite speaker. Usually this is 79dBC.

10. Solo the LFE channel and set LFE Adjust to +10dB. This adjusts the LFE channel for film mixing, which is 10dB louder than the other speakers.

11. Using the LFE Gain adjustment, shown in Figure 8.21, calibrate level to somewhere between 89 and 92dBC. Again, the SPL meter will not be as accurate as an RTA when calibrating just the low-frequency subwoofer. Some experimentation might be necessary.

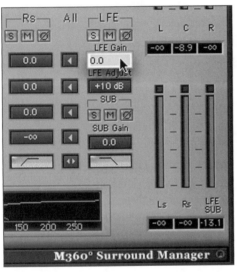

Figure 8.21 With the LFE adjust set to +10dB, use the LFE Gain adjustment to fine-tune the calibration for an SPL meter reading of somewhere between 89 and 92dBC. Make sure to use the Slow mode on the SPL meter, as it will swing back and forth when registering low-frequency signals. Use the middle point of the swing as your true reading.

12. Turn off the pink noise generator and unmute every channel. You should be ready to go.

Time Alignment

The Waves M360 plug-in is capable of meeting other calibration needs as well. In some studio situations it's not possible to have all speakers at the same distance from the mix position. In these cases, it will be necessary to use time delays to properly align the speakers so that sounds from different speakers will arrive at the listener at the same time. A common situation is having the center speaker forward from the left and right speakers due to soffit mounting of the main speakers, or perhaps placement of a viewing screen, as seen in Figure 8.22.

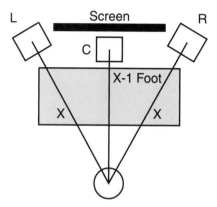

Figure 8.22   The center channel speaker is forward of the main left and right speakers, and therefore, sound from the center speaker will arrive earlier than sound from the left and right speakers.

The solution to this problem is to apply a small delay to the signal being sent to the center speaker so that sound from it arrives at the same time or "in phase" with sounds coming from other speakers. Use a tape measure to calculate the difference in distance between the two speakers. Knowing that sound travels at roughly one foot per millisecond, you can calculate the approximate delay needed to align the speakers.

Let's say the center channel speaker is one foot closer to the listener than any of the other speakers. This means that a delay of one millisecond is to be applied to the center channel in order to align it with the other speakers. The Waves M360 plug-in provides a delay adjustment for each speaker to accommodate this, as shown in Figure 8.23. In this example, the setting of one millisecond would correct the problem. This adjustment goes down to tenths of a millisecond for very precise adjustment of speaker alignment; this is necessary in order to maintain an accurate sound field in which to mix.

The M360 plug-in has several other parameters that work in conjunction with the Waves surround panners and imagers used on individual channels. These parameters can control the imaging of sounds within the surround field. Suffice to say, many interesting effects can be achieved through the use of these parameters, but they are beyond the scope of this book. Refer to the Waves literature for more details.

ANSI/SMPTE 202M X-Curve   In large theater-size mixing rooms or dub stages—those larger than 5,300 cubic feet—an EQ curve is applied to the speakers to compensate for the sound's interaction with the room itself. In smaller mixing rooms (less than 5,300 cubic feet) where material is mixed that will be played back in larger rooms such as movie theaters, a modified X-Curve 222M is applied to help mixes translate well to these larger spaces. The application of room EQ in this manner is complex, and opinions vary among acousticians as to the best methods. More information is available at www.dolby.com. I would advise consulting with an acoustician when setting up a mix room for film, TV, or DVD mixing.

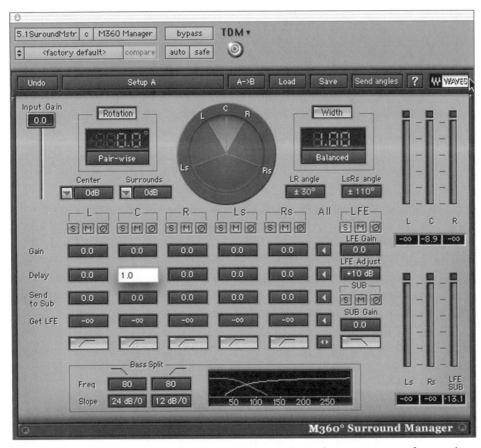

Figure 8.23 The channel delay adjustment in M360 is used to compensate for speakers that are not physically aligned properly. Here, the center channel has been delayed by one millisecond to compensate for the position shown in Figure 8.22, which is one foot closer than the other speakers.

Film-Style Mixing Workflow

Film-style mixing is such a complex and involved subject that it deserves an entire book unto itself. With track counts as high as 450 channels at mixdown, understanding the workflow of a project of this magnitude can help you plan and execute smaller projects and even integrate your work into larger projects.

How Many Tracks?   The film *Black Hawk Down* was reported to have used 450 tracks during the final dub, maxing out the Euphonix System 5 console on which it was being mixed. Now that's a big mix!

The Lord of the Rings: Fellowship of the Ring used 13 effects pre-mixes, three ambience pre-mixes, three foley pre-mixes, plus dialogue pre-mixes. This does not include all the individual channels. Pre-mixes could be in LCR stereo up to 5.1 surround. That's easily over 100 channels of pre-mixes alone!

Swordfish effects editor Joe Milner explains, "For example, as an editor, my 90 or so gun tracks on *Swordfish* were condensed into Travolta's gunshots, bad guys' gunshots, gun mechanisms, bullet metal hits, glass hits, and bullet-bys."

From Edit to Print Master

In a large, feature-film production, the original recordings go through the editorial process, where they are sliced and diced and placed in their proper positions in sync with picture. Each element in the soundtrack—dialogue, foley, ambiance, effects, and music—is considered a sound "unit." These units are brought to the dub stage in the form of Pro Tools sessions, Tascam DA-88s or MMR-8 multi-track recorders, or other forms of multi-track audio. Today, Pro Tools is the choice for source material on the dub stage, as it allows immediate editorial changes to take place at the discretion of the director or producer.

The re-recording mixers audition this material and determine if any pre-mixes are necessary to correct any problems in the recordings. Pre-mixes might also be necessary to consolidate tracks due to limitations of the film mixing console. With over a hundred available inputs on a film mixing console, the task of figuring out what tracks to combine and what tracks to leave separate in a pre-mix can take some time.

Once any pre-mixing has been completed, it is time for the final dub. This is the stage where all final creative mixing decisions occur. Any type of processing—whether EQ, dynamics, reverb, or other effects—will be applied at this time. Sounds will be panned in accordance with the picture. The routing of different sounds to different speaker channels takes place as well. For instance, 99 percent of the time, dialogue is routed solely to the center channel. Reverb and other effects applied to the dialogue might find their way into the left and right or even surround speakers. Matching every subtle element to the screen takes an experienced and artistic ear.

Once the mixing process is completed, all the individual tracks and pre-dubs are routed to individual multi-track machines that will record mix stems. The term "stem" is shortened slang for *STEreo Master*. A stem is created for each facet of the sound track:

dialogue, foley, ambience, effects, and music. With the advent of surround sound, the stems are no longer just stereo but 5.1 surround.

Typically, four 8-track recorders are used to capture the stems. Each stem can have a combination of the surround channels, individual channels for principle character dialog, and three-track stereo (LCR) for source music and foley. Figure 8.24 shows the process in a graphic manner. It can be likened to a funneling down of many tracks into more and more subgroups until final print masters are made.

Pro Tools now has an option to run in "crash" record mode to act like a stem recorder. In this mode, Pro Tools becomes a destructive recorder just like a tape machine. Re-recording mix engineers will often punch in to stem recorders to fix a section of the mix without having to print the entire length of a film. This saves time and money on the dub stage.

Usually, an additional Pro Tools system will be used as a dedicated stem recorder. That system will be set to 9-pin remote mode so that the re-recording mix engineer can punch into the stem tracks remotely from a console or a PEC-Direct paddle controller used in traditional film mixing. Visit http://www.colinbroad.com/html/pd1.html for an example of a modern PEC/Direct panel system. Think of a PEC/Direct controller as a multi-track tape machine remote control with record-enable and input monitoring functionality, just like you use multi-tracking and overdubbing in a music session with an analog tape machine.

Film-Style Mixing Isn't Just for Films Anymore: The TV Series *24* This type of mixing is not exclusively for film productions. The TV series *24* uses a film-style mix setup when dubbing the show at Enterprise Post in Burbank, California. The dub takes a day and half to complete. Emmy-nominated re-recording engineers Mike Olman and Ken Cobett handle the duties on a Neve Capricorn digital mixer with 202 channels. The sources are primarily from Pro Tools systems. With 111 source channels at final mix, they have their hands full. With Mike handling dialogue and music and Ken handling the effects mix, they print stems to four Tascam MMR-8 digital hard disk recorders. On Day 2, the producers come in and make notes for changes. The changes are made to the different stems, and then the Neve is reconfigured for compositing stems to the final print masters.

Pre-Mixes or Pre-Dubs

When you finally sit down to mix your project, you might find that there are so many tracks of different audio parts that the task of blending them all together at once seems impossible. All the audio tracks used in a film production could easily exceed the

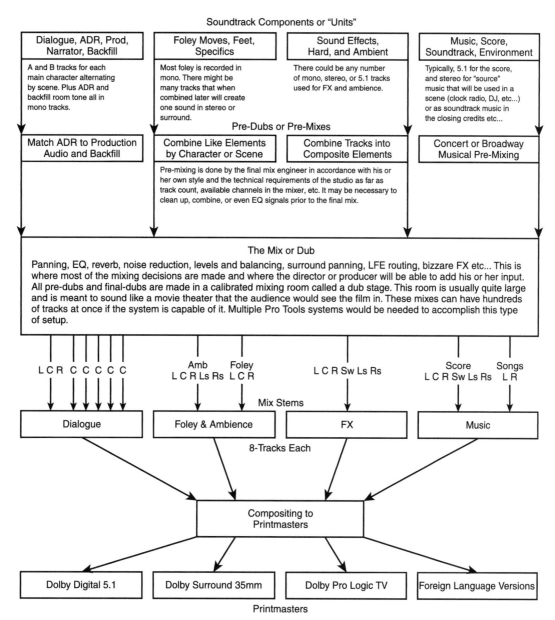

Figure 8.24   A workflow diagram of the film mixing process as it is done today. It can start with hundreds of tracks that are condensed and funneled down to 32 tracks of stems and finally to print masters for each release format. The stem process facilitates alterations such as foreign language versions with little difficulty.

200-track mark. With a track limit of 256, several systems might have to be linked together to provide complete playback of all source audio tracks. In fact, most feature film dub stages have several Pro Tools systems connected to the mixing console. It is common to have one complete system for each sound unit (dialogue, effects, and music). There might be additional systems available on the stage for editors to make last minute changes during the mix.

Due to the large size and complexity of post-production audio recordings, the technique of submixing related tracks together prior to a final mixdown is used to help simplify this daunting task. These submixes are called pre-dubs or pre-mixes.

Large film productions have several sound teams that work on different aspects of the film's soundtrack. Each team might generate one or more pre-mixes of their work that a mix engineer can use on the dub stage to create the final master or "dub" for the film. Often, mixers will prefer to have each individual track dry and without volume automation in order to combine and EQ them to their liking. This is especially true with dialogue tracks. Matching the ADR dialogue with production audio can be more accurately done on the dub stage with a calibrated monitor system, in the environment in which it will be heard by an audience. EQ-ing dialogue, or any other sound, in a small editing suite that might have substandard monitoring and lots of environmental noise is probably not a good idea.

Find out ahead of time what is expected of you as it relates to the overall sound production. If you are doing the entire sound editing and mixing job yourself, you can make up your own rules. If the mixers are expecting dry, unprocessed tracks and you provide entirely pre-mixed material without any options, you might not work there again. If you are mixing in a limited environment with only so many channels available, and the editors provide 500 tracks for you to mix in two days, you might not appreciate it. Again, communication between all members of the production staff is the key to getting any project to completion. The responsibilities and job descriptions of editors and mixers are hotly debated topics among post-production professionals, and each situation will be different.

Typically, multiple pre-mixes will be created for each facet, or unit, of the sound production. Dialogue, foley, sound effects, and music will each have its own set of pre-mixes. In addition to each pre-mix, certain key elements will be transferred to the final mix stage outside of the pre-mix, allowing for more detailed manipulation during the final mixdown. Principal characters' dialogue would be an example of tracks that you would want to keep separate and not mixed into a pre-dub.

From a music recording perspective, think of pre-dubs as preparing multi-track recordings for the final mix. This would include compiling multiple vocal takes into a final lead vocal, blending background vocals together, editing noises from guitar tracks, eliminating extraneous tracks that will not be included in the mix, and so on. This process minimizes the number of tracks at the mix. As you can imagine, doing this to a feature film's dialogue tracks can make a huge difference in the number of physical tracks present at mixdown.

The Dub Stage   The *dub stage* is a studio that is basically built into a movie theater, such as Enterprise Post's Stage A, shown in Figure 8.25. This mixing room has the same basic acoustic characteristics as a typical movie theater. This way, a mixer can hear what the movie will sound like when it is played for an audience. Dub stages have very accurately calibrated monitor systems that allow total control of the mix. Although it is possible to mix a film in a small room, it's always preferable to mix film in a theater-like setting.

Figure 8.25 Enterprise Post's Stage A. Centered around a Neve Capricorn digital console with 202 inputs, the studio is connected to a machine room that has several Pro Tools systems and MMR-8 digital dubbers. This is a top-tier dub stage. The TV series *24* is mixed here, using 111 channels at mixdown.

Mixing Dialogue

Mixing dialogue that sounds natural and intelligible and maintains enough dynamics to convey the emotion of the performance is a challenging task. Often, one of these aspects is in direct opposition to the other. For example, to make dialogue more intelligible, compression is often used to increase the volume of quiet passages. This works directly against the principle of retaining dynamics within dialogue that convey the emotion of the scene, as compression is designed to remove dynamics. Many times, the dialogue has to fight through a bevy of sound effects, music, and even explosions, while still sounding natural and clear. Making sure it does is what dialogue mixing is all about. With experience, you will be able to reduce the dynamic range of dialogue tracks to maintain clarity without losing the emotional impact. Sometimes the only way to do this is to minimize the impact of the other sounds around the dialogue—turn the effects and music down! Everything is driven by the script.

Pre-Dub versus Final Mix

The task when creating a dialogue pre-mix is to keep everything very natural so as to not limit your options during the final mixdown. You also might be creating this pre-mix for another engineer to use during the final dub, in which case keeping the dialogue as natural as possible is very important. He should be able to turn up the dialogue tracks and hear every line, every nuance of the dialogue in a smooth, even, and yet dynamic mix. If you are preparing pre-dubs for a mix engineer, each character might have his own track, with additional tracks for supporting characters. Even within one character's dialogue there might be separate tracks for ADR takes and production audio. Dialogue pre-mixes need to have as much flexibility as possible. Don't forget the background fill and ambience.

When creating a final mix, levels should be balanced between different characters and lines that correspond to the camera angles used during a scene. It should all make sense to the viewer. If, in one angle, a character is on the other side of the room saying his line, the sound should be slightly lower and perhaps more distant, with reverb perhaps. If the camera angle changes to a shot that is much closer to this character, even in the middle of a line, the sound should change to reflect the new camera angle: louder, more intimate, and with less reverb than before. This should happen on the exact frame that the camera angle changes. Automation is a real help when it comes to this type of task. Automation will be covered later in this chapter.

Another common technique for altering dialogue tracks by camera angle is the use of *checkerboarding*. Checkerboarding requires two dialogue submix channels. Let's call them A and B. As camera angles change, the character's dialogue will jump from

Track A to Track B. Both the A and B channels have entirely separate processing chains of equalizers, compressors, reverb, and so on. One dialogue chain can be set up for sound that correlates to a certain camera angle, and the other dialogue chain can be set up for another camera angle. In this way, jumping back and forth between these two dialogue chains makes the sonic transition from one camera angle to another. The name *checkerboarding* comes from the way cue sheets used to be drawn, with the alternating sound files on each track. Figure 8.26 shows what checkerboarding looks like in Pro Tools.

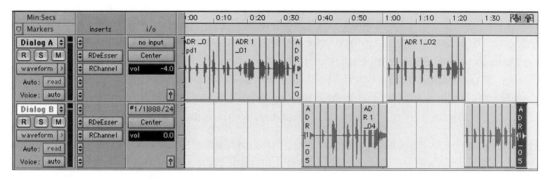

Figure 8.26 Checkerboarding in Pro Tools. One character's dialogue uses two channels with distinct processing chains in order to assist in making transitions between camera angles.

Off-Camera Boom Track   Checkerboarding dialogue to match camera angle changes brings up the case for recording an off-camera boom microphone. When the situation allows, have the production sound mixer record a second boom microphone that is facing away or is more distant from the subject. This recording can be used for a very natural off-camera sound during editing without the need for fancy reverb processing in the mix.

ADR

When mixing ADR tracks with the production audio tracks, it will be necessary to maintain the same background ambience heard on the original tracks. Hopefully, the production sound mixer has recorded for each scene long stretches of ambience, or "room tone," that you can use as filler underneath the ADR tracks in order to make them sound more natural and sonically related to the scenes. ADR room tone should appear on a separate track in a dialogue pre-dub. This allows your engineer to tweak the ADR line without affecting the background ambience.

If you do not use the same microphone when recording the ADR tracks as was used during filming, you'll most likely have to apply a certain amount of EQ to match the

ADR track's timbre to the original. You might have to add reverb as well to match the space you see on-screen. Once completed, the ADR tracks should blend seamlessly with the original production audio so as not to draw attention to themselves. The background ambience should be consistent throughout the scene without any abrupt changes in level or tone.

Animation

As animation dialogue is always recorded entirely in the studio, it will need more treatment than usual to make it sound like it fits within the scene. Reverb will typically be needed in order to make a dry dialogue track sound like it was recorded in a room or at a certain location. Any change in an animated camera angle might result in the apparent change of its related audio track. As the dialogue is always read straight into a microphone, making it sound as if a character has turned around, walked away, or is sitting across the room will require some EQ and other processing.

There is a scene in *Monsters, Inc.* in which the character Sully is standing in an empty closet in his bedroom trying to explain to the small child, Boo, why there are no monsters in the closet. When he walks forward out of the closet towards the bed, you can hear a change in the quality of his voice that really makes you believe he's actually moving from the closet into the room. The reality is that John Goodman recorded all those lines in a very neutral-sounding recording studio, standing in front of a microphone. The techniques used to achieve that subtle effect are what make great dialogue mixing a true art form. Listen to that scene, and try to notice the acoustic clues that lead you to believe he is actually in the room. Then try to figure out what techniques you might use to create that same effect.

How Loud?

How loud dialogue is in a film or TV show is a very subjective thing. A good rule of thumb is to make sure that the average level of dialogue that occurs during normal conversation is registering somewhere between −27dBFS and −22dBFS using a VU- or RMS-calibrated meter. This is equivalent to 78dBC to 83dBC on an SPL meter. This will leave plenty of headroom for "shouting matches" and explosive car chases that will exceed the reference and will keep the signal-to-noise ratio acceptable. Again, this is only the average level of the dialogue. Certain scenes and lines will register much louder and much softer in the course of a dynamic production. Also, don't be afraid to have passages of dialogue that are *much* quieter than the reference level. It all depends on what the scene calls for. It is, after all, drama. What you hear in a calibrated mixing room should correlate to what you see.

Any critical adjustment of each EQ or ambience should be done in the same studio environment in which the final mixdown will occur, or at least in a calibrated, high-quality mixing room. Many re-recording mix engineers prefer to have all dialogue tracks delivered raw and unprocessed. This gives them the most flexibility during the final mixdown. If you are performing all of the editing and mixing duties yourself, processing dialogue in a pre-mix or pre-dub session can save lots of time in the final mix. Be careful not to paint yourself into a corner by limiting your ability to make changes in the final mix. The director might want to make changes to elements that you have already pre-mixed. In this case, you will have to return to the original tracks to address this issue. Try to anticipate items that might change in the final mix and leave those isolated on their own tracks.

Mixing Foley

Foley tracks are tied to the screen. Even though most foley sounds will remain in the center channel, pre-mixes destined for a 5.1 mix should be made in 5.1 surround or at least in LCR format. You might have a separate pre-mix for moves, footsteps, and specifics in order to allow more control in the final dub.

The better the foley sounds and mixing are, the less they will be noticed, adding to the feel and vibe of the scene. Foley sounds should make the audience believe they're actually watching the scene unfolding before their eyes. It should help to suspend disbelief, allowing the audience to feel as if they are actually there. Crazy panning moves (footsteps coming from behind and panning across to the front, for example) can distract from the visual and should be used only when they serve the story.

Although most foley sounds will be confined to the front three speakers, effects applied to them to create ambience and space, such as reverb, can find their way into the surround speakers as well. Someone walking through a large space such as a train station would create reverb that could envelop the listener using the surround channels if this was the desired effect. The bottom line is that most foley sounds are heard only in the center channel, along with the dialogue. Only when things get very specific or the script calls for something out of the ordinary do foley sounds start to move around the speaker array.

Monsters, Inc. **Foley Track**   This movie contains a fabulous example of top-notch foley recording available on the DVD release. Under the options, there is a choice to listen to the 5.1 sound effects and foley track by itself without any music or dialogue. This is a fascinating exercise in perceiving the subtleties involved in creating a truly impressive foley track, and well worth a listen.

Mixing Effects

Effects offer the greatest opportunity for creative panning in surround. As is typical of sci-fi movies these days, sound effects such as fly-bys, robots, lasers, and spaceships provide an opportunity for the sound designer to use the full palette of surround speakers to create enveloping and surreal soundscapes.

When used for dramatic effect, the surround channels can provide an unprecedented degree of envelopment when panning an object from behind the listener across the sound field to the front. This type of hard panning, however, should be used in moderation because overuse can become distracting and often exhausting for the listener. Audiences typically prefer a natural sound field most of the time. If dramatic surround panning is over-used, its dramatic effect will be lessened and won't work as well when you truly need it to.

Hard Effects

Hard effects, such car crashes, airplanes, explosions, and other singular sound events, benefit from a 5.1 surround mix. As they are not occurring all the time, they can take advantage of the added dramatic effect of the surround channels.

Effects that have a large low-frequency content can be directed to the LFE channel to enhance their impact. For example, an explosion can have its low-frequency content directed to the subwoofer, where it will certainly be felt by the audience as well as heard. As the LFE channel in a theater (and in your mix room) is calibrated +10dBC higher than the others channels, sounds in the LFE channel have a large amount of headroom *relative* to the other channels. Using the available headroom will not affect the other channels in the system. This allows for a greater "punch" factor when sounds are directed to the LFE channel.

Ambience

Ambience elements, such as crickets, wind noise, rain, *walla* (background crowd noises, mumbling, and so on), traffic noises, and so on can take full advantage of the surround speakers. The subtlety of ambient sounds allows them to be used in surround speakers more often because they are not distracting and merely provide a sense of envelopment to the mix. Most ambient pre-dubs are 5.0, as they do not usually require the LFE channel.

Mixing Music

Music comes in several forms within a film or video production. Depending on its use, it can be mixed in a variety of ways. Sometimes music will transition from one form to another. For example, many times a soundtrack song will start off as an environmental sound within the scene, such as a jukebox or clock radio. Then, as the scene progresses, the music morphs into a full-blown soundtrack piece that is no longer a part of the scene and is mixed at full volume stereo, becoming the focus of the soundtrack. The transition from environmental to soundtrack can be a tricky one.

The Score

The score typically is mixed in one environment and does not transition. Usually, the score will be mixed to the left and right speakers in stereo. Sometimes composers will provide a 5.1 surround mix of their music that has certain elements or ambience directed to the surround speakers in order to create a more enveloped musical texture. The line between score and sound design is blurred everyday with music that also adds sonic textures that could be considered music or sound effects. This type of score might take advantage of the surround speakers more than a traditional orchestral score.

The score's level may need to be automated so that when other elements that have priority are present, the score does not overshadow them. Conversely, when the emotional impact of the piece is served best by the score, its level might need to be raised to heighten that impact. Most composers will compose their music to function this way by design. When mixing, you might have to augment this design with subtle amounts of automation and fader moves.

The composer might also deliver musical stems of the score for use in the final mix. These stems might break the score down into percussive elements, ambient sounds, melody, and background instruments. These stems could make up the pre-dub for the score, allowing you to combine them during the final mix to blend all the other elements together. Perhaps during one scene, the melody needs to be muted for a section to allow a particular dialogue line to be heard more clearly or to accentuate the emotional moment.

Environmental, or Source, Music

Environmental music will always require processing in order to make it sound as if it is within the filmed scene. Typically, this requires band-passed filtering of a full-fidelity mix to mimic the response of a small speaker system such as a car radio or boom box. Additionally, panning, reverb, and a short delay might need to be added to position that sound within the space of the scene.

For instance, a live rock band playing inside a large club will require some amount of slap back echo and reverb to make an audience believe that the music is being played inside a large room and over a large P. A. system. A typical studio recording of music is far too pristine to be believable in this context. Also, when the camera is not showing the stage and band, the music should correspondingly be lowered and set to a more ambient sound. If a character goes to the restroom, usually the band can still be heard through the walls. Obviously, the sound would change drastically. Checker-boarding of the music might be needed in the context of this type of scene in order to facilitate camera angle and scene changes.

When small radios, car stereos, or even walkman-style personal music players are used within a scene, the sound coming from them will most likely need to be panned in order to follow the device on-screen. Usually, a mono source is preferable in these situations.

Most source music will be separated in the mix and on the music stem in case of last-minute changes due to artistic decisions or publishing rights problems. If a song needs to be replaced—even after the mix is completed—you can return to the stems and just replace that one song without much trouble. This is one example of how punching into stem recorders can save a huge amount of time and money. The entire mix does not have to be recalled in order to change this one song. Punching the song into the stem recordings and then recombining the stems into print masters takes a fraction of the time that a total recall would need.

Soundtrack Songs

Soundtrack songs should be heard in their full studio quality sound without any alter-ation of EQ, dynamics, or ambience. The classic example of this is the music used in the closing credits of a film. The only adjustment that should be made in this case is level. Dialogue and other sounds might be present while a soundtrack song is playing, requir-ing adjustment. Those sounds still need to be heard above the song. It's all a judgment call by the mixer.

LFE Channel

The LFE channel is a powerful tool in the surround mixer's palette. Due to its +10dB calibration, a large amount of headroom is available for very dynamic and high-energy, low-frequency sounds. Most often this channel is used for hard effects such as airplanes, explosions, car crashes, earthquakes, space ships, and other such massive sounds. Typ-ically, dialogue, ambience, and music will not be routed to the LFE channel.

Keep in mind that when downmixing a 5.1 surround mix to either Dolby Surround (Pro Logic) or stereo, the LFE channel is optional and is discarded by the automatic downmixers in DVD players. This means that on certain systems, signals sent to the LFE channel will not be heard during playback when downmixing to other formats. Any "story vital" element sent to the LFE channel should be duplicated in one or more of the other speakers. This way, the essential aspects of the sounds will still be heard when downmixing, resulting in a pleasing mix. It is always advisable to preview downmixes in order to make any adjustments necessary. You may even manually create your own downmix and choose whether or not to include the LFE channel and to what degree.

Using Automation While Mixing

Automation is the most powerful feature for mixing in Pro Tools. It allows one operator to act as four or five in a traditional film-mixing situation. With this powerful set of automation tools, you can handle any number of tracks that are before you. Doing it yourself might take more time than having four or five operators on a gigantic mixing board, but automation allows you to accomplish what would otherwise be impossible.

In addition to being able to adjust levels of so many tracks, you can do more interesting things such as automate equalizers to compensate for mic positioning in a scene. Automating sends provides reverb and ambiance dynamically as the scene changes.

Levels

Writing levels or automating the faders is the simplest form of automation and is the most widely used. Pro Tools offers several modes with which to write fader automation. These modes determine how the fader functions when writing automation. Following is a list of modes and how they operate:

- **Write mode.** In this mode, the fader will record its current position as automation data. As you change the fader position, those changes are recorded exactly as you perform them into the automation playlist of the track. This mode is useful when you want to override complex automation completely. Automation is written whether you are touching the fader with a mouse or not. When you set a channel to the Write mode, as shown in Figure 8.27, it will stay in Write mode the entire time you are playing the session. Once you have stopped, any channels that are in Write mode will automatically change to Touch mode in order to prevent accidental erasure of automation data.

- **Touch mode.** Works just like Write mode except that you are writing automation data only when you are clicking and holding a fader or touching a fader on a control surface.

- **Latch mode.** Similar to Touch mode except that once you have touched or clicked on the fader, you will continue to write automation data until the transport is stopped.

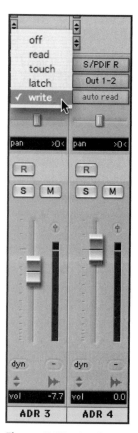

Figure 8.27 Setting a track to Write mode using the Automation pull-down menu.

- **Read mode.** Works just like the name says. No automation is written during Read mode, no matter what you do. The automated parameters will "play back" the moves you have already encoded.

- **Trim mode.** Available only on TDM systems. In this mode, the fader will remain stationary even if the volume automation data is fluctuating. The reason for this is that Trim mode enables you to either add or subtract gain to the automation data already present on that track. When in Trim mode, the volume indicators in both the Edit and Mix windows will show the amount of gain you are adding or subtracting (the *delta* value), while displaying a triangle to the left of the gain indicator, as shown in Figure 8.28. Trim mode can be useful for adjusting the *balance* of the mix without affecting the *fader moves* that correlate with the action on-screen. Being able to subtly adjust the balance of things without affecting quick fader moves that have been programmed is a great benefit.

Figure 8.28 The Trim mode's gain adjustment indicator, a triangle next to the dB reading in the edit window.

- **Off mode.** Off mode means no automation is played back or written, and all parameters remain static. No automation data is lost.

Automating Panning

Unlike music mixing, where most instruments remain static in their panned positions, film and video post-production involve a great deal more dynamic panning with motion left to right or back to front. This is especially true of surround-sound mixing where there are so many different angles and positions for panning. Panning can be automated as well. Make sure that the Pan parameter is write-enabled in the Automation window, as shown in Figure 8.29. Stereo and surround panners can both be automated.

Figure 8.29 The Automation window. Here you can determine what parameters will record automation data. This can be helpful when you want to automate fader and pan moves but still be able to adjust aux sends without writing automation data for them. You may also suspend all automation here as well. In this figure, only the Volume and Pan parameters are enabled.

Automating EQs

Automation of EQs can help you accomplish several tasks while mixing for video or film. In sessions that exceed the possible track count for your system, automating EQs can allow you to have different sounds contained on one track.

For instance, you could have a certain character's dialogue on Track 1 in one scene and then on that same track have another character's dialogue in a later scene. Using automation, you can change the parameters of the equalizer to match the character in each scene. You might have an equalizer preset for the first character that you use whenever he is on-screen and another preset for the second character. So long as those two characters are never in a scene together, this technique will work, thereby freeing up other tracks.

You could automate a single band of an equalizer to compensate for mic placement that changes within a scene in order to even out the response. Using a hi-shelving EQ, you could raise its gain as a character turns away from a microphone in order to compensate for the dissipating high frequencies.

Heavy "s" sounds, called sibilants, can be controlled by automating a narrow high-frequency band centered around the sibilant frequency, dipping when the sibilants are too strong and returning to normal when they aren't. Another example of this would be using a high-pass filter to eliminate microphone pops by momentarily engaging the filter when the pop occurs and then turning it off for normal speech. These are very surgical types of uses for automated equalizers.

Following is a step-by-step example of how to use an equalizer (Waves Renaissance EQ2) to compensate for a mic pop.

1. Instantiate the Waves EQ on the track in question.

2. Set up the first band as a high-pass filter, as shown in Figure 8.30. Play the affected dialogue part and adjust the frequency until the pop sound is minimized. (By "pop" sound, I'm referring to the sound made when wind from the person speaking catches the mic, and a bad low-frequency "boom" occurs. Bumping the mic can also cause this type of sound.)

3. Press the Auto button in the upper-right side of the plug-in window to open the automation parameter-enabling window.

4. Select Band 1 On/Off and press the Add button. This allows that parameter to be automated by Pro Tools. Click OK.

5. With the plug-in window still open, place the track in Auto-Touch mode.

6. Press the Band Enable switch to disable the band while the transport is stopped.

7. Play a few seconds before the problem spot and get the mouse positioned over the EQ's Band1 In/Out button, as shown in Figure 8.31. Right before the pop occurs, press the Enable switch to engage the high-pass filter.

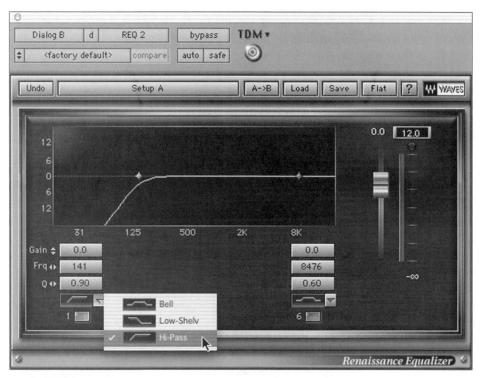

Figure 8.30   Setting up a high-pass filter in Renaissance EQ2.

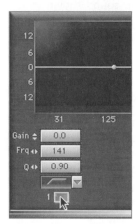

Figure 8.31   The mouse is placed over the Band1 Enable switch in preparation for automating this parameter.

8.   After the pop has passed, disable the band to return to normal. You might have to choose a moment when no dialogue is present to engage the filter, as turning it on might produce a slight click or pop itself.

9. It is possible to edit this automation by choosing the Band1 In/Out parameter in the Track view pull-down menu, as seen in Figure 8.32.

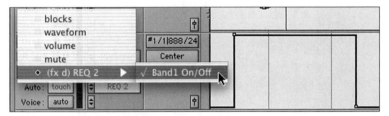

Figure 8.32 The Track view pull-down menu. This menu allows you to choose what type of data you will see on that track. In this case, we are selecting the Renaissance EQ2's Band1 In/Out parameter.

10. You can drag the automation points to change the time when the band is engaged and disengaged, as shown in Figure 8.33.

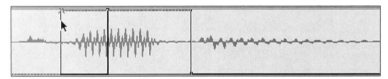

Figure 8.33 Dragging the automation points to help fix an improperly executed automation move. Here, the Band1 enable is being moved so that it occurs prior to the pop sound shown in the waveform.

Building Dynamics

Building dynamics in a mix is an art form. There is no way for me to explain how to artistically create a compelling mix for a film, video, or commercial. Time, experience, and the study of other people's mixes are the only teachers of this subject.

That being said, use your reference level as a clue to where you sit dynamically in a mix. If you are building a scene up to a climactic point, notice what your average VU meter reading is as you build to the climax. Once you've reached this climax and need to return to normal, the VU meter can help guide you back to normal level. Conversely, you will find that the average levels of sensitive and intimate moments drop well below the −20dBFS point.

Always using a calibrated volume setting in your studio can help you control dynamic fluctuations in the mix. If you're constantly adjusting the volume while you listen, it will be harder to tell how the dynamics are working within your mix.

Obviously, you do need to check your material at different volumes to see how it plays if it is intended for home or television broadcast. But always have a reference point to return to.

Using a favorite movie or program to use as a reference can be extremely helpful. Checking your mix against others is one of the most challenging tests you could impose on your work. Music engineers have known this for years and constantly use reference CDs to improve their own mixes. When referencing another mix, make sure that the volume of your reference mix is set up properly. If it is too loud, psychoacoustic principles at work will tend to make you perceive it as being "better." Level matching will give you a more accurate comparison between two different mixes. A calibrated mixing volume should make this much easier.

Be aware that if you are using a commercially released DVD as a reference for a theatrical film release, you might find the calibrated mixing volume you are using will make the DVD mix seem much louder. This can be due to the remastering of film mixes for the DVD release. Because home viewing should use a calibrated level of 78dBC instead of 85dBC, the resulting mixes from a DVD played back at 85dBC can be considerably louder. Adjusting the level of the DVD down by 7dB (85–78) as a starting point can help eliminate this issue.

Try recording your mix once it has been broadcast over TV, satellite, or cable systems and compare it to the original mix in the studio. You will be able to clearly hear the effects of the broadcast signal processing. This might not help you with that particular mix, but you will learn things that you can use in the future to improve your mixing for broadcast media.

Control Surfaces

When working on a complex film or video post-production mix, the number of tracks and controls that need to be accessed can become daunting. Tactile control surfaces provide a method for accessing more parameters of a mix than the mouse and keyboard will allow by themselves. Digidesign offers several control surfaces for use with Pro Tools.

The Digidesign Command 8, shown in Figure 8.34, is the smallest addition to the Pro Tools control surface family. This control surface can operate Pro Tools parameters such as faders, aux sends, pans, and even plug-in settings through the use of knobs and faders instead of the mouse.

The C 24, shown in Figure 8.35, is the next level up in control surfaces designed for Pro Tools. This work surface has 24 moving faders, along with a slew of parameter knobs,

Figure 8.34 The Digidesign Command 8 functions as both a control surface and a control room monitor system with external inputs.

Figure 8.35 The C 24 provides many faders, rotary encoders, and function keys dedicated to the operation of Pro Tools.

Figure 8.36 Digidesign's flagship control surface, the ICON D-Control ES. This unit is expandable, with additional fader packs, surround sound modules, and other functions.

transport controls, and many function keys that provide dedicated controls for many Pro Tools operations. This larger control surface gives the user a better look at more channels at once.

The ICON D-Control ES, pictured in Figure 8.36, is Digidesign's flagship control surface. It is expandable and can accommodate up to 80 individual channel strips, along with surround sound panners, function keys, a control room monitor section for surround monitoring, and a host of other features that can speed up the operation of Pro Tools in a complex post-production environment.

Many third-party control surfaces exist that can also control Pro Tools, including the popular Mackie Control Universal.

Many popular digital mixers that feature motorized faders have also implemented control-surface functionality into their hardware. The Yamaha 01V96 comes standard with a template for controlling Pro Tools. This can be a popular option for studios wanting to expand their mixing and routing functionality while adding A to D and D to A converters *and* a control surface in one box. The internal EQ, dynamics, and effects processors of the dedicated digital mixer can augment the functionality of the Pro Tools system and provide a control surface at the same time. In a complex surround sound film mix, these features will be very useful.

TDM and RTAS Plug-In Delay Compensation

The DSP algorithms used in both TDM and RTAS plug-in architectures require a certain amount of time to process. Every time an audio signal is processed by a plug-in or routed through additional mixer channels (such as internal busses, aux tracks, and master faders), the audio itself will be delayed by the amount of time it takes to process the plug-in or routing pathway before it can arrive at the output converter and be heard. The delay caused by DSP processing of any kind creates latency and will affect the playback of audio by delaying each audio signal by a differing amount, depending on the amount and type of processing being applied to it. The problem arises when all audio signals are combined to create a final mix. The combination of the various delays imposed on each signal will wreak havoc on phase relationships between signals and even audible timing in extreme cases. Pro Tools HD systems have the ability to compensate for this latency automatically. LE systems are not capable of this and must be manually adjusted to compensate for processing delays.

In its subtler form, plug-in latency will affect tracks that are related acoustically, such as the different mics used to record one orchestra. If two mics are used to record an orchestra and a TDM or RTAS plug-in is applied to one of those mics during mixdown, the audio channel processed by the plug-in will be delayed by a small amount, thereby affecting the time relationship between those two microphones. This time relationship, in a recording of this nature, is critical. Even a few samples of latency can cause a dramatic shift in the stereo image generated by those two microphones. This latency should be compensated for in some manner. The simplest way is to apply the same plug-in to the unprocessed channel. This plug-in can have all its parameters set in such fashion that it will not affect that channel in any way besides generating the equivalent latency of the other channel, maintaining a proper phase relationship between the two.

Delay Compensation for Pro Tools LE Systems

In extreme cases, plug-in latencies of several thousand samples can grossly affect the timing of such things as dialogue and foley tracks. The most common occurrence of this is when using noise reduction plug-ins that require very long DSP cycles to accomplish. A good example is the Waves plug-in, X-Noise.

X-Noise generates 5120 samples of latency when used as an RTAS plug-in. This latency is enough to throw off lip-sync. Because this plug-in is used to remove environmental noise from production audio, dialogue will be affected the most. The latency in this situation does not affect the relationship between two audio tracks but rather the relationship between the audio and video. Because there is no way to apply an equivalent plug-in to the video track, another method must be used to compensate for this latency.

The following steps outline a method that utilizes track slipping and alternate playlists to compensate for any amount of plug-in latency in Pro Tools LE.

1.   In order to compensate for plug-in latency, it is first necessary to determine the amount of latency that is present. Pro Tools LE offers a very simple way to find out what the cumulative delay is for all processing that occurs on one track. If several plug-ins are applied to one track, the latency generated by each plug-in will add to the total latency of that track. Pro Tools has a display mode that shows the total latency in samples for all processing on each track. Command-click on the volume indicators in the Mix or Edit window as shown in Figures 8.37 and 8.38.

Figure 8.37 The volume indicator in the Edit window. Command-clicking here will cycle you from volume to peak level and finally to delay or latency value in samples.

Figure 8.38 The volume indicator in the Mix window. Command-clicking here will cycle you from volume to peak level and finally to delay or latency value in samples.

2. Command-clicking on the volume indicator once will toggle the display, show-ing the peak amplitude value for that track. Command-clicking on this again will cause the processing delay value to be seen. It is displayed in samples of delay as shown in Figure 8.39.

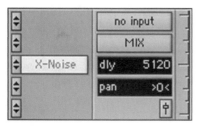

Figure 8.39 The DSP delay display as seen in the Edit window. This can also been viewed in the Mix window.

3. Set the Nudge format to Samples and manually set the value found in the delay latency display into the Nudge value as seen in Figure 8.40.

Figure 8.40 Manually entering the latency value for the track into the Nudge setting.

4. Create a duplicate playlist of the track you are working with. Name this duplicate playlist with a suffix that describes the plug-in you are compensating for. For instance, if the track in question is named Dialog 1 and you are applying a Waves X-Noise plug-in on that track, name the duplicate playlist Dialog 1-XN to indicate that this playlist compensates for the latency of X-Noise. This will help identify which playlist has been altered for delay compensation and which is the original. If you remove the X-Noise plug-in, you should return to the original playlist to maintain correct timing of the track.

5. Select all regions on the duplicate playlist by clicking in it with the Selector tool and pressing Command+A (Select All). Be sure you have not inadvertently selected other regions on tracks that do not have the X-Noise plug-in. You only want to move the audio that will be processed by the plug-in you are compensating for.

6. Press the minus (−) key *once* to nudge the selected audio earlier (to the left) in time by the nudge amount, which is equal to the delay value of the plug-in, in this case 5120 samples for X-Noise RTAS.

7. Press Play, and the audio should be back in sync, exactly where it was prior to applying the X-Noise plug-in.

This method of plug-in delay compensation yields accurate results with any amount of delay. The other method of applying equal amounts of delay to other tracks in the session has two disadvantages. One is the need for additional DSP to delay all the other tracks in a session to compensate for one track that is using a DSP intensive plug-in. The second involves the delay as it relates to video that is in sync with your session. In the case of X-Noise, the delay value of 5120 samples is close to three video frames of delay, which when applied to dialogue will throw lip-sync out the window. If all tracks in the session are delayed by the three frames needed to compensate for X-Noise, the whole sound track will now play back three frames late in relation to the video. This is obviously a problem. The track slipping method outlined here does not suffer from these dilemmas and is relatively simple to use.

Automatic Delay Compensation in Pro Tools HD

Pro Tools HD systems have an additional feature that compensates for plug-in and routing delays automatically. The system works by analyzing all the tracks in the mixer and finding the one with the greatest processing delay. Pro Tools will then add an appropriate amount of delay to every other channel so that each audio signal is being delayed by the same amount when they are combined at the final mix buss. All of these calculations happen automatically in the background as you mix and add processing to various tracks.

You must enable Delay Compensation for this to work. Choose Options > Delay Compensation in order to turn this feature on. There are a couple of options. Because Delay Compensation creates a buffer in the TDM system for additional delays, it consumes some DSP. With that in mind, there are three choices for the size of that buffer, as seen in Figure 8.41. You can choose None, Short, or Long for this buffer setting. The Long setting is for plug-in chains that use the highest amount of processing delays. Short is much more efficient.

If your plug-in chains get particularly insane, and even the Long buffer cannot compensate, Pro Tools HD allows you to enter another manual offset to bring greatly delayed tracks back in line. On a track-by-track basis, the delay compensation can be defeated, and manual control over the track offset can take its place. Using the Delay

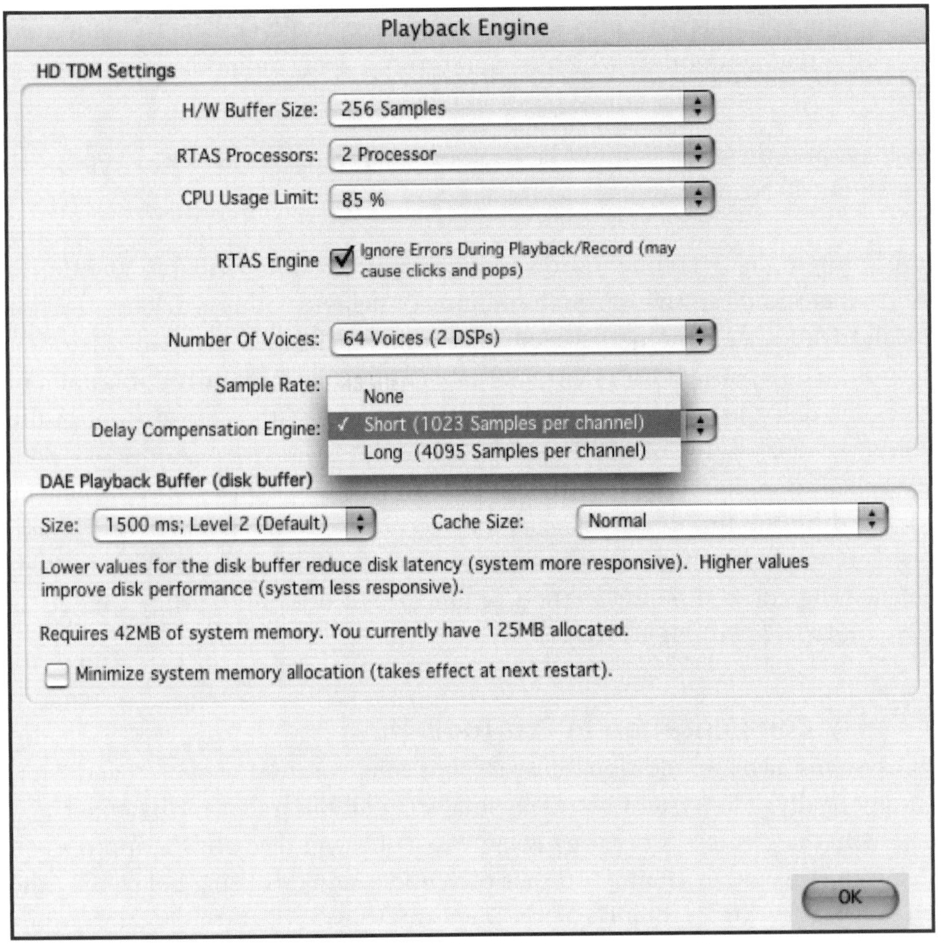

Figure 8.41 The Delay Compensation pop-up menu in Pro Tools HD, showing the options for the buffer length.

Compensation view from the mixer, you can control each track's delay compensation and manual offset.

Exceeding the ADC Buffer Once a channel's plug-in chain has exceeded the amount of delay that ADC can compensate for, Pro Tools will automatically disable ADC on that channel. For example, Waves X-Noise has more latency than can be compensated for by ADC's Long setting of 4095 samples. You must manually set the delay compensation setting for these channels.

---

9 Delivery of Master Recordings

When you consider the time and effort expended in creating master recordings, you'll realize that they are seriously valuable property. So when the time comes to deliver them to a video post house, optical mastering facility, or simply to the Web designer you're working with, you must take care to provide the right format, reference levels, time code, track layout, and documentation necessary for the project. This is the last time you will have any control over the recording you have created. Don't make mistakes here that will affect the final product.

Mix Stems

Mix stems are used to create the final print masters for film and high-end TV productions. A different print master is created for each format in which the film will be released. If done correctly, mix stems should be combined at unity gain (all at the same level) without any adjustment. Adjustments should be made only when downmixing to a format with fewer channels such as Dolby Pro Logic®. A typical adjustment would be to compensate for the −3dB level for surround speakers in theaters, or to vary the amount of LFE channel that is mixed into a Dolby Stereo/Pro Logic print master. Print masters for foreign-language versions will not include dialogue, because they will be dubbed in that language. However, the dialogue stem will be mixed to a mono reference track that can be used by foreign language editors.

Music stems often contain a separate mix of soundtrack songs or source music. This music is often subject to publishing issues and, thus, last-minute changes. With these tracks separate on the stem, it is simple to replace a song if the rights cannot be secured or if a better choice is available. Be prepared for last-minute changes to your masters.

Reference Levels

Have you ever wondered why television commercials are always so much louder than the movie or show? I always have to turn the TV down when the commercial break comes on and then turn it back up again when the program resumes, to hear the dialogue clearly. This is an obvious sign that reference levels are not being adhered to. If they were, the average level of all the program material on the television would be about the same, and you would not have to constantly turn the volume up and down to maintain a consistent volume.

In this case, commercials are usually mixed with a much higher average or RMS level than movies or episodic one-hour shows. Their purpose is to sell stuff, and with that in mind, advertisers want to have their message as loud as possible. Unfortunately, I wish the advertisers and broadcasters would realize that many viewers actually turn down or otherwise avoid especially loud commercials when they come on, thereby defeating their purpose. If there were adherence to industry reference levels, these problems would not exist, and the volume buttons on my remote would not be totally worn out!

The Purpose of Reference Levels and Tones

A reference level, or nominal operating level, is an average program level of an audio signal, as defined by a specific measurement (usually a sine wave tone at some decibel level). Obviously signals will go above and below this level in the course of a normal program, but the nominal operating level is used as a reference so that signals will be interchangeable between the different pieces of equipment, including broadcast systems, theaters, DVD players, and TVs. In analog systems, this level is measured using a VU meter. A VU meter is not a fast-reacting meter like the peak meters found in many digital systems. Extremely short transient peaks will not register on a VU meter, and therefore, it is important to realize that the actual level is exceeding the VU reading for very short peaks. The interesting thing is that human hearing perceives volume more like a VU meter reads audio signals. Watching a peak meter does not necessarily give an accurate reading of how your ear perceives the volume of that signal. It is because of this fact that VU meters are used to calibrate nominal operating levels.

VU Meters   VU meters are used to calibrate volume levels. VU stands for *Volume Units*. VU meters' slow reaction time makes them less sensitive to transient peaks. As a result, they give a reasonable representation of the overall perceived volume of a signal rather than the instantaneous level.

When mixing, you must use some point of reference to judge the average level of your mix. As discussed in the calibration section of Chapter 8, speaker systems for film and theatrical presentations are calibrated to specific volume measured by an SPL meter. The digital level used to calibrate this volume is −20dBFS. This level corresponds to 0VU. Working backwards from the sound pressure level, 85dBC = 0VU = −20dBFS. Figure 9.1 shows how reference levels relate to the overall signal.

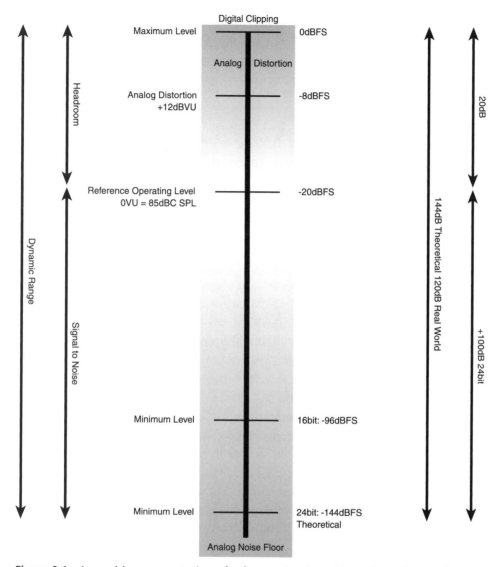

Figure 9.1   A graphic representation of reference levels and how they relate to dynamic range of a system. The gray areas represent analog noise and distortion artifacts as they increase the farther you get away from the reference level.

As normal signals will include transient material exceeding 0VU quite often, any recording or reproduction medium must be capable of passing those peak signals without distortion. This capacity is called *headroom*. The amount of signal that can be passed prior to distortion above 0VU or the reference level is the amount of headroom available to that system. With analog recording systems, distortion artifacts start to creep in gradually. Tape saturation will typically begin around +12dBVU, depending on how the tape deck is calibrated. As the level gets higher, the distortion will increase until the point at which the system can no longer output a higher level; then total clipping results. With digital systems, there is no gradual increase in distortion. Once a signal reaches the 0dBFS, it enters complete clipping and distortion.

85dBC or 83dBC It should be noted that many mix rooms are calibrated to 83dBC for film mixing and 79dBC for TV. True 85dBC coming from all three front speakers can get pretty loud. Dolby Laboratories suggests 85dBC as the reference, whereas Tomlinson Holman recommends 83dBC. If you mix primarily loud, bombastic action thrillers, you might consider using 83dBC just to protect your hearing! Smaller mixing rooms can benefit from a lower SPL setting due to the damping effect of having less air in the room.

Knowing how much headroom is available in any given recording medium is imperative. With digital systems, the amount of available headroom is determined solely by the reference level that you use to record, in this case −20dBFS. That leaves 20dB of headroom above the reference level before digital clipping occurs. With an analog tape recorder, it's safe to assume that only 12dB above the reference level is available before some amount of distortion will be introduced. This means that when you are recording a digital master referenced to −20dBFS, and this master is going to be transferred to an analog recording medium such as Betacam SP video or VHS, the peak level should not exceed −8dBFS. If the final medium is going to be digital, such as DVD or a Dolby Digital film print, the entire 20dB worth of digital headroom is available for you to use. Understand that even though you have all this wonderful headroom at your disposal, the final playback system must be able to reproduce all the dynamic range you are using. If you constantly have peaks that reach 0dBFS, only the hardiest of playback systems will accurately reproduce these without distortion or failure while maintaining an average playback level of 85dBC.

On the low end of the scale is the noise floor. The difference between the reference operating level and the point at which program material becomes indistinguishable from the inherent noise of a system is called the *signal-to-noise ratio*. Digital systems are capable of recording signals at much lower levels before reaching the noise floor. Analog systems typically have a higher noise floor.

Using Reference Levels

The way to establish your reference is by generating a 1kHz sine wave at the prescribed level. Using the Signal Generator Audiosuite plug-in, you can generate a 1kHz sine wave at −20dBFS, as shown in Figure 9.2. This tone can be recorded prior to any mix on to the tape deck, DAT machine, or even digital file, so that anyone receiving your mix will have a reference tone they can use to align other equipment for 0VU. When this tone is used to set the proper recording level, the transfer will maintain the optimal signal to noise ratio and headroom. Digital transfers will not suffer from the lack of a reference tone. However, it is always prudent to include a reference tone because you don't always know where your mix will end up.

Don't Process Reference Tones   Make sure that reference tones are not being processed by any plug-ins in the chain. Processing the master fader is no exception. When recording reference tones on a master recording, disable any processing or plug-ins.

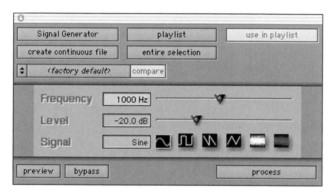

Figure 9.2   The Signal Generator plug-in set up to generate a 1kHz tone at −20dBFS.

Film and Dolby Encoding

When mixing film, always use a reference level of −20dBFS. Pink noise at that level should play back through a single speaker in your system at 85dBC on an SPL meter. Both surround channels should be individually referenced at 82dBC. This compensates for the fact that theaters calibrate the surround channels 3dB lower than the main channels. The reference level on tape remains the same, −20dBFS. Only the speaker volume is reduced by 3dB so that the mix you create for the surround channels sounds right to your ears but is recorded on tape +3dB louder than the other channels. The theater calibration will reduce the output of the surround speakers by 3dB, thereby playing your mix exactly the way you heard it.

The two types of test signals and what they are used for are as follows:

- Pink noise at −20dBFS RMS is used to calibrate speaker volume to 85dBC.

- 1kHz sine wave at −20dBFS is used as a recorded reference tone, *not* for volume calibration.

DVD Authoring

When preparing mixes for DVD authoring, the methods are the same as for film except that the surround channels should *not* be referenced −3dB from the others. All speaker channels should use the 85dBC reference volume while mixing except for the sub-woofer, which should be +10dB louder in the monitoring chain, as usual. A 1kHz sine wave should be recorded at −20dBFS on all channels as a reference tone. You might consider referencing 83 or even 79dBC for volume if the DVD is intended primarily for home viewing.

Broadcast Video

Broadcast video is an interesting topic these days. With HDTV entering the fray, there are many choices for mixes that will be broadcast. On the one hand, commercial television has progressively become louder and louder with respect to the normal reference level of −20dBFS. TV spots are overly compressed and suffer from the same problems that FM broadcast and music mastering have faced. Clients want their audio to be louder than the competition's. This forces audio engineers to maximize the perceived volume of their mix while sacrificing headroom, through the use of digital peak limiters that, in essence, clip off the transient peaks of waveforms, allowing the overall level to be increased without over-modulating the signal. Radio broadcasters also employ severe peak limiting in the signal chain so that their transmission signals appear to be louder than competing stations without exceeding FCC modulation limitations. All this processing is detrimental to the overall sound quality. The result is a mix with severely limited dynamic range and a large quantity of harmonic distortion.

However, HDTV brings the promise of renewed fidelity and dynamic range in audio. Hopefully, the trend will be to use this dynamic range for creative purposes instead of trying to maximize level for perceived loudness. Only time will tell. Hopefully, you'll decide to maintain integrity within the audio mix instead of yielding to clients' demands for volume that results in the loss of quality. Clients, however, also pay the bills. Their demands will be met somehow. Education of the client in this area can help.

One thing many clients do not realize is that even though your mix might be limited and compressed and very loud in the studio, once it hits the broadcast chain, the same type of processing will be applied to it again, resulting in even more distortion and loss of fidelity. If properly mixed, a commercial with a reasonable amount of dynamic control can sound better than an overly compressed mix once it has been processed by the broadcast signal chain. Experience will help you find a way to accomplish this. Louder is not always better.

Hopefully, you can reach a compromise between the needs of clients to be perceived as louder and the desire for high-fidelity sound. Sticking to the prescribed reference levels for all program material will help end the volume war. Perhaps standards enforced by the FCC or other governing body could help accomplish this.

Be aware that various broadcasters have certain requirements for audio that need to be met in order for the master tape to be acceptable. This might involve reference levels, channel configuration and even dialogue levels. Make sure to contact the broadcaster to ensure that you will meet these specifications before you deliver a final mix.

Internet Media

As most Internet media will be highly data-compressed in order to reduce the bandwidth necessary for transmission, it will require more dynamic control than even a broadcast commercial. Most computer users still listen to audio on small, low-fidelity, multimedia speakers that are connected directly to their computers. It is advisable to at least preview your mix on a similar set of speakers to ensure that it will play the way you want it to.

Referencing mixes on small speakers is not unusual, especially in the music-mixing world. Top mix engineers like Bob Clearmountain and Tom Lord-Alge both check their mixes on simple consumer playback systems. This is similar to the use of Auratone speakers in the past. Auratones were designed to mimic the band-limited sound of small AM radio speakers. If you can get your mix to sound good on a tiny set of speakers and still sound incredible on larger, hi-fi speakers, you are doing a great job.

Find out the type and settings used for the data compression that your Internet audio will be processed with. If you are able to, run your mix through this processing to hear what it sounds like. You might be able to compensate for losses with mix alterations. Always try to listen to your mix in its final form, through whatever processing, compression, and data reduction it might go through.

Times are changing, and the age of the multimedia PC is here. Computer users and home video enthusiasts are using personal computers to process video and audio for viewing in the home theater. Multimedia that is transmitted via the Internet might find its way onto a higher-quality playback system in the near future. Always make sure you know who the intended audience is and on what type of system they will be listening to your mix.

Something you mix to be heard on a two-inch multimedia speaker might be heard on a 5.1 home theater surround system with a 15-inch subwoofer. You never know.

Recording a Mix on a VTR

Even though many video layback operations are performed in a video post-production facility, it is preferable to lay back the audio yourself if you have access to a compatible videotape deck. Sony Digital Betacam is the current industry standard, although analog Betacam SP is still widely used. Laying back audio to videotape decks requires SMPTE synchronization and compatible audio connections.

Synchronization can be as simple as feeding analog SMPTE into your SMPTE to MTC converter and allowing Pro Tools to lock to that incoming time code. The Machine Control option can provide another level of functionality by allowing you to remotely control the videotape deck. Either way, Pro Tools and the videotape deck must be in perfect sync when laying back final mixes. This requires hardware that will resolve the speed of Pro Tools to the VTR. Refer to Chapters 3 and 4 for more detailed information on synchronization.

Using Digital Connections

When laying back to Digital Betacam, it is preferable to use digital I/O instead of going through an analog conversion stage. Because Digital Betacam is capable of recording four tracks of 20 bit, 48kHz audio, several choices are possible for stereo or surround sound recording.

When printing a stereo track, it is possible to separate the dialogue stem on Track 3 and the music and effects stem on Track 4, both in mono. This gives options for editors who will use that videotape later. You could also print an encoded multi-channel mix such as Dolby E (see Note) on two tracks and a stereo mix (Dolby Pro Logic) on the remaining two tracks. Be sure to properly label your tape so that anyone can see what exactly is on each track.

Dolby E   There is also a data compressed format known as Dolby E, which encodes a 5.1 mix into a stereo pair of AES digital signals. This format is used to carry multi-channel audio over existing two-channel cabling and equipment and survive multiple encode and decode stages before broadcasting. Like Dolby Digital, which is primarily used for broadcast signals, Dolby E requires a dedicated encoder and cannot be listened to directly without decoding. With a Digital Betacam VTR, Dolby E can be encoded onto Tracks 1 and 2, while a stereo downmix is recorded on 3 and 4 as a reference that you can listen to without decoding. The TV series *24* uses this method of layback, providing broadcasters with a six-channel discrete mix on a four-channel VTR, including a stereo-compatible reference mix. Isn't technology great?

If you are mixing in 24 bit resolution, it will be necessary to dither your outputs to 20 bits to avoid truncation errors and quantization noise when laying back to Digital Betacam. Because this is a digital format, you will not need to worry about distortion as long as your levels do not reach or exceed 0dBFS. Keep in mind, however, that a digital master tape might be used to create analog copies, whereas peak levels beyond −8dBFS might cause distortion. Even analog routing and playback equipment might not be able to handle levels approaching 0dBFS. Make sure you know exactly what the master tape will be used for.

Professional digital videotape decks will have AES digital inputs and outputs. This type of digital connection is the most reliable. Figure 9.3 shows the rear of a Digital Betacam deck wired up for digital I/O. The AES ins and outs have transformers in them that convert the XLR connection to a coaxial BNC type that can run longer lengths from the machine room to the audio suite in a facility.

Figure 9.3 The rear connections of a Digital Betacam deck shown with BNC transformers connected to the AES ins and outs in the lower-right corner.

Your Pro Tools system must be resolved in some way to the videotape deck or to the same master sync reference to which the video deck is resolved. To resolve Pro Tools to the video deck using a Sync I/O or Universal Slave Driver, you may take a coaxial BNC cable and connect the analog video output from this deck to the video reference input of the Sync I/O and then choose Video In as your clock reference in Pro Tools. To resolve to a dedicated "house sync" used by the video deck, connect the sync source to the Sync I/O and choose Video Reference as your sync source.

Another method utilizes the clock signal embedded in the digital outputs of channels 3 and 4 to clock your Pro Tools system. Connect this AES signal to a compatible input of your Pro Tools interface and choose that digital input as your clock reference. If you are recording to channels 1 and 2, their outputs cannot be used as a clock reference because that would create a digital loop. When recording to Tracks 3 and 4 of the VTR, it will be necessary to re-route the clocking channels to outputs of 1 and 2 for the same reason.

Panasonic's D-5 Cinema Mastering HD Format   As more content is being created in HD with full surround sound as a standard, video tape formats are undergoing a revolution in formats. Current state-of-the-art resides with the Panasonic D-5 format. It can record uncompressed HD video at full resolution along with eight channels of 24 bit digital audio at 48kHz. This allows you to record a 5.1 surround mix on the first six channels and then a stereo downmix on the last two channels. What the future holds is anyone's guess. I would anticipate that in the future, all media will move to a data format such as optical discs or even solid-state memory similar to the kind found in most digital still cameras. The sheer amount of data required for HD keeps the formats tied to tape. However, as technology changes, that limitation will disappear. Perhaps as Internet connection speeds increase, we will no longer need a "physical format" to transport our media. We'll just go online and download it!

Using Analog Connections

When using analog connections to lay back to a videotape deck, make sure you align your reference tone of 1kHz@−20dBFS to 0VU on the videotape deck. Also be aware that in analog recording mediums such as Betacam SP, peak levels that exceed −8dBFS begin to induce distortion artifacts in the recorded signal.

It will not be necessary to dither your outputs to bit resolutions lower than 24 in this case. Take advantage of the full dynamic range of your system when using analog connections. This might not make a noticeable difference because the analog recording medium has a limited dynamic range, but it doesn't hurt.

With analog VTRs, it is still necessary to clock Pro Tools and the VTR together. Because no digital clock source is available from the VTR, video or house sync will be used as a clock source.

Check It Again   Always listen back to your master recordings from the VTR or other recoding medium. You must be absolutely sure that your mix recorded perfectly to the master. This is your last chance. Check it twice!

Creating Multi-Channel Surround Masters

Multi-channel surround sound mix stems and print masters are typically recorded to modular digital multi-tracks such as the Tascam DA-88 or MMR-8. There are three common layouts for recording to 8-track machines.

The common abbreviations used for each speaker channel are as follows:

- **L.** Left.

- **C.** Center.

- **R.** Right.

- **Sw.** Subwoofer or LFE.

- **Ls.** Left Surround.

- **Rs.** Right Surround.

- **Lt.** Left Total (Total refers to the phase-matrixed result of Dolby Stereo or Pro Logic, the total of both left and part of the surround and center channels. When decoded, the two tracks make four: L, C, R, and S.)

- **Rt.** Right Total.

Following are three common layouts for 8-track print master tapes:

- **The ITU-R format.** L, C, R, Sw, Ls, Rs, Lt, Rt, where the first six tracks are for Dolby Digital, and the last two tracks are encoded Dolby Stereo or Pro Logic.

- **Dolby SR-D.** L, Ls, C, Rs, R, Sw, with Lt and Rt on 7 and 8.

- Another possible layout is L, C, R, Ls, Rs, Sw, Lt, Rt.

Practices may vary. Be sure to use the specified format from a production coordinator, mastering facility, or broadcast network. With an 8-track master tape, all standard formats are covered: Dolby Digital, Dolby Stereo/Pro Logic, stereo, and even mono.

As most MDMs will support Machine Control and synchronization via MIDI time code, recording a multi-track master is similar to recording to a VTR. The MDM can be synchronized to Pro Tools, ensuring time code accuracy, and the two can be clocked together via digital audio connections.

Documentation of the master tapes is crucial. Figure 9.4 shows Dolby Laboratories' Mix Data Sheet, which can be used to clearly document the masters you create.

Bouncing to QuickTime Movies

It is possible to bounce a mix directly into the current QuickTime movie you have in your session. This mix file and resulting movie file can only be encoded in mono or stereo. Surround is not yet supported in this feature. You could create a stereo downmix and bounce that into the QuickTime movie. Make sure that the video track containing the movie you want to export to is the current active video track. Choosing File > Bounce to > QuickTime Movie will open the Bounce dialog box, as shown in Figure 9.5.

Creating an Audio File or Data CD Master

Many times in commercial production, regular data CDs will be used to transfer mixes to and from video post houses, allowing clients to make approvals and even deliver masters to radio broadcasters. CD-Rs can be used to transfer any data format between editors or facilities. Data files can even be delivered via the Internet over FTP connections. Email works for MP3 files.

There are so many ways to deliver digital media in data format that the industry could possibly see the end of tape machines altogether. The advent of cheap CD-R media, DVD media, and burners has allowed us to move large amount of audio between places without the need for reels of tape. Even the iPod is a terrific way to take your Pro Tools session to another studio with 160-gigabyte models available.

When creating these data files that are, in essence, your master tapes, you must take into consideration factors such as synchronization, sample rates, and file format issues. Time code spotting information should always be included with any audio file that you deliver. Include a text file that clearly describes what the file contains, its reference level, a timestamp, and any other pertinent info. This way, the receiving party will have a better idea what to do with it.

ᗪᗪ Dolby   Mix Data Sheet

Date _____ / _____ / _____

Project _____	Project # _____
Client _____	Producer _____
Studio _____	Engineer _____

Sampling Frequency ☐ 32 kHz   ☐ 44.1 kHz   ☐ 48 kHz   ☐ 96 kHz

Bit Resolution   ☐ 16-bit   ☐ 18-bit   ☐ 20-bit   ☐ 24-bit

Time Code Format   ☐ 25 fps   ☐ 29.97 NDF

Tape Format   ☐ ADAT   ☐ DA-88   ☐ Ω" Digital   ☐ Data Cartridge (JAZ)

Surround Level SPL   ☐ Equal to Front   ☐ -3 dB to Front
Calibration

CH1	CH2	CH3	CH4	CH5	CH6	CH7	CH8

Time Code	Program
: : ;	
: : ;	
: : ;	
: : ;	
: : ;	
: : ;	
: : ;	
: : ;	
: : ;	
: : ;	
: : ;	
: : ;	
: : ;	
: : ;	
: : ;	
: : ;	
: : ;	

Notes: _____
_____
_____

Figure 9.4 Dolby Laboratories' Mix Data Sheet, which is used to provide accurate information regarding multi-channel master tapes.

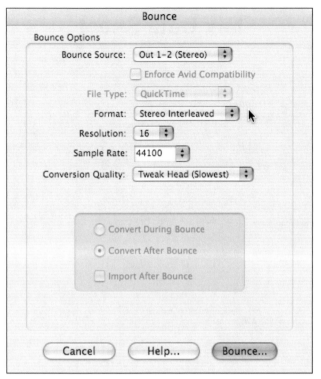

Figure 9.5 The Bounce dialog box. Here you can choose to encode your mix into the QuickTime movie in either mono or stereo.

Redbook Audio CDs

Although it is not preferable due to sample rate conversion to 44.1kHz, Redbook audio CDs can be an alternative method for creating stereo master recordings of your work. Make sure to include a 2-beep for synchronization, because audio CDs cannot support time code.

It is even possible to put a complete 5.1 surround mix onto a Redbook audio CD for transfer to another playback system. The way to do this is to record pairs of channels as individual tracks on the CD. Each track on the CD will have a 2-beep at the beginning to allow for synchronization in another workstation. You could pair left and right channels, center and LFE channels, and the surround channels, each pair on a track of the CD. When bouncing these files, be sure to maintain the same selection so the files can be lined up sample accurately later. This is certainly not the preferable way of doing things, but it will work in a pinch. Be aware that typical video workstations are set up to import audio from Redbook CDs at the fastest and lowest quality available. If an analog transfer from the CD is used, calibration issues arise. Try to avoid the use of audio CDs as a method of transfer unless absolutely necessary.

Preparing Audio Files for Internet Streaming

Preparation of mix files for Internet use usually requires using a higher reference level. As with music recording, the Internet does not have a standard reference level. As most files that will be used on the Internet are going to be data compressed, a higher reference level should work better. It has been my experience that lossy data compression used for Internet streaming sounds better when starting with a file that is as loud as possible. This goes against the grain of preserving the highest fidelity, but often the softer mixes don't translate very well once they have been compressed by an algorithm such as MP3 and played back on tiny laptop speakers. You should experiment with each codec to find the combination of settings and levels that yields the highest quality.

Another factor to consider is the environment in which people will listen to this mix. Small multimedia speakers placed close to a CRT monitor and a loud whining desktop computer do not make for an ideal listening environment. Many less expensive playback systems (cheap car stereos, smallish bookshelf systems, and so on) have such a large amount of self noise that their dynamic range is limited by their design. Reducing the dynamic range to fit these limited playback scenarios can work well.

QuickTime provides its own Internet streaming compression for video files bound for the Web. The Web designer will make the choices concerning audio compression here, as the compression type depends on the available bandwidth and video data rate as well. Try to obtain a copy of the finished file, or a Website where it can be viewed, in order to check the content creator's work. It is not uncommon to find that your mix has been horribly mutilated by data compression. You might want to speak with the programmer to find out what compression was used and if there's a way to improve the situation.

If the end file is to be an MP3, try to do the encoding yourself to ensure quality. Applications such as Peak can encode MP3 files in a high-quality fashion, as shown in Figure 9.6. Consumer MP3 encoders tend to sacrifice quality for speed. Be wary of them. Apple's iTunes tends to sound pretty good, however. Be aware that the default encoding method for iTunes is AAC and not MP3. It can be changed in Preferences.

If you know your mix file is destined to be encoded into a Flash file for the Internet, send the programmer a Redbook audio CD. The Flash program will encode your audio file into an MP3 format that is embedded within the Flash file. Sending an already encoded MP3 does not help in this case.

Figure 9.6   The export dialog box in Peak showing options for MP3 encoding. 128kBps should be the minimum bit rate used to encode MP3 files that retain any decent fidelity.

Archiving and Backing Up the Final Mix

Once your mix is completed, it is time to properly back up and store your data for possible future use. Carefully consider what the possible uses for this material are. For instance, foreign language versions of a film or television show might require a different set of foley tracks. The reason for this is that some foley elements are captured along with the dialogue when it is recorded on the set. As that dialogue is being removed for a foreign language version, certain foley elements might need to be included in order to replace those lost with the dialogue tracks. If a movie is to be subtitled in a foreign language, most likely the original print master will be used because only the visuals will be altered.

It is a common practice to gather additional foley sounds while recording in anticipation of a foreign language dub of the film. When you are creating mix stems, you might need to create an alternate foley mix stem to compensate for the elements lost with dialogue tracks. This would have to be archived in a proper format so that it is clear what it should be used for. Paperwork is boring but necessary.

Mix Stems: Dipped or Not Dipped

In commercial video production, it is common to have mix stems or subgroups that vary in gain (are "dipped") to accommodate dialogue or narration. When these mix stems are printed by themselves, the retained dynamic changes make them unusable for revisions that include changes in the dialogue or narration. It is always advisable to print stems that have no volume automation or gain riding, in order to provide usable mix components for future revisions.

Sometimes, *side-chain* gain reduction is applied to the music stem in order to "duck" the dialogue when it enters. If the mix stem is printed with this type of processing applied, it can sound very unnatural and become relatively unusable for future use. At least make a pass with and without this type of processing applied in order to provide choices later. Be sure to document all this information carefully with the mix stem master recordings.

Pro Tools Data

Archiving of the Pro Tools data is imperative. It is possible that mix stems and print masters will all be recorded inside Pro Tools. All of these files must be archived dependably. Additionally, copies must be sent to the relevant video or film mastering facilities for proper encoding to the actual picture master itself. Current practices will vary, depending on the facility involved. DVD-ROM is a convenient way to transfer the large quantities of data that result from several print masters and their associated mix stems. Be wary of using proprietary formats, such as Retrospect data, or tape storage systems unless the mastering facility specifically requests it. DVDs have the advantage of being able to record data in a raw form that can be accessed by nearly any computer system with a DVD drive.

All final mixes, mix stems, print masters, and any other file associated with your mixdown should have reference tones printed along with two beeps for synchronization. Be sure to properly document any CD, DVD, or multi-track master tape so that people involved with the project will have a clear understanding of what is contained in that media.

Hopefully, the art you create with sound and picture will outlast the current data formats. For that reason, consider how future uses of the material will take place. Having all your data in Pro Tools format only could limit future uses. Mix stems offer the best chance of future possible use as they are continuous audio files that are not dependent on the Pro Tools format in order to be used. Periodic copying of precious data from older formats to newer ones can help ensure their longevity.

Harness the Power of Cinema

Understanding the workflow and standard practices of the industry can help you create a more professional product efficiently with the tools that Pro Tools offers. So many areas in audio post-production have benefited from the ability to record, edit, and mix entire productions within one medium, Pro Tools. Tools that were once available only to those with very high budgets are now accessible to just about anyone. But while the tools have become available and somewhat simpler, the process itself remains complex and challenging.

I hope that this book has helped you to understand better the principles of audio post-production and the correlating features in Pro Tools that allow you to accomplish these tasks. I have covered the most basic areas and have pointed toward some of the more complex and subtle abilities that Pro Tools has in relation to film, video, and multimedia. With these directions as a basic roadmap, you will be able to explore the diverse and creative universe that is cinema.

Today is an important time in the development of multimedia technology. Never in history has there been this much power available to the average person. With digital technology, anyone can grab a camera and microphone and go film a movie, edit it, create the soundtrack, and voila! A film is born. It still takes talent to make it good, however. As its name implies, Pro Tools is just a tool. How you use it is up to you. Now go out there and make movies. I'm going to get some sushi.

Appendix A

SuperSuds :30TV "Country Fresh Scent"

We open on a farmyard scene with idyllic sunshine and unnaturally clean barn area with a couple goats, white ducks and a horse. As we pan across this scene, out of the house comes a woman in an apron.

Sound FX:
barnyard ambience, chickens, goats, horses, dogs and misc. birds.

She is an idealized farm mother, nurturing, healthy and beautiful. She is carrying a woven basket with the laundry in it on her hip.

She walks over to a table with a wooden tub set up on it and a box of "Supersuds Soap" next to it.

Mother: When I need to get my family's farm clothes fresh and clean I use Supersuds Soap for that farm fresh scent.

She dunks clothes into the tub and swirls them around in the huge mountain of suds.

Sound FX: Big sudsy bubble sound

Mother: These suds last and last. They're "Supersuds"!! My family loves the way their clothes come out farm-fresh clean.

Here boys!

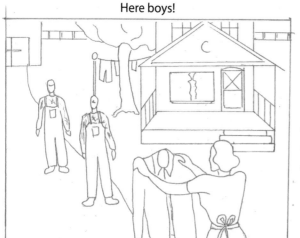

She turns to hand her two sons some clean shirts as they come up to her after working in the fields. The shirts they are wearing are filthy with dirt and dust. Their faces are covered with dirt as well.

The boys: Thanks, mom. We love our country fresh shirts!

They run off to change. We fade to a scene of the whole family standing on the front porch in their clean clothes with Mother looking very proud.

Music: Up comes the Supersuds country style music.

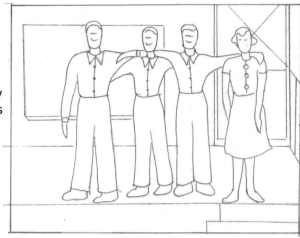

Announcer: If you want that country fresh clean in your laundry then you need to try Supersuds Soap, the soap that makes suds that last and last. Plus, that extra country fresh smell keeps your family proud and happy.

Fade to Supersuds Logo with farm scene background.

Announcer: Supersuds Soap, for that country fresh scent.

Music: "Supersuds, for that country fresh scent!"

Appendix B

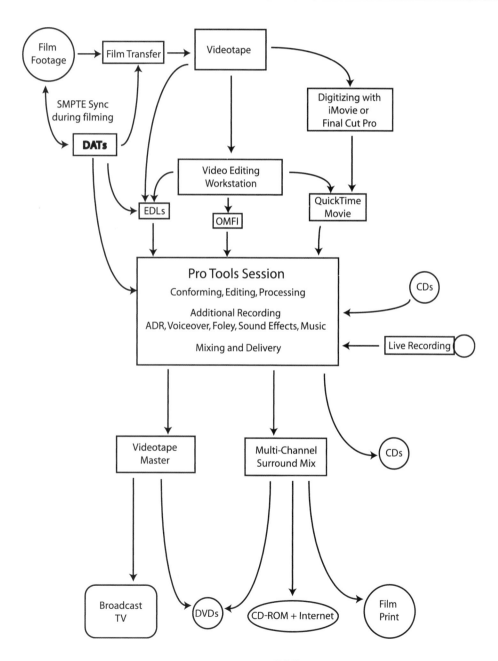

Index

2-3 pull-down, synchronization, 54–59
  24p HD video, 58–59
  film transfers, 54–57
  pull-down sample rates, 55–56
  pull-up sample rates, 56–57
24, 278
24fps HD to film synchronization, 62–63
24p HD video, 58–59
24p HD to video synchronization, 62
5.1 surround speakers, 250–251, 259–261
83dBC, 305–306
85dBC, 305–306
9-pin Machine Control, 71–78
  connections, 72–74
  operation, 74–77
  remote deck emulation, 77–78
  settings, 72–74

A

AAF files, 122–124
acquisition, audio, 31–32
action sounds, *see* foley
ADC buffer, 302
ADR, 134–142
ADR dialogue replacements, 37
Advanced Authoring Format (AAF), 33
Advanced Video Coding (AVC), 15
advantages, Pro Tools, 25–27
Ampex, 9
analog broadcasts, 11–12
analog connections, 312–313
animation dialogue, 35, 144–145
animation voices, 20
Apocalypse Now, 10
Apple Computer, 13, 15
archival, pre-production, 34
archival, master recordings, 318–319
artists, foley, 21
aspect ratios, 12

audio clock source, 69
audio; *see also* production audio
  exchange, pre-production, 30–34
  importing, 103
  transferring, 36–37
  video interchange, 32–33
audio files, master recordings, 314–318
audio to picture editing, 39–40
Audio Region List window, 137
Audiosuite plug-ins, 223–248
  compression limits, 233
  dialogue, aligning, 236–248
    Difference button, 244
    EQ, 248
    noise reduction, 240–247
    noise removers, 242
    noise samples, 241
    restoration, 240–247
    VocALign plug-in, 238
    X-Hum, 246–247
    X-Noise, 242–243
  expansion limits, 233
  files, reversing, 224–230
  pitch changing, 235–236
  Pitch shift, 235
  time compression, 230–234
  Time Compression Expansion
      Trimmer tool, 234
  time expansion, 230–234
  Time Shift, 236
  Trimmer tool, 234
automatic dialogue replacement (ADR), 18
automation features, 26
automation, mixing, 289–297
  control surfaces, 295–297
  dynamics, building, 294–295
  EQs, 291–294
  Latch mode, 289
  levels, writing, 289–291
  Off mode, 291
  panning, 291

automation, mixing (*continued*)
    Read mode, 290
    Touch mode, 289
    Trim mode, 290
    Write mode, 289
Avid Mojo, 90–91
Avid video, 16

B

Backdraft, 23
backups, 161–167
    automation, 164–165
    mass storage media, 166–167
    master recordings, 318–319
    planning, 163–165
    pre-production, 34,
backup recorders, 144
bass management, 264, 269–270
beeps, 136
Bell Laboratories, 2–3
Big Brother, 133
bit depths, new sessions, 84–85
Black Hawk Down, 277
Blonder-Tongue TVC-1-C Vidicon camera head, 9
Bounce dialog box, 316
bouncing, QuickTime movies, 314
broadcast video, reference levels, 308–309
Broadway Theater, New York, 5
burn-in windows, 91
Burtt, Ben, 10
busses, mixing, 254–255

C

calculators, time code, 49
calibration, 270–274
Carthy Theater, Los Angeles, 5
CDs, importing from, 159
CD-ROM, importing from, 159–160
change node, 216
Change Session Start Time dialog box, 87
Chiariglione, Leonardo, 14
Cinema Audio Society, 132
Cinemascope, film sound format, 7–8
Cinerama, film sound format, 7
clock source, audio, 69
clock speed, 44
Close Encounters of the Third Kind, 10
codecs, 10–11
color coding, groups, 186
color video, 48–49
compression limits, 233
control surfaces, mixing, 295–297
Coppola, Francis Ford, 11

counters, editing, 186–189
co-workers, 29–30
Create Group dialog box, 182
cue lists, 35–36
    memory locations, 197–199

D

DAT tapes, 124–127
    24fps shoot, 125–127
    29.97fps shoot, 127
    importing from, 159
    SimulDAT, 125–126
data CDs, master recordings, 314–318
decks, remote, arming, 76
delay compensation, 298–302
delivery, pre-production, 33–34
dialogue, aligning, 236–248
    Difference button, 244
    EQ, 248
    noise reduction, 240–247
    noise removers, 242
    noise samples, 241
    pre-mixes, 282–285
    restoration, 240–247
    VocALign plug-in, 238
    X-Hum, 246–247
    X-Noise, 242–243
dialogue looping, 135
dialogue, recording, 134–147
    ADR, 134–142
    animation, 144–145
    backup recorders, 144
    beeps, 136
    dialogue looping, 135
    file management, 138–142
    loop record, 135–138
    markers, 146
    MIC placements, 143
    narration, 139–140
    plosives, 143
    pop filters, 143
    rough tracks, 145–147
    takes, picture changes, 221
    technique, 142
    timelines, 146
    timing delays, 145
    undoing, 139–140
    voiceovers, 142–143
dialogue, soundtracks, 17–20
    animation voices, 20
    automatic dialogue replacement (ADR), 18
    lip sync, 19
    narrators, 19

production audio, 17–18
talent, 19
voiceovers, 19
wild takes, 18
digital clock, 44
digital connections, 310–312
digital field recorders, 127–134
Cinema Audio Society, 132
iXML metadata, 130–131
metadata, 129–130
multi-channel takes, 132–134
production sound mix track, 131
workflow, 129–132
digital multimedia formats, 13–16
Avid video, 16
DV codecs, 14–15
Flash, 16
H.264 files, 15–16
MPEG codecs, 14
MPEG-4 files, 15–16
QuickTime, 13–14
Shockwave, 16
DigiTranslator, 119–122
directors, 29
Disney, Walt, 3–6
Dolby "Baby-Boom" Six-Track, film
    sound format, 8
Dolby Digital, film sound format, 8, 10,
    250–251
Dolby Discrete Six-Track, film sound format, 8
Dolby E, 310–311
Dolby encoding, reference levels, 307–308
Dolby Laboratories, 10
Dolby Laboratories Mix Data Sheet, 315
Dolby Pro Logic, 250
Dolby "Split-Surround" Six-Track, film sound
    format, 8, 10
Dolby Stereo, film sound format, 8, 250
Don Juan, 2
downmixing, 251–252
DTS, film sound format, 8
dubbing stage, 68, 281
duration counter, editing, 188
DVCAM, Sony, 81–82
DV codecs, 14–15
DVCPRO, Panasonic, 81
DVD authoring, reference levels, 308
dynamics, mixing, 294–295

E

Edison, Thomas, 1–2, 13
edit decision list (EDL), 32, 108–117
automated conforming, 115–117

CMX 3600 EDL, 108–109
manual conforming, 110–115
Virtual Katy, 115–117
Edit Preview mode, 76
Edit window, 177–180
editing, 25, 169–195
audio to picture, 39–40
counters, 186–189
duration counter, 188
global modifiers, 174
grid values, 191–195
groups, 180–186
    color coding, 186
    creation, 181
    disabling, 183–184
    enabling, 183–184
    renaming, 184–186
    tracks, re-grouping, 184–186
Keyboard Focus mode, 180
locating, Edit window, 177–180
picture changes, 217
rulers, 186, 189–191
    Bars:Beats, 191
    Feet:Frames, 190
    Markers, 189–190
    Meter, 191
    Minutes:Seconds, 190–191
    Samples, 191
    Tempo, 191
    Time Code, 190
Tab key, 178–179
Tab to Transient function, 179
tracks, resizing, 172–174
tracks, show/hide, 169–172
zooming, 174–177
editors, 30
effects, mixing, 286
Engle, Josef, 2
Enterprise Post, 20
environmental audio, 35
environmental music, 24
EQs, mixing, 291–294
equipment, set up, 65–84
audio clock source, 69
dubbing stage, 68
home or project studios, 68
Machine Control, 9-pin, 71–78
    connections, 72–74
    operation, 74–77
    remote deck emulation, 77–78
    settings, 72–74
MIDI Machine Control (MMC),
    78–79
    connections, 79

equipment, set up (*continued*)
    operation, 79
    settings, 79
  multi-room facilities, 66–68
  single-room studios, 68
  Sync HD, Digidesign, 69–70
  Sync I/O, Digidesign, 69–70
  third-party synchronizers, 70
  time code burn-in, 70, 84
  time code reader, 71
  video playback monitors, 80–84
    Avid solutions, 80
    DV decoders, 81–82
    Firewire, 81–82
    third-party video, 80–81
  video recorders, dedicated hard disk, 84
  Virtual VTR software, 83–84
expansion limits, Audiosuite plug-ins, 233

F

Fantasia, 3–6
  DVD, 6
  "Fantasia Road Show," 6
  Fantasound, 4–6
  innovations, sound, 6
  Moviola machine, 3–4
  panpot, 5
  re-releases, 6
Fantasound, 4–6
Federal Communications Commission (FCC), 9
field recordings, 153–154
file management, 138–142
files, reversing, 224–230
film composers, 160
film crew contact, 34–35
film to 24p HD synchronization, 36
film encoding, reference levels, 307–308
film to film synchronization, 61
film to NTSC video synchronization, 60
film sound formats, 7–8
film-style mixing, 266–268, 276–278
film time codes, 46–47
film transfers, synchronization, 54–57
Final Cut Pro, 93–99
Firewire, 15
first frames, determining, 93
Flash, 10, 16
foley artists, 21
Foley, Jack, 20
foley sounds, 17, 20–22, 147–153
  artists, 21
  FX libraries, 150–151
  location sounds, 21–22, 151–153
  mixing, 285

post-production, 38
sampling, 21
sound effects libraries, 21
stages, 21, 147–150
  footsteps, 148–150
  microphone technique, 150
  moves track, 148
  specifics, 150
foley stages, 21, 147–150
  footsteps, 148–150
  microphone technique, 150
  moves track, 148
  specifics, 150
Fostex PD-6, 18
Fox Film Corporation, 2
frame counts, new sessions, 85–86
frame rates, new sessions, 85–86
FX libraries, 150–151

G

Garity, William, 5
global modifiers, editing, 174
The Godfather II, 151
Grid mode, 101
grid values, 191–195
groups, editing, 180–186
  color coding, 186
  creation, 181
  disabling, 183–184
  enabling, 183–184
  functions, 215
  renaming, 184–186
  tracks, re-grouping, 184–186

H

H.264 files, 15–16
handles, 111
Happy Days, 17
hard effects, *see* sound effects
HD, synchronization from, 63–64
HDTV, 11–13
The Hollywood Edge sound effects library, 150, 155
Hollywood standard, 27
home or project studios, 68

I

IEEE-1394-1995, 15
iLink, 26
IMAX, 10
iMovie, 92–95
Import Audio dialog box, 151
innovations, sound, *Fantasia*, 6

inserts, mixing, 255–257
International Standards Organization (ISO), 14
Internet media, reference levels, 309–310
Internet streaming audio files, 317
Internet video, 10–11
I/O Setup, mixing, 252–257
iPods, 13
iXML metadata, 130–131

J

The Jazz Singer, 3
jingle, 24
Jolson, Al, 3

K

K19, 152
Keyboard Focus mode, 180
Kinetoscope, 2

L

Latch mode, 289
latency, mixing, 257
Law & Order, 23
layback, 40–41
LE systems, 102–103
levels, writing, 289–291
LFE channel, mixing, 288–289
Lights of New York, 3
libraries, sound effects, 21, 154–155
Lindbergh, Charles, 2
link edit, 219
lip sync, 19, 103–104
location sounds, foley, 21–22, 151–153
Logitudinal Time Code (LTC), 71
loop record, 135–138
Lord of the Rings: Fellowship of the Ring, 19,
    216, 21, 277
Lord of the Rings: The Two Towers, 19, 216
loudness calibration, mixing, 264–269
Low Frequency Effects (LFE) channel, 264
Lucas, George, 13

M

Machine Control, 9-pin, 71–78
    connections, 72–74
    operation, 74–77
    remote deck emulation, 77–78
    settings, 72–74
Machine Control tab, Peripherals window, 78
markers, 146
    memory locations, 197
    placement, 205

Markers ruler, 201–205
master recordings, 40–41, 303–320
    analog connections, 312–313
    archiving, 318–319
    audio files, creation, 314–318
    backups, 318–319
    Bounce dialog box, 316
    bouncing, QuickTime movies, 314
    data CDs, creation, 314–318
    digital connections, 310–312
    Dolby E, 310–311
    Dolby Laboratories Mix Data Sheet, 315
    Internet streaming audio files, 317
    mix stems, 303, 318–319
    multi-channel surround, 313–314
    Panasonic D-5, 312
    Redbook audio CDs, 316–317
    reference levels, 303–310
        83dBC, 305–306
        85dBC, 305–306
        broadcast video, 308–309
        Dolby encoding, 307–308
        DVD authoring, 308
        film encoding, 307–308
        Internet media, 309–310
        signal-to-noise ratio, 306
        usage, 306–310
        VU meters, 304
    side-chain gain reduction, 319
McKay, John, 116, 221
Media Composer, Avid, 123
memory locations, 195–205
    creation, 195–197
    cue lists, 197–199
    Marker, 197
    marker placement, 205
    Markers ruler, 201–205
    Memory Locations window, 199–200
    None option, 197
    recall, 199–205
    Regions/Markers mode, 205
    Save As operations, 202
    selection, 196–197
    selection markers, 201
Memory Locations window, 199–200
metadata, 129–130
Mic placements, 143
Mickey Mouse, 3
MIDI Machine Control (MMC),
    78–79
    connections, 79
    operation, 79
    settings, 79
Milner, Joe, 277
MiniDV, 81

mixing
   ADC buffer, 302
   automation, 289–297
      control surfaces, 295–297
      dynamics, building, 294–295
      EQs, 291–294
      Latch mode, 289
      levels, writing, 289–291
      Off mode, 291
      panning, 291
      Read mode, 290
      Touch mode, 289
      Trim mode, 290
      Write mode, 289
   calibration, 270–274
   delay compensation, 298–302
      RTAS plug-in, 298–302
      TDM plug-in, 298–302
   film-style, 266–268, 276–278
   pre-mixes, 278–289
      dialogue, 282–285
      dub stage, 281
      effects, 286
      foley, 285
      LFE channel, 288–289
      music, 286–288
   preparation, 252–276
      5.1 surround speakers, 259–261
      bass management, 264, 269–270
      busses, 254–255
      inserts, 255–257
      I/O Setup, 252–257
      latency, 257
      loudness calibration, 264–269
      Low Frequency Effects (LFE) channel, 264
      mix stems, 255
      outputs, 252–254
      pink noise, 265
      speaker systems/layout, 258–264
      stereo speakers, 258–259
      subwoofers, 264
      surround speakers, 261–263
   stereo and surround formats, 249–252
      5.1 surround, 250–251
      Dolby Digital, 250–251
      Dolby Pro Logic, 250
      Dolby Stereo, 250
      downmixing, 251–252
      multi-channel processing, 251
   time alignment, 274–276
   tracks, 40
mix stems, 255, 303, 318–319
Modify Groups window, 185
Monsters, Inc., 149

Motion Picture Experts Group, *see* MPEG
Moviola machine, 3–4, 47
movie offsets, 100–103
Movietone newsreels, 2
MP3 files, importing, 161
MPEG codecs, 14
MPEG-4 files, 15–16
multi-channel mixing, 27
multi-channel music, importing, 161
multi-channel processing, 251
multi-channel surround, 313–314
multi-channel takes, 132–134
multi-room facilities, 66–68
Murch, Walter, 10
music
   film composers, 160
   importing, 62, 159–161
      CDs, 159
      CD-ROM, 159–160
      DAT, 159
      MP3 files, 161
      multi-channel music, 161
      tape, 159
   mixing, 286–288
   post-production, 38
   soundtracks, 23–25
      environmental, 24
      jingle, 24
      score, 24
      soundtrack music, 24–25

N

Nanosync HD, Rosendahl, 70
narration, 139–140; *see also* dialogue, recording
narration, soundtracks, 17–20
narrators, 19
National Television System Committee
      (NTSC), 9
new sessions, 84–88
   bit depths, 84–85
   frame counts, 85–86
   frame rates, 85–86
   sample rates, 84–85
   start times, 86–88
New Session dialog box, 84–85
NHK, 11
None option, memory locations, 197
NTSC, 47–48
NTSC video to NTSC video synchronization, 59–60
Nudge commands, 206–209
   Nudge values, 206–207
   regions, aligning, 207–209
   subframe, 209

O

Off mode, 291
OMNIMAX, 10
Open Media Framework Interchange
        (OMFI) files, importing, 117–124
    AAF files, 122–124
    video workstation guidelines, 118–120
Ott, Fred, 1–2
outputs, mixing, 252–254

P

PAL (Phase Alternate Line), 47–48
Panasonic D-5, 312
Panasonic VariCam, 58–59
panning, mixing, 291
panpot, 5
Pearl Harbor (the movie), 128
picture changes, 215–221
    change node, 216
    dialogue takes, 221
    edits, large, 217
    link edit, 219
    QuicKeys, 216
    re-balancing, 217–221
    timeline selections, 219–220
    Virtual Katy, 216, 221
pink noise, mixing, 265
pitch changing, Audiosuite plug-ins,
    235–236
Pitch shift, 235
planning, pre-production, 28
playlists, 212–215
plosives, 143
pop filters, 143
Porter, Terry, 6
post-production, 36–41
    ADR dialogue replacements, 37
    audio transferring, 36–37
    cue lists, finalizing, 36
    editing, audio to picture, 39–40
    foley, 38
    layback, 40–41
    master recordings, 40–41
    music, 38
    sound effects, 38
    tracks, mixing, 40
    voiceovers, 37
Postscores, 24
pre-mixes/pre-dubs, 278–289
    dialogue, 282–285
    dub stage, 281
    effects, 286

    foley, 285
    LFE channel, 288–289
    music, 286–288
pre-production, 28–34
    acquisition, audio, 31–32
    archival, 34
    audio exchange, 30–34
    audio and video interchange, 32–33
    backup, 34
    co-workers, 29–30
    delivery, 33–34
    directors, 29
    edit decision list (EDL), 32
    editors, 30
    planning, 28
    producers, 29
    production sound mixer, 30
    scripts, 29
    session document, 32–33
    Web designers, 30
producers, 29
production, 34–36
    animation dialogue, 35
    cue lists, 35
    environmental audio, 35
    film crew contact, 34–35
    sound mix track, 131
production audio, 17–18, 107–134
    AAF files, 122–124
    DAT tapes, 124–127
        24fps shoot, 125–127
        29.97fps shoot, 127
        SimulDAT, 125–126
    digital field recorders, 127–134
        Cinema Audio Society, 132
        iXML metadata, 130–131
        metadata, 129–130
        multi-channel takes, 132–134
        production sound mix track, 131
        workflow, 129–132
    DigiTranslator, 120–122
    Edit Decision List (EDL), 108–117
        automated conforming, 115–117
        CMX 3600 EDL, 108–109
        manual conforming, 110–115
        Virtual Katy, 115–117
    handles, 111
    Open Media Framework Interchange
        (OMFI) files, importing, 117–124
        AAF files, 122–124
        video workstation guidelines, 118–120
production sound mixer, 30
pull-down sample rates, 55–56
pull-up sample rates, 56–57

Q

QuicKeys, 216
QuickTime, 13–14
    movies, opening, 89–90
    support, 25–26
QuickTime Pro upgrade, 14

R

Read mode, 290
re-balancing, 217–221
recall, memory locations, 199–205
Redbook audio CDs, 316–317
reference levels, master recordings,
        303–310
    83dBC, 305–306
    85dBC, 305–306
    broadcast video, 308–309
    Dolby encoding, 307–308
    DVD authoring, 308
    film encoding, 307–308
    Internet media, 309–310
    signal-to-noise ratio, 306
    usage, 306–310
    VU meters, 304
regions, aligning, 207–209
Regions/Markers mode, 205
Relative Grid, 211–212
remote decks, arming, 76
rough tracks, 145–147
RTAS plug-in, 298–302
rulers, editing, 186, 189–191
    Bars:Beats, 191
    Feet:Frames, 190
    Markers, 189–190
    Meter, 191
    Minutes:Seconds, 190–191
    Samples, 191
    Tempo, 191
    Time Code, 190

S

sample rates, new sessions, 84–85
samplers, sound effects, 156–159
sampling, foley, 21
Samsung LTM405W LCD screen, 12
Save As operations, 202
score, 24, 159–161
    CDs, importing from, 159
    CD-ROM, importing from, 159–160
    DAT, importing from, 159
    film composers, 160
    MP3 files, importing, 161

multi-channel music, importing, 161
    tape, importing from, 159
scripts, pre-production, 29
SDDS, film sound format, 8
selection, 196–197
selection markers, 201
Sennheiser MKH-416 microphone, 36
sessions, see new sessions
session document, 32–33
Session Setup window, 86
Shockwave, 16
Shrek, 20
side-chain gain reduction, 319
signal-to-noise ratio, reference levels, 306
SimulDAT, 125–126
Singer, Philip, 21
single-room studios, 68
The Sneeze, 1–2, 13
Society of Motion Picture and Television
        Engineers (SMPTE), 9
Sony TVR-17 DV camcorder, 15
sound design, 22
Sound Designer title, 10
sound effects, 153–159
    ambience, 23
    exaggerated, 23
    field recordings, 153–154
    imaginary, 23
    libraries, 21, 154–155
    post-production, 38
    samplers, 156–159
    synthesizers, 155–156
sound formats, film, 7–8
Sound Ideas sound effects library, 150
soundtracks, 17–25
    dialogue, 17–20
        animation voices, 20
        automatic dialogue replacement
            (ADR), 18
        lip sync, 19
        narrators, 19
        production audio, 17–18
        talent, 19
        voiceovers, 19
        wild takes, 18
    music, 23–25
        environmental, 24
        jingle, 24
        score, 24
        soundtrack music, 24–25
    foley sounds, 17, 20–22
        artists, 21
        location sounds, 21–22, 151–153
        sampling, 21

sound effects libraries, 21
  stages, 21
narration, 17–20
sound design, 22
sound effects, 22–23
  ambience, 23
  exaggerated, 23
  imaginary, 23
special effects, 17
soundtrack music, 24–25
speaker systems/layout, 258–264
special effects, soundtracks, 17
Spot dialog box, 139
Spot mode, 101
spotting, 65
stages, foley, 21
start times, new sessions, 86–88
Star Wars, 10, 23
Star Wars: Attack of the Clones, 13
Star Wars Episode I, 27
Steamboat Willie, 3
stereo speakers, 258–259
stereo and surround formats, 249–252
  5.1 surround, 250–251
  Dolby Digital, 250–251
  Dolby Pro Logic, 250
  Dolby Stereo, 250
  downmixing, 251–252
  multi-channel processing, 251
Stokowski, 5
subframe nudging, 209
subwoofers, 264
surround-sound panner, 27
surround speakers, 261–263
Survivor, 128
Swordfish, 277
sync points, 210–212
  creation, 210
  Relative Grid, 211–212
  usage, 211–212
sync tones, 87
Sync HD, Digidesign, 69–70
Sync I/O, Digidesign, 69–70
synchronization, checking, 103–106
  audio, importing, 103
  lip sync, 103–104
  time code burn-in window, 104–106
synchronization, SMPTE time codes, 43–64
  2-3 pull-down, 54–59
    24p HD video, 58–59
    film transfers, 54–57
    pull-down sample rates, 55–56
    pull-up sample rates, 56–57
  24fps HD to film, 62–63

24p HD to video, 62
calculators, time code, 49
clock speed, 44
color video, 48–49
current practices, 52–59
digital clock, 44
film to 24p HD, 36
film to film, 61
film to NTSC video, 60
film time codes, 46–47
from HD, 63–64
music, importing, 62
NTSC, 47–48
NTSC video to NTSC video, 59–60
PAL (Phase Alternate Line), 47–48
parameters, time code, 49–52
  drop-frame time code, 51, 53–54
  non-drop frame, 51–52
  frame count, 50–52, 54
  frame rates, 49–50, 54
playback rate, 44–46
positional reference, 44
synthesizers, sound effects, 155–156

T
Tab key, 178–179
Tab to Transient function, 179
talent, 19
tape, importing from, 159
TDM plug-in, 298–302
Tektronix SPG-422, 67
telecine machine, 54–55
televisions, 9
  analog broadcasts, 11–12
  aspect ratios, 12
  HDTV, 11–13
third-party synchronizers, 70–71
Thornton, Douglas, 24
time alignment, 274–276
time code burn-in, 70, 84
time code burn-in window, 104–106
time code reader, 71
time compression, Audiosuite plug-ins, 230–234
Time Compression Expansion Trimmer tool, 234
time expansion, Audiosuite plug-ins, 230–234
timelines
  dialogue recording, 146
  selections, 219–220
Time Shift, Audiosuite plug-ins, 236
timing delays, 145
Todd-AO, film sound format, 8

Touch mode, 289
tracks
  main, 90
  mixing, 40
  multiple, 99–100
  re-grouping, 184–186
  resizing, 172–174
  show/hide, 169–172
transference, audio, 36–37
transport-master/time code-slave mode, 75
Transport submenu, 74, 79
Tri-Ergon process, 2
Trimmer tool, 234
Trim mode, 290

U

undoing recording, 139–140
Universal Pictures, 20

V

Vertical Interval Time Code (VITC), 71
video files, importing, 88–103
  Avid Mojo, 90–91
  burn-in windows, 91
  Final Cut Pro, 93–99
  first frames, determining, 93
  Grid mode, 101
  iMovie, 92–95
  LE systems, 102–103
  main tracks, 90
  movie offsets, 100–103
  QuickTime movies, opening, 89–90
  Spot mode, 101

tracks, multiple, 99–100
  Virtual VTR, 91, 99
Video Import Options dialog box, 89, 104
video playback monitors, 80–84
  Avid solutions, 80
  DV decoders, 81–82
  Firewire, 81–82
  third-party video, 80–81
video recorders, dedicated hard disk, 84
video recording, 9
Virtual Katy, 216, 221
Virtual VTR software, 83–84, 91, 99
Vitaphone, 2
Vogt, Hans, 2
voiceovers, 19, 37, 142–143
Volkmann, John, 3
VU meters, reference levels, 304

W–Y

Warner Brothers, 2–3
Warnerphonic, film sound format, 8
Web designers, 30
wild takes, 18
Windows Media Player (WMV), 14
workflow, 28–41
  pre-production, 28–34
  post-production, 36–41
  production, 34–36
Write mode, 289

Z

Zaxcom DEVA, 18, 32, 128
zooming, 174–177